# Women and Power in the Middle East

# Women and Power in the Middle East

Edited by
SUAD JOSEPH and
SUSAN SLYOMOVICS

**PENN**

University of Pennsylvania Press     Philadelphia

Copyright © 2001 University of Pennsylvania Press
Printed in the United States of America on acid-free paper

10 9 8 7 6 5 4 3 2 1

Published by
University of Pennsylvania Press
Philadelphia, Pennsylvania 19104-4011

Library of Congress Cataloging-in-Publication Data

Women and power in the Middle East / edited by Suad Joseph and Susan Slyomovics.
    p.   cm.
  ISBN 0-8122-3579-7 (cloth : alk. paper): ISBN 0-8122-1749-7 (pbk. : alk. paper)
  Includes bibliographical references and index.
    1. Women in politics — Middle East.   2. Women — Middle East — History.
3. Women — Middle East — Social conditions.   4. Feminism — Middle East.
I. Slyomovics, Susan.   II. Title.
HQ1726.5.W659 2000
305.42'0956 — dc21                                        00-060200

# Contents

# Introduction

Suad Joseph and Susan Slyomovics

The Arab-Islamic world is a mixture of social classes, racial and ethnic groups, religious affiliations, nationalities, and rural, urban, and linguistic communities; any discussion of gender must first account for the tremendous diversity in the Middle East and North Africa. Essays in this collection address relations among gender, politics, and class in Morocco, Algeria, Tunisia, Egypt, Sudan, Palestine, Lebanon, Kuwait, Saudi Arabia, Yemen, Iran, and Turkey. In this region, people may live in cities, provincial towns, and rural villages. Migrations of peoples from Africa, Europe, and Asia have brought about movements of ideas, values, and structures, and a mixing of peoples and cultures. The past century has been a period of intense upheaval, escalated change, and revolutionary transformation. There is no moment from the past that we can point to as a time in which Arab (or Arab-Islamic) culture was fixed.

Given this historic social and cultural fluidity and tremendous diversity, and the recent escalation of change, we have to be very careful before generalizing about gender issues or any other aspect of social organization, or assuming that these issues are the same across ethnic, religious, racial, national, regional, or linguistic groupings. With this caveat in mind, it is nevertheless possible to suggest a framework within which to understand broad patterns of gender in the region, even without asserting that they apply everywhere. Furthermore, with few exceptions, most of the patterns described in our introductory section are not uniquely Arab or Muslim.

## Core Unit

The family lies at the core of Middle Eastern and North African society — in political, economic, social, and religious terms.

This privileged position is enshrined in the constitutions of many Arab or Muslim states (which assert the family to be the basic unit of society), and is reproduced at almost every level of political life. Economies recognize the centrality of the family in many ways, including through worker recruitment and discipline, wages and benefits. Religious institutions consider themselves the guardians of family integrity and hold families responsible for safeguarding religious sanctity. People are keenly aware of each other's family memberships, identities, and status. Access to institutions, jobs and government services is often through family connections. The centrality of family to social, economic, political, and religious life has profound implications for gender relations.

## Patriarchy

The gender system in the Middle East and North Africa is shaped by and works through the institutions of patriarchy which affect much of the social order. Two Arab scholars have even argued that patriarchy is a — or the — core obstacle to equality and democracy in the Arab world.[1]

Patriarchy privileges males and elders (including elder women in the Arab-Islamic world) and justifies this privilege in kinship terms. Females are generally taught to respect and defer to their fathers, brothers, grandparents, uncles, and, at times, male cousins. Young people are taught to respect and defer to their older kin. In turn, males are taught to take responsibility for their female kin, and elders are taught to protect and take responsibility for those younger than themselves. Gender and age privilege generally enhance the power and authority of elder males, although elder women also come to have a degree of authority over those younger than themselves. Once males reach adulthood, they generally have more authority and power than even elder females.

These patriarchal rules are widely held and observed in Middle Eastern and North African families, but like all social rules, there are many exceptions and many interpretations. A younger brother can come to have more authority than an older brother, for example, if the younger brother is more financially or politically successful. A sister can exert authority over her brothers if she acquires independent wealth or influence. The authority of paternal uncles can readily be challenged when unsupported by economic, political, or social resources. And if elderly fathers falter in health or wealth, they can lose authority to their sons.

Patriarchy has generally fostered patrilineality, patrilocality, and endogamy. Patrilineality means that descent is established through the father. Lineage membership is passed down through sons who bear the responsibility, not only of reproducing the kin group, but also of protecting its members. In the cultural ideal, a married woman remains attached to her father's lineage rather than her husband's. The reality is more complex. At times maternal relatives are more important than paternal relatives as sources of political clout, social status, or emotional support. Paternal kin sometimes do not fulfill the duties of the cultural ideal. As a result of global economic and political pressures of the past century, the extended patrilineal family ideal has been transformed in many parts of the Middle East and North Africa, particularly urban areas, into joint, nuclear, single-parent, or other family arrangements. So while the patrilineal cultural ideal is upheld, in reality there are numerous family patterns today.

The patriarchal privileging of males and seniors combined with patrilineality enhances the power of male elders in the father's kin group, particularly their power over women of the lineage. A father's brothers can have authority over their nieces and nephews, and male cousins can have authority over their female counterparts. The intersection of patriarchy and patrilineality increases the range of men with authority over women—an authority nested in kinship terms. After a couple marry, it is preferred that they live near the male's family (patrilocality). In the contemporary world, most Middle Easterners would not volunteer patrilocality as an ideal. Postmarital residence patterns tend to conform more to local economic and sociological pressures than to patrilocality. Patrilocality, when practiced, can enhance the power of men over women. When combined with endogamy, it can also counterbalance the power of husbands over women by locating women near their natal families.

Endogamy refers to a cultural preference to marry within the father's kin group, and therefore one's own religious, ethnic, and national group. Endogamy, when practiced and when combined with patrilocality, means that both husbands and wives have their natal families near by. In these marriages, wives and husbands are part of the same lineage. Family elders, male and female, can exercise considerable authority over the couple. Women in this situation are subject to greater control from both families, but also have greater protection from possible in-law excesses. Arranged marriages are still common, although much less so in urban areas and among educated middle and upper classes. Arranged marriages are a vehicle to establish or reinforce relationships between families rather than just between a couple.

Marriage patterns, in reality, vary greatly in the Middle East and North Africa. Non-kin marriages outnumber kin marriages almost everywhere. In addition, interethnic and interreligious marriages are relatively common. In Arab countries, marriages among Arabs of different nationalities and between Arabs and non-Arabs were common throughout the twentieth century. Patrilineal parallel cousin marriages, the ideal marriage, account for fewer than 10 percent of marriages in most countries. Marriages to matrilineal extended relatives seem to be at least as common.

Family Resource

In most countries in the Middle East and North Africa, the family is a source of economic security. Families generally feel obligated to take care of their members financially. Given the lack or inadequacy of government programs for unemployment compensation, health insurance, and retirement benefits, most people must look to their families for those assurances. In addition, family members often work together in the same businesses, help each other find work, own shops or land together, lend each other money, and share other economic resources.

The importance of family as the primary source of economic security has given weight to the patriarchal structuring of family. The authority of men and elders has economic consequences for women and juniors. Many women, for example, never inherit their share of their patrimony, even though state law and Islamic custom entitle them to a share.[2] Some women choose to leave their inheritance with their brothers as insurance, so that they can return to their birth families if their marriages dissolve.

Family is also a key political resource in most Middle Eastern and North African countries. This is in part because of the frequent inadequacy of government social service programs, and partly because governments privilege family relationships in offering access to governmental resources. Family provides a person with his or her basic political network: family contacts are usually the starting place if one needs access to a government agency. Political leaders, in turn, want to know of a person's family connections and support of family members. Politicians and administrators often allocate resources to persons through heads of family, and favor their own families in the process. This constant emphasis on family in the state arena turns family relationships into powerful political tools. And since family is patriarchal, politics also privileges patriarchy.

These political uses of family create kinship continuities between the state (the public sphere), civil society (the sphere of private organizations), and the family (the domestic sphere). Some have argued that for democracy to develop, civil society must be separate from the state and autonomous. This model of democracy and civil society is based on the (somewhat idealized) experiences of Western states. In Arab-Islamic countries, there often are greater continuities among the public, private, and domestic spheres that are linked to the centrality of the patriarchal family.

For women, these continuities among family, civil society, and state mean that they confront patriarchy in every sphere. Patriarchy is thus reproduced in multiple sites in many Middle Eastern and North African countries — a phenomenon not unique to Arab-Islamic societies. The outcome is that women and juniors must be embedded in familial relationships to make most effective use of the institutions in these spheres and are therefore subject to patriarchal norms and relationships even in public spaces. Yet most women and juniors would argue for retention of these familial relationships because the ties also provide support.

With the exception of Tunisia and Turkey, family and religion are legally intertwined. Most Arab-Islamic countries defer personal status laws (also called family law) to religious institutions, as does Israel. Laws concerning marriage, divorce, inheritance, and child custody are under the aegis of the legally recognized religious institutions. There is no civil recourse: no civil marriage, divorce, or inheritance rules. Marriages between persons of different religions require the conversion of one of the partners, usually the wife, and the permission of the clergy performing the rites. Needless to say, this acts as an impediment to intersectarian marriages, although not a total barrier, since agreeable clerics can usually be found.

By placing family law in the domain of religious institutions, most Middle Eastern and North African states have given control over issues that dramatically affect women to institutions that are gender biased. Clerics — Jewish, Christian, or Muslim — are all male, and their hierarchy is quite patriarchal. Feminist activists in a number of countries have lobbied for years to change family law. Though there have been small successes in countries like Iraq, Morocco, and Yemen, and for a while Egypt, these activists have seen some governments retreat in recent years in the face of conservative or radical religious mobilization to undo family law reforms.

## Gender and Family Values

Family values are highly diverse, but certain patterns are widely shared. Among these are concepts of generosity, hospitality, reciprocity, pride, dignity, valor, strength, emotional openness, indirection, communication, conflict-avoidance, and the use of mediators to negotiate relationships.

Perhaps the value most widely known outside the region is that of family honor. Family honor is crucial in the Arab-Islamic world and in Mediterranean societies generally. Family honor implies that one's sense of dignity, identity, status, self, and public esteem is linked to the regard with which one's family is held by the community at large. The cultural assumption has been that a person's actions reflect on his or her family as a whole, and the reputation of the family as a whole is borne by each of its members. Children are taught that the good of the family comes before personal good. Sacrifice by individual family members to benefit the family as a whole is expected. Family members are supposed to be responsible to and for each other.

It is the historic centrality of the family for social, political, and economic security that accords family honor a role in controlling the behavior of family members. Just as honor has offered a measure of protection to family members, it has also been a means of controlling behavior, especially women's. The notion of family honor reinforces patriarchal power by circumscribing women's sexuality, movement in social arenas, and, to some degree, economic opportunities. It enhances the power of fathers, grandfathers, uncles, brothers, and male cousins over women. Though these cultural beliefs generally prevail, enactments of family honor vary considerably. In the past few decades, extended kin, particularly in urban areas and in middle and upper classes, have been less able to use honor to control the behavior of distant relatives. Even the hold of nuclear families on their members has become equivocal in certain social strata.

Much of the scholarship on personhood and family has been divided into two camps. Some scholars have argued that the Arab-Islamic world is highly individualistic, with persons strategizing for individual gain and committed to little beyond self interest. Others reject this view, arguing that the person is totally submerged in family and community. While neither view captures the totality, both identify aspects of the relationship between personhood and family. Generally, socialization practices do not support individualism, the creation of autonomous, separate selves. On the other hand, neither do socialization practices entirely conflate the person with the family as a fixed, bounded entity. Rather, persons are encouraged to view themselves as always linked with, reciprocally shaped by, and mutually responsive to family and relatives.

This relational construct of self is encouraged in both men and women (although other notions of self are also supported). The implications for women, however, are somewhat different from those for men. The relational self, when combined with patriarchy, produces "patriarchal relationality."[3] Women, more than men, are expected to put others before themselves and to see their interests as embedded in those of others, especially familial others. In practice, this means that women are particularly encouraged to see their interests linked to their male kin. This often has the effect of reinforcing patriarchal hierarchy.

As in any society, family members can be and are quite competitive with each other. Siblings, especially brothers, can compete for status or affirmation from parents or extended kin. Yet brothers and sisters are generally socialized to love, support, and sacrifice for each other. It is in the tension between competition and generosity, between love and power, that the dynamics of family are often played out. The tension provides spaces for negotiation, maneuvering, direct and indirect empowerment. While women negotiate and maneuver as much as men, they, more often than men, find themselves in the subordinate position.

## Family as Idiom

The centrality of family is often expressed through the use of idiomatic kinship: acting as if a person is a relative even when they are not socially recognized kin. In using family idioms in such relationships, people call up the expectations and morality of kinship. The use of idiomatic kinship is important not only in intimate circles, but also in political and economic spheres. Political leaders at times put themselves in the position of being family patriarchs. They expect to be treated as heads of families, with the deference and loyalties due to family elders. They use family idioms to justify the power relationships between themselves and their clients or followers. Idiomatic kinship relationships can be created for short-term purposes. People who need each other's services for political mediation, brokerage, or gaining access to resources, will often call themselves by kin terms. In doing so, they bring family morality to bear on the transactions between them. Idiomatic kin relationships are often found in the economy as well. Owners of business, particularly owners of small businesses, often use kinship terminology to create a relationship with their workers. Workers then come to expect their employers to treat them with kinlike concern.

Women as well as men use idiomatic kinship to create affective and instrumental relationships. They, like men, create short and longterm bonds by assimilating people into the moral domain of family. For women, however, there are other consequences. In evoking kinship, women intentionally or unintentionally also call forth the values and institutional arrangements associated with patriarchy. Insofar as idiomatic kinship is successful, it reinforces patriarchy in public and private arenas of social life.

Gender and family systems, like all aspects of social life, are continually shifting in response to dynamic transformations in culture and society, locally and globally. The diverse family patterns are shaped by class, ethnic, racial, religious, national, and linguistic dynamics. Yet certain patterns tend to be reproduced. Key to these patterns is the centrality of family, in its multiple forms, to one's notion of self, one's social position, one's economic security, and one's political possibilities. Family relationships tend to be upheld in state constitutions and supported in most arenas of social life, including all the religious institutions. Given the centrality of family, its patriarchal structure is crucial in understanding gender relationships in the Middle East. Family both supports and suppresses women. This paradox of support and suppression, love and power, and generosity and competition compels both attachment to and struggle within families. Many features of these gender and family systems are found in many non-Arab-Islamic cultures, yet the combination expresses dynamics that are also culturally and historically part and parcel of Middle Eastern and North African societies.

## Gender, Citizenship, Civil Society, and State

The Western construct of nation-state, which became the compulsory political form for the rest of the world, is based on the concept of citizens as individuals, as detached from communities. In fact, in the Middle East, North Africa, the Third World, and much of the West, persons are deeply embedded in communities, in families, in ethnic, racial or other social groupings. The Western construct of citizen — a contract-making individual — implies a degree of detachment and autonomy that is not universal. The capacity to make contracts emerges from the fact that this individualized self is conceived of as a property owner, first of all as owner of himself, the male citizen.

The Western liberal notion of citizen implies a masculinized construct.

Males were the property owners. Carol Pateman argues that the contemporary state is in fact a fraternal patriarchy. In the discourse that established the philosophical basis of liberal bourgeois society, the dominant idiom is that of brothers. The social contract is entered into by free men who constitute themselves as a civil fraternity. The social contract creates an association of autonomous, individualized, contract-making persons, and contract-making is possible only for property owners. The assertions that underlie this philosophical base are assertions of exclusion. Women and many minorities are not contract-making persons, because they are not property owners, in the classical liberal contractarian view of civil society, citizenship and state. Civil society was conceived of as a fraternity, not a sorority, and not a family, according to Pateman.[4]

Liberal feminist thought has had as its goal the integration of women into the state, not challenging the basic structure of the state. Marxist feminists have argued that the liberalist approach only resolves the gendering of citizenship for elite women. Class, race, patriarchy, and other forms of exclusion continue to constrain the active political participation of women (as well as working class and minority men) and limit the benefits they receive as citizens. Full inclusion would require transforming the gendered, racial, class-based structure of society.

Some feminists argue that class and patriarchy are dual systems of oppression that operate autonomously. Others argue that they are woven into each other, thus requiring political movements to take account of class embedded in patriarchy. Feminists have not reached a consensus on the primary source of oppression: gender, class, or race.

The contemporary exclusion of women is in part, but not exclusively, the outcome of this compulsory model of nation-state, a model which has built into it the marginalization of females and female activity. The nation-state with its gendered concepts of citizenship has been imposed upon already gendered systems of social stratification in much of the previously colonized world. There was patriarchy in the Middle East and North Africa prior to colonization. Precolonial and postcolonial patriarchies have intersected in contemporary nation-state building projects. There appears to have been great fluidity in the patriarchies that existed in the region in the seventeenth, eighteenth, and nineteenth centuries. Judith Tucker's work on Nablus courts, dealing with issues such as custody and divorce and child support cases in the eighteenth and nineteenth centuries, indicates that women made use of the courts effectively and actively, and across class lines. Women were very assertive in claiming their rights within what might be considered a

public domain in Palestine.[5] Research on medieval Egypt up to the nineteenth century indicates that women were active property owners. Julia
Clancy-Smith's work on colonial Algeria indicates that women were active
in religious movements, and were looked up to and sought out as saintly figures.[6] Such critical historical research appears to reveal more fluidity in gender hierarchies in the precolonial period than had been previously imagined.

Contemporary representations of the Middle East and North Africa
often depict more rigid gender hierarchies and greater exclusion of women
from public domains, to an extreme degree in some states. Western and
Eastern theorists and popular opinion often represent the position of women
as the litmus test of the character of the state in the Middle East and North
Africa. Women and women's bodies have become a central locus of tensions
among internal and external discourses; Islamist and secularist persuasions;
progressive and repressive forces. Hisham Sharabi argues that the postcolonial period has produced a "neopatriarchy." While patriarchies obviously
predate colonialism, contemporary patriarchies are products of the intersection between the colonial and indigenous domains of state and political
processes.[7]

These dynamics are not necessarily unique to the Middle East and North
Africa. While the gender/state dynamics analyzed in this book must be situated culturally and historically, there are important parallels to other societies. The Middle East and North Africa share important patterns with
China and India, for example. The three regions all have long histories of
state formation, periods of colonial control, and periods of attempted modernization. In all three regions, the literature seems to indicate consolidation
of gender domination for women in the contemporary period: increasing
control by men, families, communities, and the state. The contemporary
period in some ways has created new controls over women that are much less
fluid than those of earlier periods, linked both to the gender and class character of capitalism and to reactions to capitalism.

Edward Said argued, in *Orientalism*, that the East is feminized in relationship to the West.[8] Many scholars subsequently argued not only that the
Orient is feminized, but that the oppressed, the subordinate, the minority
are feminized. Hierarchy has tended to become gendered in contemporary
nation-states: those in the superordinate position are masculinized and subordinates are feminized, resulting in the imbuing of constructs of class and
citizenship with gendered meanings.

The individual citizen, as an autonomous, contract-making self, is an
element in a peculiarly modern and Western discourse, a discourse that has

become hegemonic as it has become universalized in various constitutions and international conventions. Chapters in this book investigate the basis of notions of civil society and citizenship in Western discourse, and the problems created by their uncritical application to Third World societies.

Rola Sharara, a Lebanese feminist, argues in *Khamsin* that women in Lebanon and in many Arab states cannot feel the impact of the state in their lives. They feel the impact of their communities, and in particular the men of their communities.[9] Lebanon may be an extreme example of citizenship funneled through communities. There ethnic, religious, kinbased communities have exerted considerable authority and claimed the loyalties of their members. In some societies, such communities have been competitive with state authority. Women may at times feel the oppression of the patriarchy of their communities more directly than that of the state. Elsewhere, such as Iraq, citizens have often experienced communities as a source of protection from a repressive state. The control of women by communities is not independent of state control. For some states, such as in Syria and Iraq, undermining local communities in order to control and claim the loyalties of their citizens is a part of the state-building project. States and communities can be competitive or collaborative forms of domination. The chapters in this volume carefully assess the political implications of preserving ethnic, religious, and tribal communities and the implications of the state "protecting" women from these communities.

Such communities have been organized through patriarchal idioms, moralities, and structures of domination. For women, in those states where communities are the primary vehicle through which they experience their membership in contemporary societies, these relations are mediated through patriarchy. In societies in which the state is more keenly felt, state forms of patriarchy penetrate more effectively into local communities. There are new, complex, shifting forms of gender domination. Insofar as the state is experienced as more repressive than the communities, then women often secure themselves in their communities, where they receive some protection from a repressive state. But to gain that protection they must submit to the control of the men of their community.

Western liberal philosophers have advanced civil society as the solution to the problem of state authoritarianism or despotism. If civil society consists of voluntary autonomous organizations capable of resisting arbitrary exercises of state power, it becomes important to assess what these voluntary organizations are. Professional associations, unions, political action groups, chambers of commerce, even religious fraternities may be considered part of civil society. All are in the "public domain." Most of these associations have been associated with men. Civil society is already identified or defined in a site from which women are thought to be excluded—the public domain. It has been characterized by sets of associations that are linked with male activity.

The construct of civil society assumes from the very beginning a split between public and private domains. It is based on an assumed three-way distinction between that which is kin-based and nonvoluntary, that which is non-kin-based, public, and voluntary—civil society—and that which is non-kin, public, and semi-voluntary—the state. That definition of what constitutes civil society is based on a gendered distinction between public and private domain. Men and male activity are associated with the public and women and female activity with the private. The civil society construct, a Western one, is now being challenged in the West by feminists and people of color. Its uncritical application to Third World countries and the uncritical use of the relative existence of components of civil society as measures of "modernity" or progress are highly problematic.

The distinction between what is public and what is private, and therefore the dichotomy that the concept of civil society rests upon, is even more problematical in the Middle East and North Africa than in the West. In many Third World countries, kinship and community are crucial organizers of social life. State institutions and civil society do not operate independently of kin-based and communal relations. A person in a position of power in a government office or a voluntary organization brings with him or her the obligations, networks, and rights of kin and community, and acts accordingly. Claims of kin and community precede those of state and civil society. Citizens may not separate public and private spheres. The boundaries in this triangulation of state, civil society, and kinship or private domain are highly fluid. People's commitments remain grounded in kin and community, and they carry those commitments with them, whether in the civil or state spheres. Men may be no less identified with kinship, and therefore private communities and obligations, than are women.

What is crucial for understanding the gendering of these relationships is not the split between public and private, or between civil society and state, or between civil society and the domestic, but rather how gender hierarchy operates. Patriarchy privileges males and elders, including elder women, but numerous other variables affect the operation of patriarchy—class, ethnicity, region.

Because men are very nested in familial and highly patriarchal communities, as nested as women, and states are often seen as repressive and external, it is in these communal-based relationships that both men and women find security. For many progressives in the Middle East and North Africa, gender issues are secondary; familial bonds are seen as sources of support and security against what is perceived as an even greater source of oppression, the state, even though many women would argue that gender oppression is as virulent as class or colonialism.

If one's rights are experienced as emerging more from being part of these familial, ethnic, sectarian communities than from being citizens of a state, then women are caught in a double vise, because these communities are highly patriarchal. The control of these communities over women's lives has in fact been reinforced by the state in many Middle Eastern states, with Tunisia and Turkey being partial exceptions. When the state intervenes actively to provide alternative arenas, at least in legal or administrative domains, for women's participation in society, it creates space for maneuvering and negotiation and, over the long run, for mobilization.

Some scholars argue that components of civil society operate as much to help the state exercise control as to hinder it. Hegemonic discourse in the West is often assumed to actually describe the empirical reality of the West. It is then used to dysfunctionalize Third World countries when those countries do not meet standards that often are not met even in the West. Distinctions between state and civil society, between civil society and the private sphere, and between the state and the private sphere are critical assumptions of Western political philosophy, but not always realities of Western political life. In both the West and the Third World these binaries are false. The problem of exclusion of women from the state has been accentuated by the attempt to separate these domains, according to many feminists. The attempts to separate state, civil society, and kinship wed women to the private domain and exclude them from the sphere of civil society and from the state.

The argument about whether there is a weak state or a strong state, a weak society or a strong society in the Middle East and North Africa, is specious. It is linked to an Orientalist perspective that sees other societies as seamless webs and the West as articulated and differentiated. The West is not as articulated and differentiated as the West presents itself to be. Citizens often do not perceive themselves as having rights as a result of their being citizens of a state. They perceive themselves as having rights because they are embedded in communities. And insofar as those communities are hierarchical and patriarchal, then the rights they perceive will be organized around those hierarchical and patriarchal structures of domination. Human rights advocates often assume universal understandings or attempt to achieve universal agreement as to the meaning of human rights. The universalization of human rights has been achieved by glossing the diversity of ways in which rights are understood. Western constructs of rights were premised on the construct of the autonomous, detached, contract-making, individualized, and masculinized person that emerged out of liberal bourgeois thought.

The construct of human rights is historically linked to the concept of the individualized citizen. For some scholars and activists, this has been problematic. A construct of citizen that is wedded to a particular concept of self may facilitate the dismissal of the rights of persons who do not share that sense of self. Creatively renegotiating the concepts of civil society, citizenship, and state not only allows for the possibility of the inclusion of women and other excluded groups, but also reveals that the ways in which men and women operate, act out their lives, maneuver, and negotiate are not inherently so fundamentally different from each other. Gender differences are constructed differences. Gender differences are historically and culturally constructed and reproduced through complex moralities, idioms, and structures of power. Feminist discourse attempts to destabilize the hegemony of these constructs and by so doing create spaces for experiments in alternate forms of relationships.

## Essays on Gender and Transformation in the Middle East and North Africa

The essays in this collection were written at different times during the life of the magazine *Middle East Reports* (previously *MERIP Reports*) published by the Middle East Research and Information Project. They capture some generalities about gender in the Middle East and North Africa at this moment. Like all aspects of social life, such gender-based analyses are continually shifting in response to dynamic transformations in culture and society. *Middle East Report* authors consider class, economic, and religious factors in understanding political dynamics as they examine topics such as the influence of state policy on women or the politics of male-female relations, not forgetting to address the question of how women themselves have acted and organized politically. Each essay encompasses a number of themes and all share the goal of analyzing the roles women have played in politics in a multi-causal way. They also raise questions about how women see themselves politically: in relation to the state, to men and to other women. They offer a range of examples of how gender issues interact with class, ethnic, religious and national factors. The reader is introduced, in these chapters, to many of the important thinkers on women's issues — Middle Eastern, North African, and Western. The bibliography also offers additional resources for further research.

The first four essays are introductory overviews that introduce trends found in later essays: the impact of rapid social change, criticisms of western political values and consumerism, the more recent disillusionment within the Arab world with the radical nationalisms of the 1950s and 1960s expressed in Nasserism, Baʿthism, and leftist ideologies, the rise of political Islamist movements, and the challenges to ideas of feminism in the region. All these political developments put pressures and limitations on how women are organized as well as creating potential for new ideas and initiatives.

Sarah Graham-Brown's essay looks at the historical context and political climate in which women's movements developed: anticolonialism, nationalism, and the development of new states. She tracks the differing histories of women's movements, such as that in Egypt which developed independently from the state, and those in Turkey and Iran which were coopted early on to serve state and national goals.

Suad Joseph critically analyzes the conditions for women's active participation in politics in the Middle East. Arguing that neither women nor men are political or apolitical in the abstract, she evaluates the conditions under which some of their activities come to carry a political charge and what counts as political change under different state and political regimes. Women can be mobilized into political action through kin, ethnic, or tribal groups, by class-based movements, gender-based movements, or as individuals drawn into the course of history in small or large actions. The forms and forums through which women participate are partly of their choosing and making, and partly shaped and constructed by the states and political environments in which they find themselves. For example, as the space for public action opens during certain historical circumstances, women tend to be more politically active, while they may appear or become more passive/inactive as state regimes actively control or regulate more of the public space. Joseph explores the questions of when women are mobilized, which women are mobilized, who mobilizes them, how they understand and participate in their mobilization, and how their mobilization differs structurally and symbolically from that of men of their societies.

Nadia Hijab challenges the assumption held commonly by both labor scholars and local men in the Arab world that women do not work. Work is heavily located in areas where it is "invisible," particularly in agriculture, in family-run businesses, in the domestic economy, and in other sites in the informal economy. The implications for women concerning their invisibility in the labor force are critical. Not only are they not recognized or acknowledged, but they tend not to receive access to training, credit, and technology. The effect is to reproduce women's invisibility, despite their centrality to national economies.

Deniz Kandiyoti, in her reassessment of issues of gender and citizenship, critiques the Orientalist tendency to view every issue in the Middle East and North Africa through the lens of religion, Islam in particular. Yet part of the conundrum for women, she observes, was the ambiguous incorporation of women into postcolonial states. Women were coded as universal subjects through the universalistic language of the formal constitutions of these states. At the same time women were coded as special subjects through the delegation of family law to religious courts and through their elevation to the special status of "privileged bearers of national authenticity." Focusing on the notion of women's rights, Kandiyoti evaluates the impact on women and citizenship of the coterminous demise of state-led models of development and the emergent critiques of modernity and developmentalism.

Mounira Charrad compares Tunisian, Algerian, and Moroccan state formation and their consequences for family law. Family law, covering marriage, divorce, child custody, and inheritance, is one of the most critical areas of law for gender politics. Tunisia is one of only two Middle Eastern/North African countries to have legislated a civil family code. Throughout the region, including Israel, family law has been left in the domain of religious law and religious courts. Yet family law is crucial to the process of state formation as it regulates reproduction of the basic unit of society, the family. Interestingly, Charrad argues, Tunisia, which made the most radical changes, was neither the most industrial (Algeria) or the most French influenced (Algeria) of the three North African countries that have shared a French colonial legacy. Charrad analyzes the family codes and the notion of the "ideal family" as an instrument in the process of state building in these three countries of the Arab Maghrib.

Since the 1980s, organized Islamist politics has become a feature of the political landscape, posing a challenge for women's organizations informed by secular leftist aspirations. In Egypt, a diversity of Islamist movements, from the Muslim Brotherhood — established in 1928 and at times engaged in the mainstream of politics — to secret militant groups such as Islamic Jihad, continue to provide child care and health care, services especially important to women but insufficiently maintained by the state. Women have also become involved in religious life and study, and in the political work of some Islamist movements. Karim El-Gawhary's interview with Heba Ra'uf Ezzat, described as an Islamist intellectual with liberal views, shows that ideas of liberation and change are not confined to secular movements.

Ellen Gruenbaum, analyzing the implications for women of the rise to power of the National Islamic Front (NIF) in the Sudan, argues that women inside the NIF have actively contributed to the new constructions of what a proper Muslim women should be. Despite the active involvement of Islamist women in the shaping of NIF policy, the NIF, in its ruling capacity, has focused primarily on "women" in the "Islamicization" of Sudanese society. NIF programs have renegotiated what is considered appropriate dress, employment, and health practices, as well as what is authorized as "authentic culture." Though clearly many women have resisted, the NIF's exercise of power through the vehicle of women's bodies and roles raises critical questions for the meanings of political Islam for women.

The Israeli-Palestinian conflict has dominated the period since World War II in the Middle East, affecting the whole region in terms of ideological perspectives and relations with Europe and the United States. Despite the pressures imposed by states, women continue to act politically and to organize in many contexts. As Rita Giacaman, Islah Jad, Penny Johnson, and Julie Peteet argue in three essays on Palestinian women, nationalist movements inspire and give legitimacy to women's movements, but they do not necessarily promote gender equality or restructure gender relations. Each essay shows how Palestinian women have organized outside the bounds of the state, whether in Lebanon or the West Bank and Gaza Strip. Indeed, Palestinian women's activism has a long history, going back to British Mandate times. However, since 1948 the experiences of those in the diaspora and those who remained in Palestine have developed differently. Stressing the multiplicity of routes such activism may take, and its complex relationship with political change, these authors describe how Palestinian women are active in response to differing situations.

The question of the politicization of the domestic sphere is raised by these essays on the political roles played by Palestinian women. In this long nationalist struggle, the domestic domain has often become part of the political terrain, both because domestic work and reproduction become political acts in support of the struggle and because there have often been violent intrusions into domestic space by soldiers and by warfare. Yet the experience of Palestinian women's political organizations suggests also that there is no simple linear movement from kin-based association to secular nationalist politics. Old structures of authority have reemerged — for example, Julie Peteet notes the emergence in Lebanon of "village associations" based on pre-1948 allegiances in Palestine — and here women play little active part. In contrast to Lebanon, Palestinian women's groups in the West Bank, and to a much lesser extent in the Gaza Strip, developed in the late 1970s with a degree of autonomy from the occupying Israeli state and from the mainstream of the PLO. Rita Giacaman and Penny Johnson offer a detailed account of the dilemmas faced by Palestinian women's groups emerging from the intifada: how are they to face the new Palestinian National Authority, itself under constant and severe pressure from Israel?

Yeşim Arat argues that, given their relatively early twentieth-century emancipation, women in Turkey have not had a history of protest against the state. The idea of liberation beyond emancipation, Arat contends, began in the 1980s when Turkish women began to defend their civil and social rights. That these feminist developments occurred at the time of the rise of political Islamic attempts to gain state power is not accidental. Despite the forward looking legal innovations in the early part of this century in Turkey, the Civil Code still considers husbands as heads of households, and women still experience citizenship primarily through their communities. And in spite of the recent experience of a woman as prime minister (Tansu Çiller), the struggle between secular and religious/communal notions of citizenship reveals the ongoing gendering of citizenship in Turkey.

Three essays on women in the Arabian peninsula stress the role of historical and nationalist contexts. Eleanor Doumato begins her essay with a discussion of two seemingly contradictory Saudi directives: banning women from taxis, yet permitting women to drive cars. Her essay shows how Saudi women are at the center of any national debate about culture and the role of the state as guardian of culture, as well as the complex ways in which nationalist, religious, cultural, and patriarchal ideologies inform and mutually support each other. Haya al-Mughni examines the development of women's organizations in Kuwait since the 1960s. Her analysis shows how the state, the male community, and elite Kuwaiti women share the same interests: to resist any meaningful changes to women's status. Sheila Carapico's analysis of Yemeni women draws on their public roles and civil rights to distinguish disparate historical contexts for women's rights. Are Yemeni women among the most "liberated" females in the Arabian peninsula, as Carapico asks, and what changes have taken place in women's lives under the newly united Yemen formed from the more conservative North and South Yemen, formerly the Arab world's only Marxist regime?

Fatemeh Etemad Moghadam also charts shifts over time in women's status by focusing on women's participation in the labor force in Iran. Covering the period from the time of the Shah's "Westernization" policies to contemporary "Islamization" during the postrevolutionary period, Moghadam argues for close attention to an array of complex factors that affect employment practices, whether they are ideologically-based government policies toward women or regional and global economic factors.

Susan Slyomovics and Lila Abu-Lughod's essays study representations of gender in the media, particularly in television. Abu-Lughod explores how Egyptian soap operas and television serials relate to rural women's lives in distant Upper Egypt, while Slyomovics reviews Algerian and Moroccan cartoonists' depictions of women and television during the Gulf War. Both authors outline the media's narrative conventions and visual cliches; both stress the multiple means by which audiences and readers rework meanings assigned to television programs and cartoon strips.

Finally, this volume raises the more general question of the relationship of organized women's activity in the Middle East and North Africa to women's movements in the West. Graham-Brown's essay notes that these relations can be problematic. In the Middle East and North Africa "feminist" is a provocative label, primarily because it signals to many people allegiance to an imported ideology regarded by many (including women) as unsuitable and dangerous. Alternatively, many Western feminists are culturally bounded in their view of Middle Eastern and North African societies. They accept stereotypes of women's roles and of Islam which emphasize passivity and deny the diversity of political experience revealed in these essays. Perhaps the most significant contribution of these articles is the questions they raise. They challenge many current theories about women's political participation in Middle Eastern and North African societies; they present us with richer approaches to what political participation has meant for women in this region and how emerging national states in the Middle East and North Africa have dealt with organized efforts by women to have their voices heard.

# Overviews

# Women's Activism in the Middle East
## A Historical Perspective

Sarah Graham-Brown

At the beginning of the twenty-first century, the Western image of Middle Eastern women's role in politics is contradictory. Individual women may be accepted in political roles but Middle Eastern women collectively are usually perceived as silenced and passive. On the one hand, through the 1990s, Hanan al-Ashrawi appeared as a sophisticated, articulate spokesperson for the Palestinians in the international arena. On the other, male politicians from Islamist groups in Algeria speak of women as subordinates who should not be allowed to work outside the home, let alone participate in politics.

These contradictory images reflect broader conflicts and debates in the Middle East over the nature of society and the status of women. These conflicts arise in part from the cumulative impact of a century of intense economic change and social dislocation, generating crises that have become particularly acute over the last decade. Women have been active political players throughout this process. They have not always won their battles, but there is no doubt that they have fought and organized for a variety of causes, including their own.

As early as 1911, Egyptian writer Malek Hifni Nasif stood up in an all-male nationalist congress and demanded that women have the right to be educated to whatever level they desired.[1] Ninety years later, women have much greater access to education and opportunities to work, in many countries they have the vote, and some positive changes have been made in the laws governing family and personal status.

Yet there has been no simple, linear "progress." Economic changes have altered expectations and patterns of family life, but not always to women's advantage. The extent and impact of economic, social, and legal changes vary greatly according to social class, geographical location and ethnic or national group. Today, struggles continue unabated over who should control women's lives, in the family and in the nation.

## Early Women's Organizations

Social and economic reform movements from the mid-nineteenth century onward frequently demanded that women should play a more active role in Middle Eastern societies. At first, these demands were put forward by men, but by the end of the nineteenth century women themselves were increasingly involved.

The earliest organized women's movements emerged from Turkey, Iran, and Egypt in the first decade of the twentieth century. Their demands, like those of male reformers, were for education and work opportunities and for reform of personal status and family law governing matters such as marriage, divorce, child custody, and inheritance. There followed pressure to end the strict segregation and seclusion of women practiced by the upper and middle classes. (Women from poor families often had to work both inside and outside the home, and complete seclusion was impossible for families sharing small and cramped living space.)

Most women involved in early reform movements came from well-to-do urban families, were brought up in seclusion or semi-seclusion, and were educated at home. They present an ironic counterpoint to the prevailing Western stereotype of such "harem" women as passive, ignorant, and subject to male whims.

From the first, the development of women's movements was intertwined with broader movements for political change and national independence. In Iran and Turkey, women's organizations developed rapidly after the collapse of autocratic regimes in 1906 and 1908 respectively. In the period of comparative openness that followed, women participated in political demonstrations and wrote in the press. Issues surrounding women's status, particularly education, were hotly debated, and women contributed to these debates.

After World War I, authoritarian nationalist governments emerged in both Iran and Turkey and began to coopt previously independent women's movements. In both countries, women were used as symbols of national modernity and secularization. While this improved their status in certain respects, the state permitted no autonomous action and thus marginalized women's own initiatives.

In Turkey, Kemal Ataturk's government initiated a major reform and secularization of the personal status law modeled on the Swiss legal code, rather than on the shari'a (Islamic religious law), and discouraged veiling and seclusion of women. In Iran, Reza Shah's regime implemented much more limited reforms of women's status: forcible abolition of veiling in the mid-1930s and improvements in access to education. In both countries, the women's movement was reduced to token official organizations.

Unlike Turkey and Iran, Egypt was under direct British colonial rule from the 1880s onward, and there an independent women's movement developed. Before World War I, women's groups had formed for a variety of purposes, from education and intellectual debate to charitable work. By the 1920s, leading women activists such as Huda Shaarawi and Nabawiyya Musa had made contact with the international feminist movement.

Women established their activist credentials during the Egyptian nationalist uprising against the British between 1919 and 1922. Women of all classes joined street demonstrations. Upper class women, still veiled, addressed crowds and confronted British soldiers. The wives and daughters of leading nationalist leaders deported by the British became involved in the leadership of the nationalist Wafd party.

The Egyptian Feminist Union, formed in 1924, was born out of the realization that very few male politicians were willing to campaign for women's demands. Over the next twenty years, the Union achieved limited practical successes: improvements in access to education, greater awareness of health issues affecting women, and minor legal changes relating to the minimum age of marriage. It did, however, succeed in making women's demands a matter of public debate and countered the image of women as passive and ignorant.

When new political upheavals shook Egypt in the late 1940s, with demands for British withdrawal from the Suez Canal zone and challenges to the corrupt monarchy, women were again active politically, but by this time the Feminist Union had lost much of its impetus. The focus had shifted again to national issues, and women activists worked mainly through political parties, including the Communist Party and the Muslim Brotherhood.

A major limitation of both the independent Egyptian feminist movement and the coopted movements of Iran and Turkey was that their work influenced only limited sections of society. The majority of women, who were poor and lived outside major cities, were scarcely touched by changes in legal status or by new educational and employment opportunities.

For the states that emerged from colonial rule in the Middle East, the "woman question" has great symbolic importance. Women are used as symbols of "modernization," or to promote "national culture," or to stress the preservation of "traditional values." Generally speaking, however, women's movements independent of the state have been allowed little or no space to develop.

State strategies regarding women differ considerably. Saudi Arabia and the Islamic Republic of Iran exemplify the theocratic imposition of strict public controls over women's appearance and behavior, enforced by agents of the state. In Lebanon, with its weak state and fragmented society, controls over women are largely enforced by community pressures. The very limited changes in personal status law in the Arab world have presented little challenge to male hegemony. Only in Tunisia and the former People's Democratic Republic of Yemen were changes made to favor women.

## Secularism and the State

Most "secular nationalist" states — for example, Egypt, Syria, Iraq, and Algeria — initiated changes affecting women's opportunities for education, health care, and improved access to employment. In these states, women's organizations have usually been closely linked with or part of the ruling political party structures. Their main role has been to mobilize women around the goals and tasks set by the party and the state. In Iraq, Suad Joseph argues, the official women's organization pursues goals set by the state: increasing women's participation in the work force when, as during the Iran-Iraq war, there were labor shortages, or, until the 1990s, attempting to loosen the bonds of tribe and family in favor of loyalty to the state and the party.[2]

Today there are more individual women's voices to be heard in the political and artistic arenas (art in the Middle East is seldom separated from politics). Yet collectively women still have little political influence. In contrast to Western feminist movements, enfranchisement has not been a major priority of women's struggles in the Middle East. Turkey has been a partial exception to this rule, but it is notable that there are fewer women parliamentarians there today than there were after women first got the vote in 1934. In general, the struggle for democratic rights for men as well as women has yet to be won in most Middle Eastern countries. In this respect, access to the right to vote is less significant than the right to organize without state direction and heavy censorship of unwelcome opinions.

One of the few women's groups to make enfranchisement its main demand was the Egyptian group Bint al-Nil (Daughters of the Nile), led by Duriyya Shafiq, in the early 1950s. Women did gain the vote in Egypt under Nasser in 1956, and subsequently the right to stand for election. Until the introduction of a multiparty system in 1979, only a handful of women were elected or appointed to parliament. Three women have held ministerial posts, all in the Ministry of Social Affairs. Since 1979, more women have been elected or appointed under a quota system of women-only seats. Almost all these women belong to the government party. Women in parliament have tended to pursue issues important to their party rather than to all women. The only occasion on which both independent opposition women and some women parliament members joined forces was to campaign against the rescinding of Egypt's liberalized personal status law at the beginning of the 1980s.

In the Gulf states, women have been denied the vote. The only exception is Kuwait, which finally granted women the vote in 1999. Some Kuwaiti women had been campaigning for enfranchisement of women since the 1980s, and women's role in resisting the 1990–91 Iraqi occupation contributed to the pressure for change.

The increasing importance of Islamist politics has not always prevented women from exercising the vote. Some Islamist groups have recognized the potential of women's votes to boost their own support. For example, women have not been deprived of the vote in Iran under the Islamic Republic despite the regime's highly misogynist attitudes, which have pushed women out of public life and limited employment in mixed work places. In Algeria, the Front Islamique du Salut (Islamic Salvation Front, or FIS) did not object to women voting but wanted to limit their employment outside the home. This policy may be motivated as much by high levels of male unemployment as by a moral or religious objection to women working.

The vote alone does not guarantee improvements in the overall status of women. Women can easily become ballot fodder for political parties, whether Islamist or secular. Where they have little liberty in other respects, they can be pressured into voting for the candidates chosen by husbands or male relatives.

## Nationalism and Women's Rights

Where nationalist struggles have been intense, violent and prolonged, for example, in Algeria and in the Palestinian-Israeli conflict, the outcomes of women's participation in political life have been more complex. Some women have risked their lives, and many have been imprisoned and tortured. Although women suffering these ordeals have sometimes been praised as heroic, fears and suspicions about their sexual vulnerability have often created painful problems when they return to ordinary life.

In Algeria, the early nationalist movement argued for improvements in women's status, but the major preoccupation was confronting French colonialism and its profoundly disruptive effect on Algerian society. Both the policies of the French colonial administration and those of the nationalist resistance had ambiguous effects on attitudes toward women. French efforts to promote the unveiling of women and the "modernization" of legal codes provoked opposition from Algerian nationalists who equated the preservation of national and cultural integrity with the "traditional" dress and behavior of women.

During the war of liberation between 1954 and 1962, women were not prominent in the leadership of the National Liberation Front (FLN), but they did play an active role in the resistance, mainly in "behind the lines" work and as couriers. While women often ran considerable risk of capture and torture, these new roles did not essentially challenge male authority. After independence, the FLN confined itself to general statements of principle on the status of women.

Some women were indeed held up as heroines, but this legitimation alone did not give women a voice in government or a base from which to put forward demands of their own. The Algerian constitution gave equal rights to all citizens, but until 1984 no changes were made in personal status codes, and social attitudes toward women receiving education beyond the primary level or going out to work remained restrictive. The 1984 changes in the personal status law were heavily influenced by male religious authorities, though modifications to the original draft were made after women protested in the streets. The present code still defines women almost entirely in terms of the family and institutionalizes family control over them.

"We don't want things here to go the same way as in Algeria" is a remark often heard among Palestinian women. Those active in demanding changes in attitudes toward women are acutely aware of the dangers inherent in putting off women's liberation until national liberation has been achieved.

Yet in the particular circumstances in which Palestinians find themselves there has been great pressure to do so.

Women have been organizing in Palestine since the end of the 1920s. The earliest women's organizations characteristically mobilized mainly urban elite women connected with the national leadership, although during the great Rebellion of 1936–39, many more women joined the nationalist resistance in both rural and urban areas. After 1948, the dispersion and exile of some 800,000 Palestinians fragmented communities and organizations. Some women remained active in social welfare roles or joined various opposition political movements in the Arab world, but not until the 1960s did formal women's organizations reemerge.

The General Union of Palestinian Women (GUPW), the main women's organization active in diaspora communities, began its work in the refugee camps of Jordan and Lebanon in the 1970s. The GUPW organized women in their communities and helped provide work and social support, especially in the many families with no male breadwinner. Generally speaking, it has not directly challenged the male-dominated leadership of the PLO or its attitudes toward women. Women have been regarded as important primarily to "serve the revolution," and are often held up as symbols of cultural integrity. The more conservative elements stress women's vulnerability to the "temptations" of mixing with men in political and military activities. At most the GUPW has mediated between these contradictory attitudes and supported women in their attempts to work and to participate in political activities outside the home.

In the Israeli-occupied West Bank and Gaza Strip, the urban and elite bias of women's organizations was gradually eroded under the pressure of occupation. New and more radical groups emerged by the end of the 1970s. Practical initiatives included supporting working women through trade unions, giving advice on labor problems, providing pre-school education and kindergartens, and working to mobilize women in rural communities, mainly around primary health care issues. The new women's committees did succeed in moving away from urban-centered and elite-dominated structures, but they were still caught up in the political factionalism dictated largely by the priorities of male political leadership.

The Palestinian uprising (intifada) in the Occupied Territories, which began in December 1987, mobilized more women than ever before, young and old, in refugee camps, towns, and even isolated villages. Heightened violence by Israeli occupation forces did not spare women, who were subjected to imprisonment and harassment. The involvement of women in the intifada, and their experience of politically motivated violence by Israeli forces, even inside their homes, even their experiences of imprisonment, have not always given them more independence or political status. In some cases, men have responded by taking a more protective and restrictive attitude. The ambiguous and not always sympathetic attitudes faced by women who suffered imprisonment and sometimes torture indicate the difficulties which Palestinian society has in dealing with this issue. While some observers feel that the political process of the intifada and women's involvement in it have brought real changes in attitudes toward women's political activism, others argue that this was at the expense of attention to women's own demands.

Until the 1980s, the secular nationalist movement had formed the mainstream of Palestinian politics. While its attitude to women's movements was certainly ambiguous, and women played little part in the leadership of the main political parties, it did allow some space for women to organize. The increasing influence of Islamist movements since the mid-1980s, notably the emergence of Hamas as a significant political force, particularly in the Gaza Strip, has set different agendas in regard to women. The most obvious feature, particularly in Gaza, has been the pressure for "modest" dress and the wearing of the hijab. However, this in itself may be less significant for many women activists than the limitations which the Islamist organizations wish to impose on the kind of work women can do, and the positions they can take on women's rights and participation in politics.

## The Politics of Personal Life

There has been a growing awareness among activist women in the Middle East that, even where women enjoy greater legal rights (for example, in Turkey or Tunisia) or improved rights to education and employment (as in Egypt, Syria, and Iraq), male control of women's personal lives and sexual behavior is little changed. This is highly controversial terrain. Women who challenge the patriarchal norms of virginity at marriage, male sexual freedom compared with control of women's sexuality, and, in some regions, genital mutilation, risk accusations of betraying their culture, their religion, and even their own sex. In the view of many, to challenge these norms is to accept Western norms of sexual and personal behavior. This is despite the fact that many women who are critical of their own culture are also critical of the West and its attitudes toward the Middle East.

While some of the ideas advanced on the politics of personal life may have been "seeded" from the West, their expression is shaped by the region's specific political and social context. Most women who regard themselves as feminists or campaigners for women's rights are acutely aware that they may be regarded as promoting ideas associated with cultures which have challenged and tried to subvert their own.

The Egyptian doctor and writer Nawal El-Saadawi has argued that women suffer severe damage from sexual repression and oppression by men, and that this internalized repression is passed from one generation of women to another.[3] While she is highly critical of genital mutilation, she points out that this practice is not in any sense Islamic and is prevalent in many non-Islamic cultures in Africa.

El-Saadawi regards Islam as having progressive potential for women, and objects to conservative interpretations which cast women only in subordinated roles. She also argues that the problems facing Middle Eastern women are compounded by the encroachments of Western cultural and economic imperialism. Women are therefore caught in the repressive social controls of their own society, while they are also prey to some of the worst aspects of Western "commoditization" of women. She also points to the impact of poverty and social inequality in determining women's status and opportunities, and contends that the overall lack of democratic rights has limited women's ability to organize.

Moroccan sociologist Fatima Mernissi has been an outspoken critic of the sexual double standards. She is critical of the role of religion, particularly Islam, in creating or legitimizing patriarchal power. She has argued that Islam regards female sexuality as active, but therefore potent and dangerous: capable of disturbing the social order and male morality. She also asserts that "Arab identity" has been conceived in a way that regards change as threatening to the moral order, and thus impedes the development of both democracy and the emancipation of women.[4]

## Islamist Influence

A prominent trend in the 1980s was the revival or creation of Islamist movements in most countries of the region. These have gained numerous women adherents, including many college graduates. These groups are far from homogeneous in their political stances, but have fairly similar views on the "woman question." They have played an influential role in setting the tone of debate in the 1980s, often putting their critics on the defensive. Their strong condemnations, not only of the encroachment of Western values in the Middle East but also of the "corruption" of indigenous moral values, has challenged exponents of women's rights in a more secular tradition.

Most Islamist groups stress the importance of male authority and emphasize the primacy of women's roles as wife and mother. They stress sexual purity and control, and the danger of losing it, as a justification for increased male supervision of women and for insisting on self-control by women themselves. Women activists working within Islamist groups clearly have to tread a fine line between political commitment and the pressure to prioritize the roles of wife and mother. The tension is not always resolved. For example, Zaynab al-Ghazali, who broke with the Egyptian Feminist Union to form the Muslim Women's Association, a group closely linked to the Muslim Brotherhood, claimed that she left her first husband over her devotion to political work. She included a clause in the contract for her second marriage that she would be free to do political work. Nonetheless, she frequently emphasized that a woman's first duty is to her family.[5]

The issue of women's dress has recently become the most visible symbolic sign of the struggle over women's identity. "Covering up," which became much more prevalent in urban society during the 1980s, can range from covering hair and throat and wearing modest clothes to full veiling and gloves. The importance ascribed to dress codes also reflects a broader concern over women's social and political roles and how these are symbolized. Many people in the region, not only Islamists and their sympathizers, regard this as a significant political issue.

Some women argue that "modest dress" frees women to move around the streets and the workplace without harassment by men. Opponents argue that it is another form of male control and male definition of women's space. They further aruge that it stigmatizes those who do not conform and denies women the freedom to decide on their own appearance: personal morality should not be confused with external conformity to norms of dress. One consequence of this visual divide has been to put considerable pressure on young women to adopt modest dress, and many do so, for a variety of reasons which may have little to do with adherence to an Islamist group or even with personal piety.

While some feminists view Islam, and indeed all the major monotheistic religions, as incompatible with women's emancipation or liberation, the majority of Middle Eastern women activists seek some kind of accommodation with religious belief, because of its critical role in indigenous culture. Some women have sought in the earliest days of Islam a model of women's role in society that differs from those which have evolved since. This has been a largely speculative and even polemical exercise, though historical research has helped to revise ideas about women's roles in Middle Eastern societies. Stereotypes of the passivity of Middle Eastern women in the face of oppression are embedded in most histories of the region written by Western and Middle Eastern male historians. Women and their concerns frequently have been omitted entirely from the historical record. Recent efforts to recoup this hidden history of women have challenged these assumptions and revealed a far more complex picture.

Recent historical work has shown that women often played active roles, and on occasion resisted oppression, both by the state and by their own menfolk. Some studies also suggest a considerable difference between the way women actually behaved and the prescriptive writings on "proper" female behavior that have come down to us from religious scholars and other male writers. Some recent films, novels, and plays have also challenged this assumption that men monopolized history and political action.

At the present time many Middle Eastern societies are going through particularly intense political and cultural identity crises, generally coupled with severe economic dislocation. In these circumstances, women's symbolic roles tend to take on added significance, to the detriment of women themselves. Women as activists and participants in political and social movements in the Middle East, continue to struggle as they negotiate and renegotiate the way they present themselves at home, in the workplace and in the larger political arenas of neighborhood and nation.

# Women and Politics in
# the Middle East

Suad Joseph

How are Middle East women political and how do they participate in states, movements, revolts, and revolutions? Few activities of ordinary people are self-consciously political. How
something comes to be seen as political at some times and
nonpolitical at others, and who gets to define it as such, are
basic questions. Neither women nor men are political or apolitical in the abstract. How their activities come to carry a
political charge must be understood in the context of their
particular histories and cultures. What counts as politics can
change dramatically as states consolidate and expand the public arena, as nationalist movements use traditional social
forms and roles to mobilize women, or as revolutionary conditions break down the barriers between the political and the
nonpolitical.[1]

Women's political participation has become an issue for
scholars mainly since the women's movement has sought to
mobilize women into political action. As a result of the wom-
en's movement, this issue is now firmly on the historical
agenda for scholars and activists alike. But women often do
not choose the moment and the context for their political involvement. Their political participation may be evoked by the
state, by rulers, and by politicians or others in authority.
Women become a subject of mobilization, targets of political
action programs, a mass to be welded into citizens or political
followers. As they are mobilized they may begin to assume,
for themselves and others, public identities apart from the
private ones of kin and community.

Depending on circumstances, women can be mobilized
as members of kin, ethnic, or tribal groups, as members of a

class or gender, or as individuals. In Egypt the Mubarak regime is attempting to recruit the support of middle and lower middle class women, while in Lebanon women have hardly experienced the state in their lifetime.[2] On the other hand, some Middle Eastern women have mobilized themselves as individuals — and at times in a gender-conscious way — as Raymonda Tawil's autobiography attests.[3]

When are women mobilized, which women are mobilized, who mobilizes them, and does their mobilization differ from that of men of their kin, class, ethnic group or region? Does the nature and impact of women's political mobilization differ if it is initiated by the state (Turkey, Iraq), by nationalist movements (Palestine), by revolutionary parties (Sudan), or by spontaneous revolt (Egypt, Iran)?[4] What happens to women when those mobilizers win or lose? Are there qualitative changes in women's status and conditions?

## Contest for Citizenship

In pre-state societies, politics, like economics and religion, is embedded in kin and communal relations. Politics becomes differentiated from kin and communal relations as states emerge. The competition for subjects often revolves around the creation and legitimization of hierarchically differentiated public (state) and domestic (kin, communal) spheres. But new states do not incorporate all their citizens equally. Some citizens are admitted to the public sphere, where matters of state policy are at issue. Others are restricted to the domestic sphere of kin and community. The more powerful public sphere is associated by some scholars with males and the domestic with females.[5]

The discourse of public/domestic domains in the study of Middle East women developed slowly compared with feminist studies of other regions.[6] More recent work has offered a more dynamic analysis of the nature of the public and the domestic, characterized by accounts of fluid and shifting relationships. The boundaries are neither fixed nor irreversible. The state expands and retreats, kin and communal groups gain and lose control over members. Women's location and the definition of their activities shifts as the boundaries move, or as they become more or less permeable.

The modern state not only formalizes politics, it also changes the nature of political conflict, diminishing the forms in which women might previously have participated. As the Egyptian state developed, formal politics expanded and women's participation declined. Periods in which the state retreated saw an expansion of informal (street) politics where women participated more actively. The strengthening of the state in Iran under the shah reduced local political factionalism and competition, an arena where women had been active. In contrast, women's informal networks can be politically significant in a weak state such as Lebanon.[7] Politics can also become an integral part of domesticity, as it did among Palestinian women in Lebanon. Women's domestic roles take on political significance, particularly as they become "producers of fighters."

The organization of society is much more contested in the Middle East than in the West. Middle Eastern states and their rulers have not succeeded as have their Western counterparts in imposing their hegemony. Kinship and communal power flourish: rulers rely on them as a mainstay of their power, while citizens turn to them to protect themselves from state repression or to compensate for inefficient administration.[8] The domestic sphere is a lively arena of social, political, and economic action in the Middle East, far more so than in the West. Locating Middle Eastern women primarily in the domestic domain does not have the same meaning or outcome as it does for Western women.[9]

## Women as Political Actors

How do women come to be seen as political — by states and rulers, by social movements, and by women themselves? In nineteenth-century Egypt, the state identified women as political, and in pre-1948 Palestine both the British authorities and the Zionist movement considered Palestinian women as agents and targets of political action. On the other hand, in the Algerian war of liberation and in the early part of the 1975 Lebanese civil war, women were able to carry out underground political activity because the authorities did not see them as political. Similarly, village women in Iran were seen as immune from harm because the authorities assumed that men were responsible for their women's political acts.

Uncovering the context of women's politicization may reveal possibilities and limitations. In Iraq, for instance, official mobilization of women has been less about liberating them and more about strengthening the state.[10] In the Palestinian struggle, women's questions have been largely muted. The agenda of the Sudanese Communist Party was to transform the polity but not the social arrangements subordinating women. Empowering women (at least in the Western meaning) does not appear to have been on the minds of the Iranian clergy.

When do women make women the issue of their political activism? Do they have to be detached as individuals from family and kin and community? Do they have to take up their own cause politically before any substantive change in their position can be achieved? Studies suggest that women's roles do not necessarily change as a result of their political participation, nor does activism inevitably bring structural changes in their lives. A potential for feminist consciousness may not lead to feminist action.

We must also ask when and how women become central to a political movement or process. In the Sudanese Communist Party women were a sort of Greek chorus; Egyptian and Iranian women have often been the emotional workers of political movements. Similarly, Palestinian women have been in secondary and supportive, not leadership positions. How can progressive movements incorporate women as both active participants and subjects of discourse at the center of their political life? Must women have a movement separate from progressive, nationalist, and liberation movements in order for them to champion successfully their own cause?

## Feminism, Nationalism, Class, and State

We need to look at the relationship of feminism, nationalism, class and state.[11] The Palestinian national movement gave women's participation in informal communal politics a national context and legitimacy. But this diluted a commitment to women's issues because the movement has carefully avoided challenging patriarchal structures, thus deflecting the emergence of feminist consciousness. In some sense, the absence of a Palestinian state inhibits the liberation of women. In Iraq, on the other hand, the presence of the state coopted the possibility of an autonomous women's movement.[12] Many Middle Eastern states have created women's organizations; their power, as with the General Federation of Iraqi Women (GFIW), derives entirely from their close ties with the ruling elite.

Politics in modern societies are linked to both gender and class. We need to ask whether working class or peasant women participate politically any less than men of their class. Some studies indicate that they do.[13] Class organization and membership affect the forms through which women participate, the processes in which they engage, the issues around which they mobilize, the social and political relationships they establish, the personal and social consequences of their political actions, and the durability of their participation. All of these questions need further study.

## Women's Political Participation

Women often seem to share patterns of political participation. For one thing, women are often found in gender-linked social spaces: in nineteenth-century Egypt, the street and the public square; in prerevolutionary Iran, in homes; in revolutionary Iran, the street. The *zar* can be seen as a prefigurative political form in the Sudan, even though women have also been active in work places. A formal definition of politics often defines women's political participation out of the picture. The informal spaces of female participation may be not only gender linked, but class-linked. Middle or upper class women may be less likely than working class women to act politically in the street, neighborhood or square. They may, on the other hand, be more likely to act through formal organizations: political parties, women's associations, philanthropic organizations, religious institutions, social agencies, and the like.[14]

Similarly, women are more likely than men to engage in certain political practices. Egyptian and Iranian women use the taunt. Because of their position in visiting networks, Iranian, Palestinian, and Sudanese women perform important emotional roles and help create social solidarity.[15] They may gather and pass on information to their men, persuade and cajole men to join factions, act as decoys and dramateurs. Women link factions, kin, and political groups.[16] Women's work proceeds even in turbulent times. They continue to perform important social rituals, hold families together and preserve social interaction.

The political participation of women described in these articles tends to be erratic, informal, and organized around men with whom they are connected in socially legitimate ways. The leadership of the Sudanese Women's Union was appointed by the male-run Central Committee of the Sudanese Communist Party. Palestinian women activists in the various revolutionary organizations take orders from their male-dominated leadership.

But we need to see the character of women's political participation in a cultural and historical context. The absence of women from leadership positions in these movements is not surprising, for women have been only minimally represented in the leadership of such movements even in the West. Furthermore, Palestinian men are also often mobilized through kin networks.

Rural Iranian and urban working class Egyptian men's political participation is also erratic. Perhaps men as well as women engage more actively in politics through informal channels. This is not to diminish the importance of the differences in men's and women's political participation, but rather to suggest the limits of broad generalizations. We always need to keep clearly in mind the specific context of both men's and women's participation.

How women's activism becomes legitimate also affects the nature and durability of their participation. Iranian women's activism was sanctioned by the clergy. Among Palestinians, and earlier among Algerians, women's activism was sanctioned by a popular resistance movement. In Iraq and Libya, the state sanctions women's participation. In Sudan, it was a political party, while in nineteenth-century Egypt women's activism was legitimated by popular social revolts.

Anthropologist Julie Peteet relates that a representative of the resistance movement may pay a visit when a Palestinian family objects to the political activism of a female member. This can be a powerful act of persuasion and legitimization. Similarly, the mass appeal of the Communist Party in the 1950s and 1960s served to legitimize women's activities in the Sudanese Women's Union.

Organized mass movements appear to have greater abilities to legitimate women's political participation than informal groups. Yet the fact that so many movements also recruit on the basis of primordial ties indicates that these affiliations and loyalties still are a significant, if indirect, avenue for legitimating women's participation.

How women's participation gains social approval affects the form and possibilities of women's activism. The fact that Iranian women gained legitimacy for their participation from the clergy, and most acted in the name of religion during the revolution, has meant that with the success of an Islamic revolution women are subjected to the clergy's definitions of what is appropriate political — and nonpolitical — behavior. That a secular nationalist movement has mobilized Palestinian women appears to have had quite different consequences.

## The Price of Participation

Women often pay a price for their political participation in ways that men do not. They may have to become "honorary males" to remain honorable and public. They may feel compelled to be more ethical than most women, as members of the General Federation of Iraqi Women reported to me. They may face negative sexual or political labeling if they raise feminist issues. They may have to drop out of political activism periodically to enjoy female-linked roles or activities.

This price that women pay for their political participation may be affected by their class membership, family background, or financial autonomy. How are women, as compared to men, rewarded for their sacrifices by kin and communal groups, by public agencies, by the state? We should try to learn how the known costs affect women's willingness to participate politically.

Much remains to be done to understand Middle Eastern women's political activism inside and outside political movements. Toward that end, further work can develop historically and culturally specific analysis. Only if we understand clearly the specificities of Middle Eastern states, classes, and ideological formations can we apprehend the necessary context for evaluating women's place in politics today.

# Women and Work in the Arab World

Nadia Hijab

According to a labor force participation survey published in the mid-1980s, when men in rural Syria were asked whether their wives worked a large proportion replied that they did not. But when the question was rephrased as, "If your wife did not assist you in your work, would you be forced to hire a replacement for her?" the overwhelming majority answered yes.[1] This was just one striking example of the invisibility of Arab women in the workforce some two decades ago. Other examples abounded: in Egypt, where women were thought to comprise 11 percent of the total labor force, samples of rural households in Lower Egypt revealed that half the wives plowed and leveled the land and between 55 and 70 percent were involved in agricultural production. In Upper Egypt, between 34 and 41 percent were involved in agricultural production and 75 percent were engaged in animal husbandry.[2]

On the face of it, the situation of Arab women at that time was not unusual in comparison with other regions; however, both then and now the invisibility of women in the Arab world appears to be more serious than that of women in the rest of the world. Does this mean that social and cultural factors are more of an impediment to women's work in the Arab world than in other parts of the world?

Before addressing this question, it is worthwhile first to review quickly perceptions about women's work in the rest of the world in the 1980s and 1990s. Research on women in both industrialized and developing countries since the 1970s had uncovered a vast army of "invisible women" whose work was neither reflected in national statistics nor compensated in monetary terms, yet who worked, on average, longer hours than men. Most of these "invisible" women worked in agriculture or other family-run businesses, in the domestic economy, or elsewhere in the informal sector. For example, in India, when the revised definition of economic activity introduced by the International Labour Organization (ILO) was applied, initial estimates that only 13 percent of all women were economically active had to be revised upward to 88 percent.[3] The consequences of invisibility were serious indeed, as feminists frequently pointed out: if the women were not even recognized as workers, they were certainly not going to be given access to the training, credit, and technology of modernizing societies.

One would have expected these revelations to result in recognition of the importance of women's economic roles, both paid and unpaid. However, by the mid-1990s the problem of the invisible woman was so acute that the subject was tackled by the annual Human Development Report published by the United Nations Development Programme in 1995, just in time to contribute to the decisions of the Fourth World Conference on Women held in Beijing in September of that year. The report estimated the undervaluation of women's economic contribution at $11 trillion a year. It said:

Of the total burden of work, women carry on average 53 percent in developing countries and 51 percent in industrial countries. On average, about half of this total work time of both men and women is spent in economic activities in the market or in the subsistence sector. The other half is normally devoted to unpaid household or community activities. Of men's total work time in industrial countries, roughly two-thirds is spent in paid activities and one-third in unpaid activities. For women, the situation is the reverse. In developing countries, more than three-quarters of men's work is in market activities.[4]

A decision to invest in national statistics that more accurately reflect women's economic activity was one of the outcomes of the Beijing Conference.

As noted above, women in the Arab world[5] either suffer from the worst case of invisibility around the world or are indeed the least economically active women. In 1970, women were reported to account for less than 10 percent of the adult work force in six Arab countries for which there were data, less than 20 percent in five countries, and less than 30 percent in another six countries.[6] By 1995 there had been some improvement, with women reportedly accounting for less than 20 percent in six countries, less than 30 percent in eight countries, and less than 35 percent in three countries.[7] However, Arab women's share of the labor force in 1995 was significantly lower than the average for other developing countries, which was 37 percent for countries enjoying high human development (the five Arab countries in this category ranged from 13 percent in the United Arab Emirates and Qatar to 31 percent in Kuwait); 43 percent for countries in the medium human development range (the 10 Arab countries in this group ranged from 13 percent in Saudi Arabia to 34 percent in Morocco); and 38 percent for countries in the low human development range (the four Arab countries in this group ranged from 27 percent in Yemen to 44 percent in Mauritania, whose share was much closer to that of other African countries than to that of Arab states).[8] Arab women's share of earned income was, in 1995 the lowest of any region around the world.[9]

## The Sociocultural Framework

Do Arab women face greater cultural or social constraints as they seek entry into the modern workforce? There are no definitive answers to this question, but it is clear that this part of the world does attach great importance to its cultural identity, and to the role of women in the family in preserving this identity, although things have begun to change, as a look across decades reveals. For example, the report presented by the Economic and Social Commission for Western Asia (ESCWA) to the 1985 Nairobi United Nations Conference on Women began with a cultural definition of the region that no other area felt necessary to emphasize: "The Strategy for Arab Women in Western Asia to the Year 2000 is based on the heritage of Arab-Islamic civilization and the religious and spiritual values of this region, the cradle of the messages of God which affirm the dignity and freedom of all human beings in this universe."[10]

The effort to define and construct Arab identities in the era of nation-states has been made more complex by the many ethnic and religious groups in the region. The majority of Arabs are Muslims, but some countries include large Christian and other religious communities that are among the oldest in the world. While the majority of the region's inhabitants believe in a shared ethnicity, there are large groups of non-Arabs who live in the Arab region, including Kurds and Berbers. Post-independence efforts to define Arab identities in ways that would encompass the diversity in the region — for example, Arab nationalism or socialism — foundered because of, among other things, autocratic rule and incompetent economic policies. More recently, weak state systems have been unable or unwilling to challenge Islamist forces who seek to impose their own definition of identity on society at large.

For women, the implications of this phase of the continuing search for identity are perhaps most stark in Algeria, where Islamist militias have targeted women as well as men in their current conflict with the government. During the 1970s and 1980s, the Algerian debate on personal status (family) law was heavily influenced by the concern to preserve an "Arab-Islamic" heritage. The struggles in Arab society over the construction of identities and heritage is tied to efforts to preserve the family and community. As in other parts of the world, such as southern Europe or Asia, where strong family ties predominate, many Arabs tend to view the family as the linchpin of society, and women as the core of the family. Many family functions have not been, and cannot be, replaced by state institutions. Besides warmth, companionship, and moral support, the family provides material benefits such as social security and employment, by caring for the infirm and the unemployed, and promoting family-run businesses or family contacts in the private and public sector.

The ESCWA report mentioned above dedicated an entire section to the family, giving it more prominence than did reports from other regions: "Constitutions, charters and legislation in the region have asserted the role of the family as the nucleus of social organization in Arab societies. It is necessary, therefore, to make available to the family the economic, social, cultural and psychological conditions that would ensure its stability and satisfy its needs."[11] The determination to support the Arab family is not, in theory, supposed to be at the expense of women's other roles. The document explicitly endorses "the right of women to choose their roles in and out of the family." Elsewhere, however, it accords "priority to the work of women who devote their time to family and home affairs and hence ensure the continuity of generations, the cultivation of values and the transmittal of knowledge and expertise from one generation to another."

How are these conflicting textual messages reflected in actual lives? Throughout the Arab world, people both see the need for social change and feel threatened by it. Libya, for example, sought to integrate women into that country's modern workforce by promoting education and employment (Muammar Qadhafi used to create a stir with his flamboyant use of female guards when he traveled abroad). Libya is also one of the Arab countries to have ratified the International Convention on the Elimination of All Forms of Discrimination Against Women. But when Qadhafi spoke to a conference on the Arab and African family in Benghazi in 1990, he dwelt at length on family problems in the West, the importance of having a stable home environment for children, and the role of mothers. He repeatedly attacked the use of day care centers as places to dump children, calling on Libyans to march against them and to bring up their children themselves. The requisites of modern society, however, are such that Libyan women continue to make use of such facilities. The day after Qadhafi's speech, one could visit a center run by the Libyan Women and Family Department and see what looked and sounded very much like a day care center, a place teeming with children and a line of mothers pulling up their cars in front of the door to drop off their offspring before going to work. "This is not a kindergarten," one woman manager carefully explained to me. "It's a children's 'club.' Children can spend an hour or two here, or all day if they like."

## Alternative Framework

By 1994, there was enough mobilization and awareness among women in the Arab world about their socioeconomic rights and conditions, that there was a virtual revolution at the preparatory meeting convened by ESCWA in November to finalize the region's contribution to the Beijing Conference. This was not apparent at the start of the meeting, when ESCWA circulated a draft plan of action based on the reports submitted by its member governments. This draft, like the 1985 document, made many references to culture and tradition. To take just one example, the 1994 draft called on Arab governments that had not ratified the International Convention on the Elimination of All Forms of Discrimination Against Women to do so, but it did not insist on removal of reservations by those countries that had made them, which is what the international women's movement called for. On the contrary, it suggested that Arab countries should lobby at the international level to change the Convention itself to bring this more into line with Arab culture and tradition.

But when the government delegates began to discuss the draft, it turned out that they were much more progressive than the national reports their governments had submitted. ESCWA had invited representatives from North African governments to participate, and they were among the most progressive. The participants made a major decision not to ground the plan of action in past documents, but rather to draw on the ten-point agenda that other regions were using for the Beijing Conference. Another important decision was to base the text on the recommendations of recent United Nations conferences "of relevance to women and children," including the 1993 World Conference on Human Rights and the 1994 International Conference on Population and Development.

The effect of these two decisions was a major shift in framework — from the Arab-Islamic heritage to the international arena, and from an Islamic framework to a secular one. The 1994 document states, once, in paragraph 4: "The Arab plan of action draws on the features of Arab civilization, the values of revealed religions, and human civilization." It is interesting that the change of the term "Arab-Islamic heritage" was proposed by the Lebanese delegation, on the grounds that there were other religions in the Arab region. This was accepted by the delegates without any difficulty. The 1994 final document also speaks of respecting "women's rights as a human being and her participation in development and its benefits as a condition for comprehensive and sustainable development." The words "rights" and "equality" had been missing from the 1994 first draft.

The delegations most active in bringing about change included Egypt, Jordan, Lebanon, Morocco, Palestine, Tunisia, Algeria, and Yemen. The Sudanese delegation made the most protests on cultural and religious grounds. Eventually, the Sudanese delegation had to be content with registering some reservations on the final text. The Sudanese reservations were balanced by the Algerian delegation, whose delegates spoke forcefully and movingly against the misuse of Islam as a tool of terror against women. The Algerian minister described how fundamentalists were seeking to impose the veil and to prevent women from participation in public life. She received a standing ovation on more than one occasion.

Part of the credit for introducing new issues into the text goes to Arab women's nongovernmental organizations (NGOs), which lobbied strongly against the initial draft, and insisted on the inclusion of issues like violence against women. Indeed, it is worth noting that NGO participation in a forum held just prior to the official meeting far exceeded the planners' expectations. They had expected some 300 participants; 900 came. This is a reflection of the increased interest in and activism on women's issues.

This grassroots activism was also expressed at the global NGO Forum held in Beijing in September 1995 alongside the official intergovernmental conference. For example, a group of Arab women lawyers and activists convened a large meeting of Arab women at the Forum — they called themselves an Islamic Parliament — in order to discuss family law in Arab countries.[12] The idea began in 1992 when women lawyers and human rights activists from the Arab Maghrib decided to prepare for Beijing by looking at the family law in their countries and seeing how it could be improved. They organized as a group called "Maghreb '95," and held a series of seminars and workshops. By the end of the process, they had proposed 100 measures and modifications to the family laws. They invited women from around the Arab world to become parliamentarians and to discuss the laws at the meeting in Beijing. The proposals were published and disseminated widely, and all the women who participated in the Islamic Parliament adopted the 100 proposals for discussion and action when they went back home. It is worth noting that Arab government delegations to the intergovernmental conference at Beijing were somewhat more conservative than had been the case at the preparatory meeting in November 1994; however, all world governments were there, and after much debate a Platform for Action was adopted by consensus on ways to achieve equal rights for women.

Therefore, considerable social and cultural change has been taking place in the Arab world. Yet the figures on women's participation in the labor force remain lower than those in other regions. Can one attribute this to culture and tradition, arguing that the region is uniquely conservative? Heritage, identity, religion, patriarchy, the family and community, and women's central role within the family are issues not unique to the Arab region. Documents from all four United Nations world conferences on women held since 1975 identify the obstacles that continue to block the advancement of women everywhere as deeply-rooted traditions, poor understanding of the significance of women's issues, and lack of financial resources to reform the position of women. Both the language and the issues in the debate on women's roles in the Arab region should be familiar to students of nineteenth and early twentieth century Europe and North America, when rapid industrialization also spawned debate about women's roles within the family and society. Current controversies in the United States under the rubric of "family values" indicate the persistence of this debate in the West.

Therefore, it is not enough to look only at cultural factors in assessing women's potential to participate in the labor force. Other factors are equally important, including those that affect women's ability to participate in the workforce, as well as those that affect their opportunity to do. An accurate picture of the situation requires an examination of three interlinked factors: the need for women's work, whether as a result of national economic development or of the need for more family income; the opportunities for women's work that are created through legislation and the removal of sociocultural barriers; and the investment in women's abilities through education and training. In fact, in the Arab world, as elsewhere, whenever there has been a need for women's work — by society or by the family — there have been no serious sociocultural obstacles to Arab women's participation.

## Mix of Factors

Unfortunately, Arab economic conditions do not encourage women's work. Arab economies have been shifting rapidly from a subsistence basis, where work is done primarily at home, to one where labor or skills are exchanged for wages in the marketplace. This has meant that both men and women, rural and urban, have had to seek work outside the home or neighborhood, often moving from the countryside to the city, or even from one country to another, to do so. As a result of rapid population growth and urbanization, governments have found it hard to generate employment and maintain health, education, and welfare services. Unlike other parts of the world, however, modernizing Arab economies had not yet created a pressing demand for women's work. Global and regional recessions, together with the global financial crisis, have brought serious unemployment to all but a few oil-rich Arab states with small populations.

As economies modernize and subsistence agriculture gives way to cash crops, women's traditional productivity is frequently undermined, without other income-generating avenues opening up. General ignorance of women's traditional productivity has repercussions not just for women but for the region at large. By the year 2000, per capita food imports were expected to rise to $300 annually. In the last years of the twentieth century, Arab states, with just 4 percent of the world's population, imported around 13 percent of the world's food output, and 20 percent of the world's cereals, using up hard currency that could be productively invested. This situation can be partly attributed to economic mismanagement and to environmental factors, but the belief that Arab women have marginal roles in agriculture is also a contributing factor.

Interestingly, those countries that have had the resources to do so have invested significantly in the education of their populations, many achieving parity between boys and girls up to and including secondary education. There is some way to go. In 1998 the Arab states had a higher combined first-, second-, and third-level gross enrollment ratio for women than Africa and South Asia (52.7 percent, 38 percent and 43.8 percent respectively), although they were lower than East Asia (62.4 percent) and Latin America and the Caribbean (68.7 percent).[13] This clearly helps promote women's access to the labor market. Jordan, for example, had made substantial investment in women's education and training by the 1970s. When the country faced labor shortages because of extensive male labor migration to the Gulf, there was a pool of skilled female labor from which to draw. The government actively pro-

moted women's participation in the modern workforce through consciousness raising seminars and legislation. At the same time, as inflation cut into
family incomes, families also actively encouraged participation of women in
the labor force.

The trend toward more female participation in Jordan's modern workforce slowed by the mid-1980s due to recession, and later as a result of the
return of many male labor migrants. The government's interest in woman's
labor has waned, as has happened in other societies in similar circumstances
(for example, in Britain and the United States after the two world wars). Yet
family need for women's income remained high. Jordan's Business and Professional Women's Club drew attention to women's pressing need for wage
employment. "At one point," the legal counseling staff explained, "600
graduates came to us wanting work, so we organized a conference on female
unemployment in 1985, which we followed up in early 1989 with a conference on women and work."

By contrast, in the Arab Gulf states, although there is a pressing need
for labor power and there have been substantial investments in education,
women's labor force participation remains low. This is because, among other
things, oil wealth has allowed governments to import foreign labor. The need
for women's income at the family level, moreover, is not as pressing as it is in
other countries. Here again, economic factors are important to an accurate
understanding of women's labor force participation.

Education sometimes has an adverse effect on women's economic productivity. Schools in the Arab region often foster dismissive attitudes toward
manual labor, which has exacerbated productivity problems. In Jordan, secondary school graduates would wait at home until "their turn" came for
government jobs. An innovative approach to this problem was adopted by a
Jordanian project manager, the director of a center for social services in the
village of Husban, who saw that many of her center's income-generating
projects (knitting, dressmaking, traditional handicrafts, medicinal herbs)
were not as successful as anticipated, mainly because of problems with quality control and marketing.[14] She also noted the relatively high net profits
cash-crop farmers secured. So she set about encouraging village women to
return to agricultural production, leasing land in the area. She convinced
male household heads to allow their wives to participate in lentil production,
not for wages but for a share in the net profits. Since the women were able to
avoid being perceived as wage laborers and were able to choose working
hours that fit their domestic duties, husbands were not threatened.

As is the case with regard to education, Arab labor laws are generally fair to women and abide by international standards. Legislation in areas such as maternity leave, time off for child care, and protection from dismissal because of pregnancy is adequate. However, as in countries elsewhere, application of the law is easier in the public than in the private sector. For example, in Egypt, where the law requires companies to have onsite child-care facilities when they employ over 100 women, many stop just short of employing that number.

The public sector generally offers the most trouble-free and respected employment for Arab women, and for women in such jobs the problems and benefits are similar the world over: the double work load, difficulty of finding good child care, and lack of husband's support with household chores. Arab women also account for a small but visible share of the professional class in the region, averaging about a third of that category for those nine countries for which data were available in 1995.[15]

## Power for Change

Clearly, Arab women have less access to the modern workforce than men do, although prevailing economic conditions have made full employment a distant dream in Arab and other societies. To what extent do Arab women have the power to address their socioeconomic position? The number of women in formal power structures is low in the Arab region, as elsewhere, and there are few formal democratic structures for either men or women in the region. Women's influence in society is primarily expressed through traditional structures, such as in family ties, where women's power and status increase with age and the number of children they bear, and through women's organizations.

There has been a change in the approach of women's organizations in recent years, moving from an agenda of nationalism, development, and feminism to one stressing the gender dimensions of socioeconomic change at the policy level. In the occupied West Bank and Gaza, the grassroots Palestinian women's committees that emerged in the late 1970s, for example, brought in a new, politicized generation of women and new organizational techniques. The committees have spread social as well as nationalist consciousness from urban to rural areas while offering services in health and education, along with a range of income-generating activities.

Recently Palestinian women in those areas have moved to set up some five independent women's research centers that articulate a frankly feminist agenda and seek to keep a distance from the factional differences that have affected the Palestinian women's committees. The centers see their role as advocates for policy reform so as to create an enabling environment for women's socioeconomic and political rights. They plan to lobby the new Palestinian authority for services rather than provide services themselves, and to train women in political and other skills to enable them to argue their case. They are tackling hitherto little discussed issues related to women's legal and economic status, such as violence in the family, inheritance, school dropout rates, and women's economic activities in the informal sector.

Organizations with a sharper feminist focus have also emerged elsewhere in the Arab world. In addition to university departments in Lebanon, Egypt, and Algeria, there are well-established women's research networks in North Africa, and a regional Arab Women's Training and Research Center in Tunisia was set up in 1992 with United Nations support. An independent Arab women's publishing house, Nour, was established in Cairo in 1993.

Social and cultural traditions certainly bear on women's status, but it is misleading to see these as the only predominant factors affecting women's entry into the workforce. In the Arab region, tradition has often served as the ready answer for those in search of simple explanations to complex phenomena, or as the excuse of policymakers unable to generate enough employment for men or women. The emerging feminist understanding in different parts of the Arab region is a sign that women are preparing to fight for their social, economic and political rights on their own terms. They will not be alone. The fourth world conference on women in Beijing was evidence, should this be necessary, of the shared problems that women face worldwide, and of their determination to keep organizing until these problems are resolved.

# The Politics of Gender and the Conundrums of Citizenship

Deniz Kandiyoti

For a long time anyone attempting to address questions relating to women's human and citizenship rights in the Middle East came up against a persistent tendency to articulate these issues with exclusive reference to Islam. With hindsight, it is possible to recognize that this was not merely the product of a lingering Orientalism but was also indicative of the profoundly ambiguous terms under which women were incorporated into the postcolonial nation-states of Muslim societies: as part-beings caught between the contradictions of universalist constitutions defining them as citizens, of shari'a-derived Personal Status codes limiting their rights in the family, and of a postcolonial malaise burdening them with being the privileged bearers of national authenticity.[1]

In this chapter, I revisit my earlier attempts to foreground the role of the postcolonial state for a more contextualized understanding of women's rights, acknowledging that this work was meant to capture a specific historical moment, namely the phase of nation-building and state consolidation.[2] Although this was a decisive phase leaving varied legacies that had an important bearing upon the politics of gender in different countries, processes of economic liberalization in the Middle East and North Africa and the ascendancy of neoliberal policies have contributed to significant shifts in state-society relations that require fresh thinking on the issues of democratization and citizenship in general and women's rights in particular. The demise of state-led models of development also coincided with critiques of modernity and developmentalism, often drawing their inspiration from poststructuralist and postcolonial criticism. This body of scholarship drew attention to the politics of modernity as a regulatory discourse creating new forms of subjection and exclusion rather than fulfilling promises of universal emancipation. The particular conjuncture of preoccupations about those marginalized or excluded from modernity, mainly understood as Westernization, and the simultaneous rise to prominence of political Islam gave discussions about civil society in the Middle East a distinctive slant dominated by contradictory pronouncements about the perils of fundamentalism on the one hand and the appearance of alternative modernities or, indeed, postmodernities on the other. Critiques of modernity found echoes in a parallel body of feminist scholarship which exposed the gender-biased and masculinist premises of universalist discourses about rights and citizenship in the West.[3] The search for alternative formulations and more inclusive conceptions of citizenship and democracy opened up a rich field of debate which revealed important disagreements among feminists over what these concepts should entail.[4] In the Middle East, this debate is considerably impoverished by the fact that it is often narrowed down to the question of whether Islamist agendas are able to accommodate or express feminist aspirations, albeit in different terms from those of the West. There is a culturalist bias in this discussion that reduces it to querying whether certain conceptions of rights and citizenship, or for that matter of feminism, may find any resonance in a Middle Eastern environment. We may inadvertently revert to treating Islam as reflective of some cultural essence that informs indigenous conceptions of rights, social justice, or citizenship rather than reminding ourselves that "there are as many Islams as there are situations that sustain it."[5] In what follows, I shall restate the case for the contingency of the relationship between Islam and women's rights and suggest that the problems we experience in dealing with questions of citizenship are partly due to the fact that we have not yet found an adequate language with which to talk about state-society relations in the Middle East.

## Islam and the Politics of Gender: A Contingent Relationship

My original argument set itself the limited objective of demonstrating the contingent relationship between Islam and women's rights. It centered around the proposition that the relationships among Islam, the state, and the politics of gender comprised at least three distinct components: links between Islam and cultural nationalism; processes of state consolidation and the modes of control states establish over local kin-based, religious, and ethnic communities; and international pressures that influence priorities and policies.

The first component, nationalism, introduced the possibility of significant variations in the deployment of Islam in relation to different nation-building projects, with important consequences for legal frameworks and social policies. Although a shared history of colonial encounters with the West can and does encourage a defensive rallying around the symbols of Islam, none being so potent as the veil, the trajectories of postcolonial states are too diverse and complex to be reduced to mere effects of their colonial histories. I found the conventional wisdom linking Muslim women's varying predicaments to the dynamics of colonial domination and indigenous resistance quite limiting.[6] I argued, instead, that cultural nationalism, itself animated by the contradictory logic of popular sovereignty and the expansion of citizenship rights, on the one hand, and the reaffirmation of authentic cultural values, on the other, assigned women an ambiguous position by defining them as both citizens of the state and the privileged custodians of national values.[7] These built-in tensions could culminate in the uncritical acceptance of versions of cultural integrity that are coterminous with the patriarchal control of women, especially at junctures when ethnic and communalist tensions erase any secularist pretensions that the state might have had.[8] I have argued elsewhere that these tensions and contradictions act to limit women's claims to enfranchised citizenry.[9]

The second component, namely the process of state consolidation, was also rich in paradoxes. The expansion of modern states resulted in various forms of encroachment upon subnational entities based on ethnic, religious, and tribal affiliations and their incorporation into the nation-state as the primary locus of loyalty and allegiance. There were not only significant variations in the strength of this unifying, secularist impulse (one only has to think of the contrast between the centralist Turkish state and Lebanon, which retained the contours of the Ottoman *millet* system and incorporated it into its modern system of governance) but the question of whether the modern nation state ever took hold in the Middle East became the subject of a heated controversy.[10] This controversy goes to the heart of whether notions of modern citizenship and political participation have any place in Middle Eastern polities, a proposition denied by those Sadowski labels as "neo-orientalists."[11]

Without having to engage with this broader debate, it is important to note the contradictions inherent in processes of nation-building from the perspective of women's rights. On the one hand, the developmentalist agenda of early periods of national consolidation encouraged women's education and labor force participation. This legitimized women's greater public visibility. It also cast modernizing elites in the role of enlightened vanguards who resorted to various forms of social engineering to confront the "obscurantism and ignorance" of local communities whose lifeways could be devalued and policed.[12] Nonetheless, the management of patriarchal sensibilities always remained high on political agendas as a central plank of populist consensus.[13] On the other hand, the expansion of women's social and political rights was promoted by authoritarian, *dirigiste* regimes that typically discouraged the development of an associational sphere where women's interests could be autonomously represented. Nonetheless, despite the circumscribed nature of the gains achieved, growing constituencies of educated, professional women did develop a major stake in both defending and expanding their citizenship rights.

Finally, conflicting international and regional pressures produced contradictory consequences at the local level. On the one hand, the United Nations system and major international aid donors exerted pressure on governments to create national machineries for the "advancement of women." This stimulated the growth of a women's NGO sector involved in a wide range of activities from service delivery and development projects to rights advocacy, sometimes providing platforms for feminist activists. On the other hand, both aid from oil-rich Gulf countries and the growth of local Islamist grassroots organizations promoted an agenda centering around the virtues of Muslim domesticity. Governments were often caught in the crossfire of these conflicting demands, attempting at times, to comply with international conventions and, at others, to placate internal constituencies opposing an expansion of women's rights.[14]

The above considerations amounted to a comprehensive repertoire of the flawed and limited nature of women's rights in the Middle East and of the obstacles in the way of their realization. The tenuousness of women's hold on the realm of citizenship is most starkly illustrated whenever the issue of their rights is opened to renewed debate and becomes the subject of contestation, sometimes through the medium of violence.[15]

The terms of this debate have been further complicated by the appearance of two phenomena alluded to earlier: processes of economic restructuring and liberalization that have curtailed the role of the postcolonial state as the principal agent of economic and social transformation, and critiques of development and modernity which have subjected the legacies of elite-led modernization to close scrutiny. The local concerns that these global developments gave rise to have been quite distinctive. In the Middle East, the debates on democratization and civil society, which generally coincided with the ascendancy of neoliberal economic policies, tended to focus on the challenge of political Islam and on prospects for political pluralism.[16] Critics of development and modernity targeted both the colonial legacy of modern states and the national development trajectories of post-independence regimes.[17] This critique encompassed the effects of state-led modernization on the politics of gender. A cleavage appeared between those who endorse state action as potentially progressive and emancipatory when it results in the expansion of women's education and employment opportunities, and others who are less sanguine about the benefits of state-led emancipation.[18] These divergences also make themselves felt in assessments of the effects of Islamist mobilization for women, variously evaluated as a threat to their civil rights or as offering alternative avenues for voice and empowerment. One of the major limitations of these debates is that they continue to take place in a framework that is implicitly informed by the concepts of tradition and modernity, each corresponding to the contradictory pulls of indigeneity and Westernism. This false dichotomy means that one is constantly confronted with the largely irrelevant question of whether Islamisms are negations or alternative expressions of modernity, rather than addressing the more pertinent issue of identifying the type of politics embodied in state or oppositional projects which make references to secularism or Islam. Equally important are the debates that surround the nature of state-society relations and whether the state or civil society constitute appropriate arenas for the articulation of more gender-equitable notions of citizenship.

## Caught in Between: Women, State, and Civil Society

There is a striking degree of ambivalence vis-à-vis both the state and civil society in discussions of feminist politics in non-Western societies. In her analysis of the Third World state, Shirin Rai argues that the reach and regulatory power of the state is limited as far as protecting women from patriarchal excesses is concerned, and that furthermore the state itself perpetrates violence against women through its coercive apparatus.[19] She is, however, equally wary of civil society, which she claims "is a deeply fraught space with hidden and explicit dangers that lurk there in the garb of national, religious and ethnic identities as fashioned by male-directed movements of various kinds." She invokes the "embeddedness" of most Third World states in civil society to argue that women are subjected to pressures from both although she does not elaborate upon the forms that this embeddedness might take.[20]

Suad Joseph expresses a similar sense of disquiet but goes much further in elaborating the specificities of state-society interactions and their implications for women's citizenship rights. She argues that rights and entitlements in the Middle East are mediated via membership in families and communities, which are hierarchical entities animated by a patriarchal logic that privileges men over women and the old over the young. There exists, in other words, no autonomous associational arena between state and society that is not thoroughly permeated by both the reality and the idiom of kin and family relations.[21] Therefore, an associational life premised on an autonomous self bearing rights in his or her own person does not have much resonance in a social context where connectivity rather than contractuality structures notions of selfhood. This applies equally to men and women, but it is women and the young who bear the brunt of the inequalities inherent in patriarchy.

This acknowledgment of cultural difference can be both illuminating and limiting, especially if the source of difference is principally located in the psychosocial realm. There is a risk of conflating the abstract notion of the individual in liberal theory with an actual empirical reality assumed to characterize an ideal-typical notion of Western individuality, which may be contrasted with an intrinsically different type of selfhood defined as relational or connective. Yet the concerns underlying this position are totally justifiable: why and how is it that communally based networks of influence and authority are able to permeate both the state and civil society?

A similar concern is echoed in Sharabi's argument that the patriarchal structures of Arab society, far from being weakened by modernization, have been reinvigorated and transformed into "neopatriarchy."[22] Neopatriarchal discourse is invariably authoritarian whether it manifests itself in its secular or religious, nationalist, or leftist forms, since it emanates from largely untransformed structures that regulate interpersonal relations at every level, from the family to the state.

The crux of the matter appears to lie in the difficulty of theorizing some residual entity — the community, patriarchy, subnational groupings, or the "people" — that is not fully captured by the dichotomy of state and civil society. In a luminous paper, Partha Chatterjee provides us with important insights about the reason for the longevity of the concept of "tradition" (and possibly patriarchy, which becomes its adjunct), which rest precisely in our inability to conceptualize the part of society in non-Western states that lies outside the domain of civil society.[23] Chatterjee finds it useful to reserve the term civil society to identify those institutions of modern associational life that originated in the West and are based on freedom of exit and entry, equality and contract. An important consideration in thinking about the relations between civil society and the state in postcolonial societies is that whereas the legal-bureaucratic apparatus of the state is able to reach virtually all of the population, the domain of civil institutions is still restricted to a fairly small section of "citizens," a narrow urban elite. However, nationalist politics could not remain contained within the confines of the civil society of urban elites, but had to reach out to the population. Chatterjee suggests that the mediation between the population and the state takes place on the site of a new political society which engages in various types of mobilization, such as political parties, movements or non-party political organizations, which do not necessarily conform to the normative standards of civil society but act to channel popular demands on the developmental state. This, in turn, has a clear bearing on our conceptions of democracy and points to a tension between democracy and modernity in postcolonial societies.

Analyzing the emergent institutional forms that political societies might take is absolutely crucial to a discussion of women and citizenship. The various ways in which the politics of gender become a stake in struggles over power, representation, or resources cannot be understood with reference to categories such as tradition, patriarchy, Islam, or indigeneity. It is only when we locate religious or communalist movements firmly on the terrain of political society that we can comprehend how they may both articulate popular demands and democratic aspirations, and simultaneously adopt a politics of gender that results in restrictive and exclusionary practices that curtail women's life options.

It is also within this framework, rather than with reference to the dichotomies of traditional/modern, religious/secular or Western/indigenous, that we need to evaluate the various manifestations of political Islam and their implications for women's rights. The contradictions at the heart of Islamic populisms' claims to be inclusive and represent the will of the people become crystallized in their exclusion of women from citizenship. This contradiction fuels women's relentless struggle to expand and redefine their rights, a struggle which is quite clearly apparent in the Islamic Republic of Iran, as in other countries in the region.[24] Apparently, women in the Middle East are not content to accept their "difference" and refuse to limit their longings for full citizenship. It is incumbent upon feminists to refrain from adopting positions that would deny them access to universalist aspirations in the name of their assumed cultural differences.

# Country Case Studies, West to East

# State and Gender in the Maghrib

Mounira M. Charrad

Women's rights as defined in family law have represented a political issue in the modern history of the Maghrib, as elsewhere in the Islamic world.[1] The issue has involved state power and conflicts or alliances in national politics. This chapter presents a structural framework to analyze the basic choices made by the Tunisian, Algerian, and Moroccan states when each promulgated a national code of family law (also referred to as code of personal status). Each national code equipped the country with a body of legislation that defined the parameters of the law for the population as a whole. Each code also set the stage for further struggles and policies concerning family law and women's rights. The focus of the chapter is on long-term structural processes of state formation and their consequences for family law. The central argument is that the relationship between the national state and kin-based tribal groups as it evolved historically shaped the structure of the state and its policies.[2] Major recent developments in family law are outlined at the end of the article.

Tunisia, Algeria, and Morocco constitute a geocultural entity. They all went through a period of French colonization, and they achieved independence during roughly the same period, in the late 1950s and early 1960s. Despite the similarities, the three countries engaged in markedly different policies in regard to family law and women's rights after independence. Tunisia made the most far-reaching changes as it promulgated its Code of Personal Status in 1956. Morocco remained most faithful to prevailing Islamic legislation when it adopted its Code of Personal Status in 1957–58. In Algeria, the law was in gridlock for over two decades, during which reform plans repeatedly aborted until a conservative Family Code was promulgated in 1984.

## State Formation and Kin-Based Tribal Solidarities

The differences in family law and women's rights among the three countries are made especially intriguing by the fact that it was neither the most industrialized country (Algeria), nor the most socialist and revolutionary regime (Algeria again), nor the society exposed to French culture for the longest period (Algeria still) that made the most radical changes. Neither level of industrialization nor official socialist ideology thus accounts for the variations in state policies among the three Maghribi countries.

Most explanations of changes in women's status emphasize factors such as economic development and revolutionary ideology. Here, however, an approach that takes the state as a key variable is more useful. In explaining changes in women's rights, it is necessary to consider the process of state formation and to relate state and gender. State interventions are not only responses to economic or class-based demands. They are also shaped by the political requirements of state stability or consolidation. At given historical moments, the state engages in actions to further its own interests of domination and hegemony.[3] The state is an institution of domination with its own structure, history, and pattern of conflict.

A common denominator of many postcolonial countries at the time of independence was that they were "old societies," but relatively "new states."[4] Even where existing ruling dynasties went back to the nineteenth century or even earlier, the precolonial state effectively controlled only a fraction of the population with respect to taxation, military service, and law and order.[5] Colonial rule frequently weakened existing indigenous political institutions. A national state had to be either formed or consolidated in the wake of colonization.

In many postcolonial nation-states, the existing social structure at the time of independence was characterized by social segmentation. Collectivities — ethnic, caste or kinship-based, tribal, religious, or linguistic — retained a degree of separate identity and had to be integrated into the nation. The establishment or extension of state domination therefore entailed a rearrangement of the nexus of social solidarities. In the Maghrib, the ties of solidarity binding local communities together have historically been grounded in kinship. Members of a community thought of themselves as relatives issued from a common ancestor. Family and kinship served as the bases for social formations striving to remain autonomous from the state. They also offered a unifying principle for contesting state power.

Germaine Tillion captures the character of Maghribi kin groupings with her metaphor of the many "republics of cousins."[6] Many tribal kin groupings survived as cohesive entities until the period of national independence. As an integral part of this process, they kept tight control over their women, jealously saving them for the men in the "republic of cousins," or orchestrating collectively useful marriage alliances with outsiders.[7] Whatever the particular pattern governing marriage ties, the control of women was necessary for the maintenance of community cohesion. Women were key resources for the alternative, tribally-organized centers of power resisting the state.

State formation affects the position of women in society in several ways. In particular, the state mediates gender relations through the law. Legislation is a key element in the panoply of strategies available to the state in its attempt to foster or inhibit social change, to maintain existing arrangements, or to promote greater equality for women in the family and the society at large. Insofar as it regulates marriage, divorce, individual rights and responsibilities, and the transmission of property through inheritance, family law is a prime example of a state policy affecting women.[8]

There is no single route to nation building and state formation. In the case of the Maghrib as a whole, the national state in formation had to take resources previously embedded in kin-based networks of obligation and redirect them toward national goals. But there is more than one way of doing this. The possibilities are several: the state may directly threaten and break tribal or kinship ties; it may tolerate them and only timidly chip away at tribal cohesion; or it may actively encourage the existence of tribes and lineages as part of a divide-and-rule stratagem. In all cases, the status of women is affected. Whatever its pattern, the process of state formation is likely to have consequences for gender relations.

## Islamic Law and Women's Legal Status

Islamic law, especially in its Maliki version that has historically predominated in the Maghrib, gives male members of the kin group extensive control over key decisions affecting women's lives. For instance, a woman need not give her consent to marriage during the marriage ceremony. It is the consent of the woman's guardian, her father, or the next male in the kinship line that makes the marriage valid. There is no legal minimum age for marriage.

Like other schools of Islamic law, Maliki law gives the husband the privilege of breaking the marital bond at will, while it specifies, and restricts, the circumstances to be considered legitimate grounds on which a woman may be granted a divorce. If a man chooses to repudiate his wife, the woman has no legal recourse. A man has the legal right to marry as many as four wives. No more than a small minority of men can afford more than one wife at a time, but the legality of polygamy threatens women and pressures them to comply with their husband's wishes.

Maliki laws define precisely who is to inherit under various conditions. A woman receives half as much as a man would in a similar situation. Under many circumstances, the laws favor distant male relatives on the man's side of the family over the wife and over female descendants. Regulations on marriage encourage kin control of marriage ties and thus facilitate marriages within the lineage and collectively useful outside alliances. Laws on divorce define the conjugal bond as fragile and easily breakable. The absence of community property between husband and wife implies that the patrimony of each spouse may remain untouched by marriage. By favoring males and kin on the male side, inheritance laws solidify ties within the extended patrilineal kin group.

The "message" of Maliki family law as analyzed above is that the conjugal unit may be short-lived, whereas the ties with male kin may be enduring. Maliki law defines the kin group rather than the nuclear family unit as the significant locus of solidarity. As such, it facilitates the maintenance of tribal communities. The law thus has implications for tribal kin groupings in the broader social structure, at the same time as it subordinates women.

## Women's Rights After Independence

Similar questions apply to the laws promulgated in each Maghribi country in the wake of independence. What is the "message" of the laws? What type of relationships do the new laws define as enduring, and what kind of family structure do they sanction? When Morocco and Tunisia became independent states in 1956, and Algeria in 1962, the previous homogeneity in family law throughout the Maghrib came to an end as each newly formed national state formulated its own policy. All three national codes consisted in a body of legislation on individual rights and responsibilities in the family, but they differed significantly in content.[9]

The Moroccan Code of 1957–58 essentially reiterated Maliki family law in a more concise and codified manner. Consent to marriage continued to be expressed not by the bride, but by her father or male guardian. The bride did not have to be present at the marriage ceremony for the marriage to be valid. Compulsory marriages remained a very real possibility. The procedure for divorce remained the same, except that repudiation, which could previously be a private act, now had to be observed by two witnesses who had to record it in writing. Polygamy remained legal. Even fewer modifications were made to the laws on inheritance.

Algerian positions toward family law and personal status oscillated for over twenty years. From the time of independence in 1962 until 1984, there were several attempts to reform the law, but the plans were aborted because of disagreements in the working committees or conflicts between liberal and conservative tendencies. Some of the slight modifications to Maliki law introduced by the French colonial regime were reconfirmed, and a few new laws were passed, but for twenty-two years Algerians lived in their politically sovereign country without an overall, comprehensive family law. Legislation consisted of a perplexing mismatch of Maliki law and secular codes until June 9, 1984, when the government finally adopted a long-awaited Family Code.

In the Algerian Family Code, the legal prerogatives of husbands and unequal inheritance between women and men remained essentially unchanged. Polygamy continued to be legal. The principle of the matrimonial guardian was reconfirmed. An innovation was that, if the father died, the mother now became automatically the children's guardian. The term "divorce" replaced "repudiation" and a divorce had to occur in court, but the husband's will to terminate the marriage was still a sufficient and legitimate reason for divorce. Algerian political leaders did not deliver on earlier promises to increase women's rights. Following a gridlock of twenty-two years, the codification of family law in sovereign Algeria remained faithful to Maliki legal principles.

Tunisian women saw their legal status change significantly when the Code of Personal Status was promulgated in 1956 and supplemented by additional laws thereafter. The bride now had to attend her own marriage ceremony and give her verbal consent for the marriage to be legally valid. Divorce could only take place in court, and husband and wife were equally entitled to file for it. Polygamy was abolished outright. It became punishable

with imprisonment and a fine. Although the new laws on inheritance maintained that the share of a woman was worth half that of a man, daughters and
granddaughters now might, under certain circumstances, receive the entire
property to the detriment of distant male kin.[10] The law also ended the legal
guardianship of man over woman and redefined the rights and obligations of
husband and wife so as to make them more equal.

## The Ideal Family

One of the key functions of a legal system is to present a summation of
objectives for the society at large. The law provides a basis for social control
and is meant to imprint on social dynamics a given rhythm and direction. The
legislation that emerged from the reforms in each Maghribi country contained an image of the ideal family as envisioned by the national state.

The Tunisian code gave greater rights to women and decreased the legal
control of male kin over them. With respect to the kinship structure, the
Tunisian code weakened the extended patrilineal kin group while it strength-
ened the conjugal unit. In contrast, in the model of the family contained in the
Moroccan code, women remained in a subordinate status. Moroccan law
sanctioned the extended kin group. It continued to allow kin to control marriages, the marital bond remained easily breakable, and inheritance rules
maintained male privileges. Like its 1957–58 Moroccan counterpart, the
1984 Family Code of Algeria kept women in a subordinate status. Viewed
with respect to kinship, the Algerian code attempted some very timid steps in
favor of the development of a conjugal unit, but on the whole it continued to
sanction the extended patrilineal kinship structure.

The Moroccan and Tunisian reforms occurred very soon after independence: within a year in Morocco and within six months in Tunisia. In both
countries, they came from above rather than as a response to pressure from
below. They were formulated by the government, as a result of political
choices on the part of the social groups in power. In both countries, individuals, mostly intellectuals or prominent figures in the nationalist movement,
raised the issue of women's rights and family law. In Algeria in the early
1980s, a small minority of women were active in obstructing the most conservative plans to make Algerian law even more faithful to Maliki law. But
nowhere in the Maghrib between the 1950s and the early 1980s was there a
sustained, mass-based, organized movement with the issue of family law and

women's rights at the core of its platform and with influence on policy outcomes.

What are some of the reasons that help explain why the political leadership in each country made the choices it did? The answer lies in part in the fact that the three countries reached independence with a different balance of power between the national state and local kin-based tribal communities, and this in turn shaped state policy on family law and women's rights. By leaving intact the integrative mechanism of kin-based communities, the Moroccan policy could only help maintain the "republics of cousins." In Algeria, there was a partial but aborted attempt to confront these communities. In Tunisia, the legal policy of the newly formed national state directly threatened the "republics of cousins."

## Strategies of State Formation

The relationship between the national state and kin-based tribal communities resulted from long term historical processes from the precolonial period to the time of independence. Even though Maghribi societies had developed some state institutions in the precolonial period, they lacked a state apparatus able to control the whole territory effectively. In the absence of bureaucratized states in the precolonial period (which was not chronologically the same for the three countries), tribal communities were major actors in the regulation of economic production and political life. Some were involved in an ongoing antagonistic relationship with whatever state existed at the time, with the goal of evading state control. Depending on the area, local revolts, for the most part aimed at avoiding taxes, occurred either occasionally or with great frequency.[11]

Precolonial Tunisia was the country where kin-based communities had retained the least political autonomy and where the trend toward the emergence of centralized institutions was most recognizable. The history of precolonial Morocco exhibited an antagonistic relationship between central authority and tribal communities, as the former struggled to extend its power either through the use of force or through tactical alliances with local groups. Algeria was the most segmented society, with local groups living in relative independence and with minimal state interference.

Colonization altered the situation. In Tunisia, the colonizers exerted their rule in large part through the administrative machinery available. They increased administrative centralization and weakened kin-based communities even beyond the loss of political leverage that these communities had experienced before colonization. In Algeria, the French dismembered entire communities by transplanting parts of them to distant areas, took the best lands, and imposed their own network of officials onto the largely segmented social structure. Algerians retreated into what was most secure, namely the solidarity of their kin-based collectivities, whenever that refuge was available. The effect of colonial rule in Algeria was to destroy some of the tribal communities, while leaving others in place and unwittingly reinforcing their internal cohesion. In Morocco, the French took the place of central authority and relied largely on a method of indirect administration in which they manipulated the local power structure. The result was that colonial rule affected tribal communities less in Morocco than in either Algeria or Tunisia. At the end of the colonial period, the state was most highly bureaucratized in Tunisia, least bureaucratized in Morocco, and was somewhere in the middle in Algeria.

Occurring in different structural settings, the struggle for national liberation and the transfer of power at independence took different forms in the three countries. In Tunisia, the nationalist strategy was to operate through a powerful party extending throughout the whole country. This was made possible by the relative integration of Tunisian society. State formation proceeded in large part without the reliance of the political leadership on kin-based tribal communities.

In the Algerian war of national liberation, factions appeared not only on the basis of ideological differences but also among groups finding their support in different regions and local areas. Several postindependence insurrections in local areas demonstrated the revival of kinship and tribal ties. Segments of the leadership had at their disposal links to local kin-based, communities that they could mobilize when necessary in the struggle for power at the central level.

In Morocco, a party somewhat similar to its Tunisian counterpart found support predominantly in urban centers, but could not penetrate rural areas. It lost out to the monarchy, which relied precisely on tribal communities in rural areas. In the period following independence, kin-based tribal communities continued to be significant in Moroccan politics in that they served as bases of political support for power struggles played out at the national level. The strategy of the monarchy was to establish systems of patronage, to act as arbiter among competing groups, and to orchestrate a complex web of factions.

National integration was accomplished throughout most of the Maghrib in the aftermath of independence, thus excluding direct competition as the predominant form of interaction between the state and kin-based tribal groups. There were no secessionist movements in which tribal communities demanded separation from the state or the creation of entirely independent political units. In Morocco and Algeria, however, these communities remained relevant to national politics after independence.

For these reasons, the three Maghribi states were not equally interested in bringing about changes in the relationship between the state and kin-based communities and, therefore, in reforming family law. In Tunisia, it was in the best interest of the government to break kin-based solidarities, and it was possible to do so because tribal groups had already lost much of their political leverage. In Algeria, it was also in the best interest of some leaders to foster a rearrangement of kinship by weakening tribal kin groupings, but other segments of the leadership depended in part on the continued availability of kin-based solidarities for political mobilization. In Morocco, the monarchy derived much of its power from its ability to maintain a balance among kin-based communities. It thus had a strong incentive to avoid any disruption of kinship organization.

## Subsequent Developments

Once the sovereign state was formed in each country, it shaped national politics and family law in the following decades. Despite some changes, the political systems and institutions that emerged at the end of colonization have remained essentially in place in all three countries of the Maghrib. The same applies to the overall orientation of family law. The trends that started when each country equipped itself with a basic legal code on the whole continued in the 1980s and 1990s. Some modifications were made in the family law of Tunisia and Morocco, but the gist of each code was respected. Tunisia kept its innovative code and added some amendments. Morocco made some adjustments while retaining the faithfulness of its code to Islamic family law. In Algeria, the Family Code of 1984 remained the legislation in effect.

Noteworthy among the amendments to the Tunisian Code of Personal Status in the 1980s and 1990s were the law of 1981 on divorce and the reforms of 1993.[12] The law of 1981 introduced the possibility of lifelong alimony for a divorced woman, instead of a lump sum. A divorced woman now could receive a regular monthly or yearly payment from her former husband until she died or remarried. The basic principle involved was to maintain in divorce the standard of living that the woman had experienced in marriage. The 1981 law also brought changes to guardianship, which is different from custody. Custody involves day to day care, while guardianship refers to legal responsibilities for the child such as authorizing a passport or signing school papers. Before 1981, if the father died the judge selected a guardian for a child among a wide range of potential candidates, including paternal and maternal relatives. The mother was considered among other possible guardians, depending on the child's best interest. The 1981 law automatically made the mother the guardian in case of the father's death, and in that case only. In the event of divorce, guardianship continued to rest with the father as it did before 1981.

The 1993 amendments dropped a clause stating that a wife had to obey her husband, a clause that appeared in earlier versions of the Tunisian code. The 1993 laws also brought further changes to guardianship. They expanded a mother's prerogatives and reduced a father's power over children after divorce, a point of great concern to women's rights advocates. In the past, the father retained legal guardianship of the child even when the mother had custody. After 1993, a mother who gained custody after divorce could also obtain guardianship if she showed that the father failed to respect the best interest of the child or that he manipulated guardianship to hurt his former wife.

In Morocco, some changes were brought to the Code of Personal Status in 1993.[13] The new laws continued to require a matrimonial guardian's consent to marriage on behalf of the bride. They made a change, however, in requiring that the bride also sign the marriage contract. The new laws in principle took away the matrimonial guardian's legal prerogative to give a woman in marriage without her consent even though, except in a few special circumstances, a bride still had to be represented by a matrimonial guardian for a marriage to be valid. But the 1993 amendment was offset by the fact that the Moroccan Code did not require a written marriage certificate in all cases.[14] A judge could consider a marriage valid even without a certificate if circumstances warranted such a recognition, thus undermining the 1993 modification concerning the bride's signature of the marriage contract.

Polygamy remained legal in Morocco after the amendments of 1993. The amendments introduced the stipulation that the notaries in charge of writing the marriage contract should receive a written statement from a judge, who would authorize a polygamous marriage after having considered fairness to all women involved. The 1993 amendments brought a minor modification to repudiation. They retained the husband's unilateral right to end the marriage at will, but required that a man repudiate his wife in the presence of a judge and after arbitration.

A development throughout the Maghrib in the 1980s and 1990s was the emergence of women's associations. In all three countries in that period, albeit to different degrees, women's agency developed as an influence to be counted in matters of family law and women's rights. Women began to take their destiny into their own hands. Women's rights advocates became active in several kinds of associations, ranging from some with a directly feminist objective to others tied to political parties or groups, to still others with a more social or humanitarian bent. In those associations, women gained increased consciousness of their situation. They sometimes used the channels of communication that the associations offered as a basis for collective action aimed at influencing policies on women's rights. Women had a measure of influence on policy formulation in Tunisia and Morocco in the 1990s. In Algeria, women's activism became hostage to broader national conflicts after the promulgation of the 1984 Code.[15]

How much effect women's rights advocates have on future state policy will depend in part on the balance of power between reformist and conservative forces in national politics in each country. Women's rights advocates are more likely to be able to influence family law policy when they have an opportunity to form an alliance with reformist forces and when the balance of power in national politics is favorable to such forces.

## Conclusion

In the aftermath of independence, family law was used as an instrument of change in Tunisia. It served the status quo in Morocco. It was held hostage to political cleavages in Algeria. In the early phase of national sovereignty, political elites had vested but divergent interests in either strengthening or undermining kin-based communities. Depending on these interests, elites made different choices in regard to family law and women's rights following the formation of the national state. Now that women's rights advocates are taking steps to capture a political space for themselves in the Maghrib, they may influence further developments in family law and women's rights. Their success will depend on how much support they can generate among political forces in the country. As in earlier periods, the policy outcome is likely to be shaped by conflicts and alliances in national politics in each society.

# Sex, Lies, and Television
## Algerian and Moroccan Caricatures of the Gulf War

Susan Slyomovics

A cartoon image is succinct and does not move when you look at it. Condensing history, culture, gender, and social relationships within a single frame, a cartoon can recontextualize events and evoke references in ways that a photograph or a film cannot. As do graffiti, jokes, and other genres of popular culture, cartoons challenge the ways we accept official images as real and true.

One of the more curious uses of images during the Gulf War was the widespread deployment of cartoons and caricature. Cartoons played a significant role in shaping not only the perceptions of that conflict but also its conduct. Whether part of a rhetoric of nationalism or militarism, or linked to strategies of resistance and critique, cartoons were everywhere. They were used by governments, media, artists, activists, and soldiers; they appeared daily in the pages of U.S., Arab, Israeli, and European newspapers and periodicals, representing every imaginable perspective and point of view. Another side to the deployment of caricature is as a kind of popular critique and as a mirror into gender representations.

American cartoons appeared on the surfaces of tactical weapons; they blanketed the deserts of Iraq and Kuwait in the form of "Surrender Pamphlets" dropped by U.S. planes. Readiness for that conflict had been secured, on all sides, through "virtual-wargaming technologies" where video-arcade enemies were selected, targeted, and destroyed; CNN diagrammed the war nightly; the walls of Middle Eastern cities were covered with posters and graffiti that disappeared overnight under a new cover of subsequent cartoons and commentary.

Every U.S. ship stationed in the Persian Gulf unofficially put its onboard printing facilities to the task of producing thousands of caricatures of Bush, Saddam, and other more generic stereotypes on T-shirts, sweatshirts, and jackets. George Bush was a cowboy, Saddam was any number of Indians, Hitlers, Stalins, or Ali Babas. A veritable industry arose of collectible military items and souvenirs: postcards, bandanas, autographed campaign badges, annotated Iraqi, Saudi, and Kuwaiti currency, official Desert Storm stationery, and the ubiquitous T-shirts. In the United States, entrepreneurs sold thousands of yellow ribbons,[1] and several companies produced Desert Shield/ Desert Storm bubble-gum trading cards; Desert Storm software packages appeared for armchair wargamers; and books, catalogues, essays, and accounts of the war were published, and continued to proliferate.[2]

In contrast with the American material, the various uses of cartoons in Morocco and Algeria frame caricature within the conventions of wartime usage, such as propaganda and other forms of persuasion that shape perceptions of the war and give both a face to the enemy and legitimacy to "our side." Cartoons operate differently in the press and media in the Arab world than they do in the West. There are affinities and a shared visual vocabulary between Western and Arab notions of caricature, but the traditions and public roles to which they are linked are very different.[3]

## The Arab Context

In the Arab world caricaturists often operate within regimes of censorship and control. The appearance or disappearance of cartoons accurately marks the shifting fortunes of the press.[4] In Morocco, for example, it is an imprisonable offense to caricature the King or his ministers. In Algeria, the government finds ways to block free expression by newspaper cartoonists through strategic "shortages" of film and newsprint and an official distribution and circulation monopoly. In Iran, cartoons and posters carry the message of Islamic revolution, while in the Occupied Territories of Palestine during the intifada cartoon graffiti were the only visible — albeit illegal — critique of the Israeli occupation.

During the Gulf War people throughout the Middle East and North Africa had access to European, and hence, American, television through recently installed satellite dishes as well as to their own government-controlled stations. It became immediately apparent that there was no independent news-gathering operation at the sites of conflict. Graphic commentaries on the media form an important sub-genre of cartoons about the war. In this context, cartoons became more important than television in representing the war and in constituting a public forum for critique and debate in many Middle Eastern cities. Cartoons became the only form of popular culture that challenged the ways television coverage of the war was accepted and framed as factual and true. The caricaturists who appeared in the daily newspapers were widely regarded as the most reliable sources of information on events in the Persian Gulf.[5] Also, during the Gulf War official attitudes toward and responses to caricature were relaxed, which brought about a remarkable flourishing of cartoons and graphic satire. In some Arab countries, notably Egypt and Morocco, caricaturists pushed the limits of censorship and produced a fascinating range and proliferation of cartoons.

Cartoons, therefore, chronicle the state of an independent press by highlighting the central relationship of image production to censorship. In the Arab world, where the glut of mass media coverage is a new phenomenon, cartoons have played a central role in examining such issues as the power of the media, political rhetoric and persuasion, censorship, and resistance. The representation of the media in cartoons in Algerian and Moroccan newspapers during the Gulf War has much to say about the lack of any genuinely independent news-gathering operations, whether Arab or Western, at the scene of Gulf War battles.

## Algeria

The Algerian press only recently experienced an explosion in freedom and diversity. From independence in 1962 until the 1988 "October revolution," the press was controlled and censored by the one-party government of the National Liberation Front (FLN). Following the 1988 introduction of a new constitution that legalized political parties, abolished government control of the press, and guaranteed journalists' salaries for a transition period of three years, the number of newspapers and journals increased from fewer than a dozen to several hundred. Two weekly cartoon newspapers, the French-language *El-Manchar* and the Arabic *Es-Sahafa* which began publication around the time of the Gulf crisis. The Algerian government could still impede free expression, either through government monopolies of distribution or by inducing shortages of paper, ink, and film. In August and September 1992 it began imposing fines, confiscating issues, and initiating libel proceedings against several newspapers, including the French-language *Le*

*Matin* and *La Nation,* the Arabic-language satirical weekly *Es-Sahafa,* and some Islamist newspapers.

The historical development of cartoons in Algeria is related to complex linguistic issues inherited from the French colonialist past that continues to shape all means of cultural production, whether they be films, plays, popular songs, novels, or cartoons. In their ground-breaking work on Arab comic strips, Alan Douglas and Fedwa Malti-Douglas offer a rare overview of cartoons within the context of Algerian bilingualism.[6] Algerian comics are unique in the Arab world because, as the Douglases point out, they are largely invisible to Arabic readers. The majority of Algerian comics are in French; even the small number of Algerian Arabic-language albums are translated from Francophone originals. In addition, these works exist in a rich linguistic interzone, "between Arabic and French," a language the Douglases call "Algerian French." This is defined as a French base "spiced" with Algerian Arabic, with the capacity to exploit a rich array of possibilities inherent in punning across languages.[7]

During the Gulf War, Algeria's bilingualism provided a critique of the ways the media of opposing sides lie to their audiences. In a cartoon by NED in the weekly newspaper *Simsar,* 9–14 March 1991, (Figure 1) an Algerian viewer channel-hops between Arabic and French-language television programs: the French one proclaims the Coalition victory, the Iraqi Arabic ones announce Saddam Hussein's supremacy. In the end, the bilingual, bicultural Algerian announces that, yes, he belongs to the category of *des informés* (the well informed). The two French words *des informés* can be jammed together into a single word yielding a punned opposite *désinformés* (the disinformed).[8] To be media-wise is to be disinformed. To know too much is also not to know because European and Arab television are diametrically opposed in the many ways they promote possible interpretations. An Algerian comic strip interrogates the bases of our information: as viewers — bilingual, bicultural, Algerian ones — we are only entitled to minimal freedoms, such as channel surfing or station zapping.

## Algeria: *El-Manchar* and *Es-Sahafa*

Coincidentally, two weekly newspapers began publication at the same time as the outbreak of the Gulf War. In keeping with Algeria's bilingual traditions, the French-language *El-Manchar* ("the saw") in Algiers and the Arabic-language *Es-Sahafa* in Oran began publication.

Figure 2. Slim, *El-Manchar,* February 1991, 3.

The Gulf War and media representation during the war were very much the topics of Algeria's premier cartoonist and comic-strip artist, Menouar Merabtene. He writes under the nom de plume Slim and he is characterized by the Douglases as Algeria's Jules Feiffer.[9] Currently in exile, he resides in France after a sojourn in Morocco where he first fled to escape Islamist attacks targeting journalists and cartoonists. His work is replete with puns that cross language boundaries between French and Algerian-Arabic, and between French and English. An example of a French-English intertextual visual pun is Slim's labeling of the American television broadcasting service CNN (Figure 2). The CNN logo was beamed throughout the televised world and was said to represent disinterested, objective Gulf War coverage. In the cartoon, which appeared in the February 1991 issue of *El-Manchar* (Figure 2), Slim inserted tiny letters to transform what the global audience understood as truth into what he perceived as CNN's genuine role, namely purveying idiocies. The war, according to Slim, is the American CNN which

Figure 1. NED, *Simsar,* 9–14 March 1991.
(French): We are the strongest, there is nothing left of Iraq! (Arabic): Iraq still stands!
(French): 80% of Iraq's military potential has been destroyed! (Arabic): The Iraqi army is not yet destroyed!
(French): We love the Arabs, moreover many of them have followed us! (Arabic): At last the masks of the Arabs have fallen!
(French): It is a huge victory for the coalition! (Arabic): There has never been such a defeat for the West!
(French): At least it must be said that we are *des-informés!*

Level 1

Level 2

Level 3

Figure 3. Slim, *El-Manchar,* February 1991.

becomes the French *connerie.* The war, television, CNN, and CNN coverage are all identified with "lies and idiocies."

Another example of Slim's complex punning technique in service against the Gulf War also appears in *El-Manchar,* February 1991 (Figure 3). It too calls upon French and Algerian Arabic to cross linguistic lines with laughter. Level one allows for two readings, a French one: "Qu'Irak?" and "La Baisse" to mean, under the heading of gas and oil, "What's with Iraq?" and its pessimistic reply: "Going down." At the same time these phonemes reproduce exactly the Algerian Arabic greeting and response: "How are you?" (*kay rak*) and its immediate optimistic reply, "Not bad," literally "no evil" (*la bas*). Level two exploits only puns in French giving us: *L'Arabie, c'est ou dites?* (Arabia? Where is it?) or with the same pronunciation, the country *L'Arabie Saoudite.* With either reading, this country is geographically findable, according to Slim, if you just follow the Scuds. Level three uses French culture to mock conservative Gulf Arab sexual mores. It reports that Saudi banks were refusing French money because the image of France — the ubiquitous, semi-nude, female figure of Marianne — adorns France's bank notes. For once, money (Saudi greed) is vanquished by sexual prudery. *Bouh,* or "shame on you," says Slim.

Many Algerian cartoonists, Slim among them, contributed puns on the word referring to the Iraqi missiles, the Scud. Slim speaks of a North-South dialogue as a "Dialogue Nord-Scud" (*El-Manchar,* February 1991, 3), thereby satirizing both sides in the bureaucratic-speak of international peace accords (Figure 4). Melouah, another Algerian cartoonist, entitles his page of Gulf War cartoons in *El-Manchar* as "Boy Scud." He further conflates the two countries, the United States and Saudia Arabia, to highlight their interchangeability as well as the complete capitulation of the Gulf states to American interests. To do so he creates the acronym USA or "United Saudi Arabia" (Figure 5).

*Es-Sahafa* was Algeria's rare Arabophone response to the overwhelming French-language bias of Algeria's cartoonists, comic strip artists, and satirical writers. It is significant that it emerged, not in the capital, Algiers, but in the country's second city, Oran, on the distant western Moroccan border. Its press run was brief: from the Gulf War until it was closed down in the fall of 1993 as a result of a government libel case. Its logo (Figure 6) exploits not only Arabic-language linguistic possibilities (*Essahafa* = "journalism" or *essah afa* = "truth is a scourge") but also the layered graphic qualities of traditional Arabic calligraphy.

In addition, the artwork in *Es-Sahafa* often followed a more complex,

Figure 4.
Slim, "Dialogue Nord-Scud,"
*El-Manchar,*
February 1991, 3.

cross-hatched inking, as opposed to the simple line techniques of the French (or European) influenced drawing style. In contrast to Slim's one-two punch style, the work of Sabri Achour (Figure 7), for example, calls for a slow reading of symbols and images. Achour litters the desert landscape with helmets, skulls, and snakes to signify the vipers of the Coalition armies. The Saudi King Fahd wears the Arab *kafiyya* (but with the Israeli Star of David) as he perches on top of a cross. An Iraqi Scud is about to descend and disrupt the King's world.

Also from *Es-Sahafa* are cartoons produced during the Gulf War (Figure 8 is an English-language version) by Nadjib Berber, who characterizes his Gulf War work as a visual campaign against the sexism and corruption of the Gulf states, against George Bush and his personality cult of misplaced machismo, against all the leaders on all sides that forced the war upon the world, against war profiteering, and against the butchery and police state terror of Saddam Hussein but in support of the sufferings of the Iraqi people.[10] As did many Algerian cartoonists before the dismemberment of press censorship in the late 1980s, Berber worked for publishing houses of children's books and comic strip albums that retold important areas of Arab, Islamic, or Algerian history in pictures. When a genuinely freer press began to flourish in Algeria, it coincided with the onset of the Gulf War. Caricaturists could protest the war through humor; more important, they were able to link anti-Gulf War sentiments within the Algerian population to a critique of the rising tide of Islamists and the power of their political arm, the Front Islamique de Salut

Figure 5. Melouah, "Boy Scud," *El-Manchar,* February 1991, 5.

Figure 6. *Es-Sahafa* logo, 13–19 February 1991, 1.

(FIS). At the beginning of the Gulf War, the FIS leaders, especially the younger, fiery Ali Belhadj, supported the Kuwaiti and Saudi governments from whom their funding was derived. Their dilemma was compounded by the massive support of their own Islamist cadres and people for Iraq. The FIS public retreat from their initial pro-Saudi position presented opportunities for cartoonists to mock secret financial funding and the evident ease with which the Islamist leaders could redirect their calls for jihad (holy war). Belhadj (Figure 9) may be the first to call for war, but he will assuredly be the last to arrive in the region.

Algeria was unique in the Arab world as a haven for political cartoonists: beginning with the demonstration and riots of 1988 that freed the press, and continuing past the army coup d'état that removed Chadli Ben Jadid, uncensored caricature, playful punning and invective, and inventive graphics entertained and enlightened the Algerian population. Political cartoons, and comic strips as well, are produced and valued by the Algerian intellectual elite, many of whom are in the world of serious art and literature as well as in the mass culture milieu of journalism. Their audience may be illiterate in Arabic or French, but Algerians are nonetheless sophisticated "readers" of graphic materials. Algerian comic strip artists, as members of an Arab, usually secular, elite, take their work seriously and often attach a didactic, moral dimension to it. Because the emergence of a free press in Algeria is coincident with the outbreak of the Gulf War, a wide variety of political, artistic materials supporting or condemning Iraq saturated the print media but not the national broadcast government-censored media. For a brief and rare moment, cultural discourse in Algeria overturned the long reign of the state-sponsored,

Figure 7. Sabri Achour, *Es-Sahafa,* 1991.

single-party FLN propaganda. Algeria's current political chaos, verging on a civil war, has destroyed the new, fragile structures of a civil society and an emerging free press. One consequence of this chaos is that, according to the Committee to Protect Journalists (an organization with ties to Middle East Watch and Amnesty International), Algeria provides the world with the gruesome statistic of the greatest number of journalists and media staffers killed since 1990. In the minds of those artists who enjoyed a rare consensus characterized by the free and playful spirit of liberated media, those all too brief years of political cartoon freedom must, therefore, be placed in the context of what was going on at the same time and what has since followed: freedom of the press existed during the Gulf war and quietly disappeared during the current, deadly, internal Algerian war.

Figure 8. Nadjib Berber, English language version of *Es-Sahafa* cartoon.

Figure 9. Nadjib Berber, *Révolution africaine,* 1991.

## Algeria and Morocco: Cartoons, Satellite Dishes, and TV

The short-lived freedom of the press in Algeria coincided with the wide-spread installation of small, cheap satellite dishes that could pull in French and American television programming: illegally for the most part, since Algerians often did not pay for access. By 1989–90, Algeria possessed not only a free press but also a television audience well versed in the images and sounds of several cultures. Algeria is directly in the path of satellite transmission, so reception, even with small dishes, is clear. In Morocco, further to the west and not in the path of a satellite, only the affluent could afford the larger dishes needed to receive French broadcasts. The regime of King Hassan II censored national television and print media. Foreign radio — BBC, Voice of America, and Radio Monte Carlo Arabic language broadcasts — were extremely important news sources for most Moroccans.

The history of contemporary cartoons in Morocco is very much tied to the life and career of the preeminent Moroccan cartoonist Mohamed Filali. Since 1973 he has founded over seven political cartoon weeklies. The first magazines were in Moroccan Arabic dialect, later ones in French. More recently, he has been the editor of and principal contributor to two weeklies, *Al-Aqrab* (The Scorpion) and *Al-Usbu 'a al-Dahik* (The Laughing Week), which feature texts in literary Arabic but speech balloons in Moroccan dialect. Authorities frequently close down his newspapers and sometimes arrest and detain him. When interviewed in January 1992 in Casablanca, he pointed out that twice in his career Moroccan press censorship was eased, both times when King Hassan II was involved in an unpopular war: in 1975 during the Green March against the Polisario to claim the southern region of the Western Sahara for Morocco, and again during the Gulf War. Only during these periods, he said, had he been able to explore the limits of cartoon satire. Both times, censorship was quickly reinstituted. In Morocco, unlike Algeria since 1988, it is against the law and punishable by incarceration to caricature the head of state, or even a government minister.

A United States Information Agency (USIA) content analysis study of Arab media coverage during the Gulf War confirms Filali's observation that the Moroccan press was relatively free from censorship during the crisis.[11] David Pollock, director of Middle East research for the USIA, found, not surprisingly, that the media in countries in the coalition against Iraq were almost totally one-sided in support of the U.S.-led coalition. Morocco was an anomalous case: The government was officially on "our" side, as Pollock put it, but the media reflected pro-Iraqi public opinion. USIA statistics show that, of 60 editorials in major Moroccan papers during the first four weeks of the war, 55 supported Iraq and were hostile to the coalition. This includes the so-called "palace press" as well as the opposition press.

Television viewers worldwide watched Baghdad under bombardment. Not unlike a video game, the war became familiar and repetitive: a target is fixed in the crosshairs, a missile hones in, the television screen is momentarily awash in white light, and an isolated object we never see is proclaimed destroyed.[12] In contrast to television's rapid movement, a cartoon can comment on a recurring image by freezing it and placing it in contexts that the television media avoid. Nadjib Berber's cartoon (Figure 10) in the Algerian *Révolution africaine,* for example, plays with President Bush's statement that this is a war only against Saddam Hussein. A cartoon frame shows General Schwarzkopf and President Bush leaning against a television monitor, its screen lit up with the aerial bombardment of Baghdad. Bush briefs the American people: "Our objective was never to remove Iraq from the map." Schwarzkopf chimes in: "Affirmative, just its population." The politician tells a lie, the general's apparent agreement actually contradicts his leader; the graphic image on the television monitor reinforces the general's statement. The actual role of television was to shape one-dimensional representations of the "enemy." A cartoon from *El-Manchar* (Figure 11, 9 February

Figure 10. Nadjib Berber, *Révolution africaine,* 1991.

1991) depicts a television set that appears to be speaking into a radio micro-phone in the manner of a human sports announcer: "and now the massacre game, your favorite broadcast, to decimate is to win, or how civilized nations have fallen so low."

For Moroccan cartoonists even foreign radio broadcasts are more news-worthy than Moroccan television, which censors not just by silence and ab-sence but also through frivolity. A 1991 cartoon by Mohamed Filali (Figure 12) in *Al-Usbu'a al-Dahik* shows a radio blaring war bulletins in literary Ara-bic while next to it a television represented as a dancing girl undulates her mid-riff screen to the music of Egyptian love songs: "O sweetheart, I love you."

## Gender Reflections

War and international crises incorporate repetitious stereotypes when women appear on television; they are victims, martyrs, mothers, or national symbols, such as the Statue of Liberty for America or Marianne for France. Charac-terizing this circumstance, Cynthia Enloe has coined the term "womenand-

Figure 11. Melouah, *El-Manchar,* 9 February 1991.

children," a phrase she notes "rolls easily off network tongues because in network minds women are family members rather than independent actors, presumed to be almost childlike in their innocence about international affairs. Rarely do *realpolitik* journalists look to women to reveal any of the basic structures of a dangerous confrontation."[13] Although many cartoons embrace cliched depictions of female sufferings, the drawn image, nonetheless, when combined with wordplay has much to say about television images of female martyrology projected into homes during the Gulf War. For example, in an Algerian cartoon (Figure 13) by Nadjib Berber, unseen American pilots appear only in word balloons representing their conversation in a plane flying over Baghdad during one of the war's infamous bombing sorties. One American pilot asks the other: "Did you see on TV how Saddam Hussein treated our pilot prisoners?" The second replies: "It's disgusting, these Arabs are barbarians!" The reader sees neither the pilots nor their planes; the frame

Figure 12. Mohamed Fitali, *Al-Usbu'a al-Dahik.*

graphically shows the devastation caused by American saturation bombing to Iraq's "womenandchildren" and Iraqi buildings.[14]

Drawings of the Gulf War showed both Western and Arab leaders enacting macho scenarios. America, as opposed to her leaders, was semiotically configured as that monumental female body, the Statue of Liberty. Until now a symbol of freedom, she has been reattired by Nadjib Berber (Figure 14). Because the encounter between the conservative oil-producing Gulf states and America is mutually corrupting in powerful ways, America and the statue's virginal maternality have undergone "Saudification": her body heavily draped in cloth, she hides her face behind a veil, her torch of liberty held aloft is replaced by a flaming oil derrick, her spiked crown is composed of Patriot and Tomahawk missiles, and in her lowered arm she carries a barrel of Exxon oil. Masculine power over the feminine is validated because only in

Figure 13. Nadjib Berber, *Révolution africaine,* 1991.

her reformed clothing can the Statue of Liberty be attractive to the pot-bellied desert Arab figure in the lower right corner. He silently declares his love to the female body made over to conform to a Saudi, male-defined, sexual economy. By altering the standard American iconography, this new "Saudified" version plays with the fluid symbolism of Liberty's image at the same time that it mimics France's original gift. The cartoon proclaims: "To thank the USA for their aid, Saudi Arabia has built for itself a Statue of Liberty, Wahabi version." Since Saudi wealth can buy anything, the Algerian cartoon

Figure 14. Nadjib Berber, *Révolution africaine*, 1991.

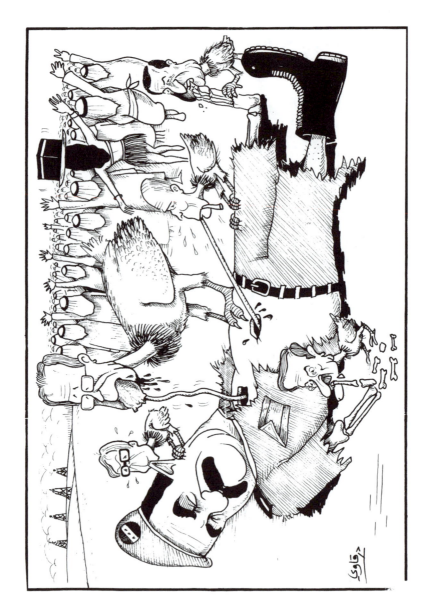

Figure 15. Derkaoui, *Al-Aqrab*, 3 March 1991.

Figure 16. Mohamed Filali, *Al-Aqrab*, 4 February 1991.

Figure 17. *Al-Aqrab,* 11 February 1992.

suggests what happens when symbols travel across countries and cultures. Female sexuality and liberty are elided in the false exchange of the gift (the Saudis buy themselves an American woman) or perhaps the Statue of Liberty, imaginatively reconstituted according to the laws of the Kingdom of Saudi Arabia, still conceals the uncontrolled wild woman. If so, she is, in this reincarnation, an Amazon warrior who is nourished by, fighting for, and illuminated by oil.

## Bush/Femme: Gender-Bending in Moroccan Caricature

Images of belly dancers and prostitutes as caricatures of coalition forces (minus Moroccans) in various scenes of debauchery proliferated in Moroccan cartoons during the Gulf War. In the foreground of a cartoon by the pseudonymous Derkaoui (Figure 15, *Al-Aqrab,* 3 March 1991), five vultures — Mubarak, Bush, Major, Mitterrand, and Asad — tear at the flesh of a prone Saddam Hussein, while Arabs turn their backs on the scene and jiggle away

Figure 18. *Al-Aqrab,* February 1991.

following the lead of a belly dancer. A mix of the profane and the sacred, the dancing girl performs the gymnastic feat of balancing the Kaaba containing the holy black stone, in Mecca, on her head. Another Moroccan cartoon by Filali (Figure 16, *Al-Aqrab,* 4 February 1991), draws upon the same themes: Bush is in drag as a prostitute, with money that has been tucked under his costume in sexually strategic places by a composite alcohol-imbibing Saudi-Israeli customer. A variation on this theme (Figure 17, *Al-Aqrab,* 11 February 1992) replaces Bush with his Arab allies, Hosni Mubarak of Egypt and Hafiz al-Asad of Syria, as belly dancers garbed in American flags, their mouths silenced by a cover of American dollars, dancing in front of Saddam Hussein. Gulf Arabs in general, as well as their leaders, were often shown as female prostitutes. In *Al-Aqrab,* 4 February 1991 (Figure 18), a wild party is taking place in an Arab city among Israelis, Arabs, and Americans. We see the Israeli leader Yitshak Shamir and a high-heeled, lipsticked Gulf Arab exchanging kisses in the midst of abundant money and liquor. The image of the prostitute

Figure 19. Mohamed Filali, *Al-Aqrab,* March 1991.

belly dancer is carried to a higher level of invective in this cartoon when she is revealed under his/her robes to be a male homosexual transvestite Arab.

Moroccan cartoonists generically stereotyped the coalition leadership, and its Arab component in particular, as women or as the lowest category of woman, the belly dancer, or as the most despised category of femininity, the male homosexual transvestite. Persons known to be male (e.g., Bush) are shown in women's clothing. Consequently, the only "real men" in the equation of war caricatures were American women serving in the armed forces in the Gulf. A Filali cartoon in *Al-Aqrab* (Figure 19, 4 March 1991) shows a voluptuous American female soldier with a purse full of money: at her feet, a Saudi male is on his knees purposefully stuttering: "We thank you, you have sexually excited us, sorry, I mean you have liberated us." The American woman soldier in uniform remains an object of sexual revulsion and attraction as she comes to embody the perverse ferocity of U.S. military capabilities.[15] An Algerian cartoon illustrating an editorial in *El-Watan* (Figure 20, 10 February 1991), by cartoonist MAZ, pictures a Saudi shrieking in retreat at the sight of a uniformed American woman soldier driving a jeep. He

Figure 20. MAZ, *El-Watan,* 10 February 1991.

shouts: "A naked woman! Even more she is driving a car, a sacrilege!" The accompanying article in the Algerian paper points out the contradictions of women defending a country with no women's rights and includes an interesting anecdote about an American woman soldier who allegedly pulled a gun on a Saudi official who objected to her uncovered hair. American women presumably could only defend American rights, and even then their fight preserves only such minimal freedoms as the right to soldier unveiled.

Caricatures explicitly reduce the political expression of a country, say Iraq or the United States, to a single individual: Saddam Hussein, Bush, or to a woman who symbolizes that country. At the same time, the graphic image allows for a speculative and interrogative dimension. In contrast, television discourages reflection upon complex issues of context, history, gender, culture, and international relations. Images are discrete and self-contained and exclude any discussion. Television, then, is a more powerful caricature, if you will, than any cartoon. As an *Al-Aqrab* cartoon (Figure 21, 21 January 1991) predicts, a person who relies on television for information ends up in

Figure 21. *Al-Aqrab,* 21 January 1991.

the insane asylum as an idiot who fuses with technology and becomes one with the idiot box. The idea that "the camera never lies" and the way we accept television images as real are challenged by conventions of cartoon drawings. Television images of the Gulf War, including diagrams, maps, and quasi-scientific graphics were neither real nor more natural than a cartoonist's drawing of something we have never seen. Political cartoons served as vehicles for imaginative projections of reality about sex and war; to quote the motto of True Comics in America: "Truth is strange and a thousand times more thrilling than fiction." If Moroccan and Algerian cartoonists can depict the arena of struggle between the television image and the cartoon graphic, then the ways that actual readers make use of newspaper humor in their own lives may provide that critical jolt to supplement TV channel-zapping with the subjectivities of cartoons.

# An Interview with Heba Ra'uf Ezzat

Conducted by Karim El-Gawhary

Heba Ra'uf Ezzat is a teaching assistant in the Political Science Department at Cairo University. Active in the Islamist movement, she is known for her academic research on women's political role from the perspective of political Islam and its theory. She formerly edited the women's page in *Al-Sha'b,* a weekly opposition newspaper published by a coalition of the Muslim Brotherhood and the Labor Party.

As a young Islamist intellectual, she is evoking a new discourse on women, politics, and political sociology that is seen as rather "liberal" inside the Islamist movement. "I don't believe that God wants to humiliate me as a woman," she has said elsewhere, explaining that, in her view of orthodox Islam, prescriptions which hold a woman's testimony to be worth only half of that of a male apply only in very special cases.

Ezzat contests any separation between the public and private spheres; rules that apply in the political arena should also be valid for the family. Within this framework, she calls for a kind of "democratization of the man-woman relationship inside a family structure." She does not cooperate with secular women's groups in Egypt, although she was one of the most active participants in a youth dialogue between Islamists and secularists organized by the Muslim Brotherhood in April 1994. Afterward, some people expressed disappointment at the lack of interest on the part of secular women's groups for such a dialogue. Ezzat is married to an Islamist student leader and has a young daughter.

This interview was conducted in September 1994.

Figure 1. Heba Ra'uf Ezzat. Photo courtesy of Heba Ra'uf Ezzat.

*El-Gawhary:* Your research deals with the role of women from an Islamic point of view. How do you approach this issue?

*Ezzat:* I declare myself an Islamist, but this doesn't mean that I accept the dominant discourse about women inside the Islamist movement. My studies focus on the need for a new interpretation of Qur'an and Sunna [the tradition of the Prophet]. We should benefit from the *fiqh* [Islamic legal theory] and the contributions of previous generations of Islamic scholars. This doesn't mean that we have to stick to their interpretations of Islamic sources while we ignore the sociology of knowledge.

*El-Gawhary:* There is a parallel effort in the West to restructure different academic disciplines with a feminist approach. Is this discussion relevant to your work?

*Ezzat:* Feminists are secularists who are fighting male domination. Many regard religion as an obstacle to women's rights and they concentrate on women's superior or special nature. Conflict is the main concept of their theory, a theory that they even want to turn into a paradigm.

My effort is quite different and even opposes such ideas. I am not an

Islamic feminist. I do believe in Islam as a worldview, and I think that women's liberation in our society should rely on Islam. This necessitates a revival of Islamic thought and a renewal within Islamic jurisprudence.

*El-Gawhary:* Would you say that orthodox Islamic jurisprudence is a patriarchal construct?

*Ezzat:* I wouldn't go so far as to accuse the whole *fiqh* of being patriarchal. I believe we need to differentiate between what is absolute and what is relative in shari'a. I am not aiming to deconstruct Islamic law and thought, but rather to reconstruct it. I am actually defending Islam from stagnation and bias.

*El-Gawhary:* What do male Islamic scholars say about your reinterpretations?

*Ezzat:* I am using the same orthodox methodology to interpret the Qur'an and Sunna. I say: "Respected ulama: I use the same tools of interpretation and reach different conclusions." The aim is to change the paradigm from within. My discourse seems to be confusing on both sides. The secularists realize that I am still standing on Islamic ground yet using a different language from the dominant Islamic one. The Islamists, on the other hand, see that my language is Islamic but filled with new ideas and different conclusions.

*El-Gawhary:* Can you synthesize your central ideas?

*Ezzat:* I am mainly refusing the public-private dichotomy that is dominant in Western and Islamic thought. This dichotomy gives either privacy — for example family life — the priority, or the contrary. In my opinion, Islam doesn't embody such a polaristic perception. Private is political, not in the feminist aggressive sense but rather in the Islamic sense of solidarity and the importance of social infrastructure and grassroots politics. Social movements cannot be understood in an Islamic social system without analyzing the extended family as a political and economic unit. The Palestinian intifada is an example.

In my study of religious sources, I found a lot of analogies between public and private. For example, the main Islamic dynamic within the political process is *shura,* which means consulting people. We have shura like the West has democracy. The same value is dominant in family relations. You can't have a totalitarian patriarchal system in a family in Islam. The family should be run by shura. The same values and laws count in the public and the private arenas. Marriage is like voting for or choosing the *khalif* [the successor of the Prophet]. We do have a family head, but he is like the khalif and should be chosen freely. If he is unfair, he should be denied the right to be the head of the family. As people can withdraw their homage to their khalif, women can divorce their husbands.

*El-Gawhary:* Doesn't your emphasis on the family reinforce the call for the return of the working women to the home, which is widely supported by the Islamists?

*Ezzat:* The issue is not black and white. Women differ according to their education, social class, age, talents, and creativity. Every woman at every moment of her life should have freedom of choice among different roles. Circumstances should be changed to help her contribute in all spheres of her life, to fulfill her economic and political duties. The family should be regarded as the basic unit of society and protected and developed. Women's role and society's respect should focus on women's active participation within and outside of their homes. Breaking the dichotomy would give housewives more social esteem and would encourage working women to fulfill their psychological need to be good mothers and wives.

*El-Gawhary:* Isn't it a paradox for you that historically women's liberation movements were secular?

*Ezzat:* We should not only study the romantic start of these movements, but the results, too. Did women really obtain their rights in Islamic societies? We are still facing many problems. The Islamists always considered women's liberation a Western idea. This prevented them from making their own interpretations about women's problems.

It is time to launch a new women's liberation movement — an Islamic one, not only for the benefit of Muslim women and Muslim societies but for all women everywhere. If Islam is a universal religion and a way of life, then this movement too should aim at universal goals. It should parallel a struggle for economic and political liberation from the colonialism of the new capitalist world order.

# Women on Women: Television Feminism and Village Lives

Lila Abu-Lughod

In January 1996, when I returned for a short visit to the Upper Egyptian village I had been working in for a number of years, I watched, with friends, some episodes of the current television serial, *Mothers in the House of Love*. Set in a retirement home for women, the episodes unfolded the stories of each of the residents, showing how they had ended up there (some tricked into it so their share of an inheritance could be stolen by a brother driven by his greedy wife, some to escape unpleasant daughters-in-law). The central drama concerned the attempt by the unscrupulous brother-in-law of the widow who ran the place to take it over so he could achieve his dream of building a twenty-two-story hotel. Armed with a newfound purpose, the women residents banded together to defend their threatened home. They forgot their squabbles about which television programs to watch, mobilized their talents to raise the money to buy out his share, and stood up to him.

The serial had been written a few years earlier by Fathiyya al-ʿAssal, a vibrant and self-confident writer and one of only a handful of women of her generation writing television dramas. Active in the Egyptian leftist party, she had occasionally been jailed and had had numerous story ideas tabled and serials cut by the television censors — civil servants working for state-owned television — and even by those higher up in government. Her serials were known for their social concerns, and she considered women's issues critical.

How did al-ʿAssal's serial, and others like it, relate to the lives of women in this Upper Egyptian village? In a region of Egypt considered "peripheral" these women live in a village that might look atypical: set in and among the Pharaonic tem-

Figure 1. Fathiyya al-ʿAssal. Photo: Lila Abu-Lughod.

ples of ancient Thebes, it has been the base for numerous foreign archaeolo-
gists, folklorists, and writers. But in being a mix of mudbrick homes and new
cement and brick structures, in having television sets in every house, men
with experience as migrants, and households whose meager incomes derive
from a combination of wage labor and farming, it is by no means unique in

Figure 2. Women's literacy class, rural Upper Egypt, 1996. Photo: Lila Abu-Lughod.

Egypt. Nor is the village women's exposure to foreign and urban worlds and lives, especially through television, unusual.

Television, in Egypt monopolized until only a few years ago by state-controlled broadcasting, is particularly useful to examine because this is a crucial place where village women and urban intellectuals meet. What happens in that encounter? How well do they speak to each other? What problems do socially concerned television producers face when they aspire, as does al-ʿAssal, to social reform? What do Egyptian feminists, by and large urban, professional, and upper middle class, have to offer to village women?

## Love and Marriage

I watched several episodes of *Mothers in the House of Love* with my village neighbors, who, though intrigued, kept up a running commentary, laughing at ludicrous characters like the compulsive knitter of pullovers. After an episode in which a sixty-year-old widow had finally consented to marry an old sweetheart, one person joked, "Now all sixty-year-old women will want to marry."

The next day, though, Zaynab, another woman I knew well, commented more realistically on this episode.[1] She simply contrasted it to local attitudes. "We say when a girl is past thirty she won't marry. . . . It is shameful. If a woman over thirty does marry, she'll do it quietly, far away, without a wedding celebration."

Zaynab's comment was revealing in so many ways. Directed to me, it posited the difference between the villagers (and Upper Egyptians in general, by extension) and the urban, wealthy Alexandrian women of the television serial as a cultural difference within a moral frame. The construction of difference was partly for the edification of the anthropologist. Zaynab's long years of watching her mother's wealth of funeral laments being carefully noted down by a Canadian folklorist, and her regular experience of being photographed by visiting tourists, had no doubt helped her objectify her own culture. Her gifts to me over the years suggested she had learned her lessons well. Her first gift was an earthen casserole dish of the sort locally made and used. The second was a traditional piece of black cloth, threaded with gold. She offered it with the confident announcement that she had got me something I would really like, something rare nowadays. The third was a black shawl, the latest local design for what "traditional" women wore on their heads. Each represented something unique to Upper Egypt and something that those eager to become more sophisticated would have rejected as old-fashioned. Yet for Zaynab, a woman very much at home in her social world, a little old before her time, and confident as one of the adult women of the village who took her social duties — sick visits and funerals, for example — very seriously, the cultural differences within which she framed her response to the serial were also personally meaningful.

The writer of this serial had strong views on love and marriage. One of the serials she was most proud of, called "She and the Impossible," was about a woman who, rejected by her husband because she is uneducated, gets herself educated. When he then wants to take her back, she refuses, even though they have a son together. Al-'Assal said of it, "My point was to emphasize the value of a home as a home. That is to say, a man and woman should only enter on condition that they love one another." Marriage for her should be first and foremost about mutual understanding and love. She, like other progressive television writers, and a long line of feminist reformers since the early twentieth century, contrasts her ideas about companionate marriage to prevailing values that place financial considerations first.[2]

Zaynab's marriage did not fit this bourgeois feminist ideal. Hers had been an arranged marriage but, following the lines of closest practical kinship, it was to a maternal rather than paternal cousin. Zaynab's mother had been a second and younger wife, widowed shortly after she gave birth to this only child. Not close to her own husband's patrilineage, she had turned to her relatives for support, and eventually for a husband for her daughter. She had inherited some land, on which she and Zaynab had later built a two-story mudbrick home. Zaynab's husband had worked on and off in Cairo since he was fourteen, leaving her mostly alone with her mother to raise her children, most conceived on his occasional visits home to give her money and to see to some of her needs. Secretly, he had married a second wife in Cairo; Zaynab now knew about it and was resigned to the fact that he would probably never return to live in the village.

As the years went by, Zaynab coped. It was tough when her milk dried up after she gave birth to a set of twins; it almost ruined her to feed them expensive formula. She and her mother were forced to sell all their livestock because they could not take care of them. Then her mother, by all accounts an extraordinary woman, died. This left Zaynab on her own. She talks about her husband's visits home this way: "He's like a guest; he doesn't know anything about our lives."

One cannot ignore the possibility that Zaynab had remarked on the episode of the older widow's wedding because it was meaningful to her own personal situation. The idea of remarriage might have been appealing. She was alone, managing a complex household, and her children provided her only company most evenings (when they all watched television together). She had no man to help her make decisions about the children's schooling, about what to plant and harvest on which strips of land, and about which domestic livestock to buy or sell. For help with the hard work in the fields, she had to call on young male relatives or pay for labor. Certainly she had no one for companionship or love.

Some people urged her to ask for a divorce. She thought it was improper. And, of course, with all these children and at her age (she was forty), she would never remarry. She had social protection in her status as a married woman, and her children this way had both a mother and a father. He might not be much of a presence, but he would give away his daughter in marriage; and, who knew, perhaps his sons would develop some bond with him.

In fact, a recurrent theme in my conversations with Zaynab was the situation of the five or six older women from Switzerland, Germany, and the United States who had married — or had affairs with — village youths they met while on holiday. Some were divorcees with grown children, a feature Zaynab remarked on several times. Over the years, Zaynab brought up this topic many times, using me as an informant about the strange behavior of foreigners. Why did these women do it? She tried to sound morally neutral, not condemning them outright but expressing puzzlement about how this might be acceptable, especially to their children. Was this the way Europeans were? She was not the only village woman to talk to me about this phenomenon, but I wondered if her curiosity about these older women who had second lives, and chances at love, might not have had a special resonance, as had the episode about the widow's remarriage. Nevertheless, as a woman whose respectability rested on her marriage, she distanced herself in moral language from what she perceived as a cultural difference between life here, in Upper Egyptian villages, and there, in Alexandria, Cairo, or other cities.

## Work and Education

In one of the first conversations I had while watching television with Zaynab, she animatedly told me about the program that had just come on the air. This extraordinary weekly show was called *The Confrontation* and consisted of interviews — more like interrogations — of actual criminals serving prison sentences. Imitating the Cairene dialect, Zaynab recounted a memorable interview with a woman drug dealer. When the interviewer asked if she would do it again, the woman had replied, "Of course. As soon as I get out I'll deal in drugs again." Asked why, she replied, "I have to eat." Zaynab explained that the woman had become accustomed to a certain standard of living and so had to keep it up. Zaynab quoted her again, "They'll jail me, and I'll get out and deal. They'll put me in prison, I'll get out and do it again. That's how I make a living."

In retrospect, that she found this female criminal so memorable seems as significant as the fact that she responded to the television theme of marriage at a late age. For Zaynab, a person of great integrity insulted by any hint of disrespect, the woman drug dealer, trying to feed herself, must have represented something strangely compelling. Zaynab's whole life was organized around trying to feed herself and her family, in the larger sense of trying to manage a household and educating, clothing, and raising her children. Work and economic management were the most persistent themes in her conversations with others and the main concerns in her day to day life. She farmed two small plots of land, far apart, as well as raising sheep, a water buffalo, chickens, ducks, and pigeons. She had to arrange for irrigation, help with ploughing, and fertilizer. Her sons were now old enough to help harvest clover to feed the animals and to help her with grazing, if they weren't at school. She had to arrange for wheat to bake bread, as well as the buying and selling of animals and vegetables. Because she had a migrant husband, she had more responsibility than many village women for managing such a complex enterprise. But many of the poorer women I knew worked just as hard, if not harder.

Women's work and social usefulness were also the main themes of the serial we watched in January. But here again, the differences between what Zaynab saw on television and what she experienced were genuine. One of al-ʿAssal's goals in writing her serial *Mothers in the House of Love* was to show that the perceptions of "old age"and "senility" in women were, at least in part, the result of their not having any social role. As she put it, regarding her script:

Rather than sitting around and waiting for death because she has already raised her children and no longer has a purpose, I wanted to create a new role for older women. I have a number of female protagonists who were able to find another path. In the retirement home itself, they started a class for teaching English, because there was a woman who had been an English professor; another woman who had been a silversmith opened a small silver workshop and taught women the skills needed for this work. They participated in the eradication of illiteracy by teaching neighborhood girls to read and write. They also gave classes on household management, and even agriculture. There was even a peasant who did the gardening and she instructed people on planting. In other words, all of their skills were put to use, not simply discarded. My message is that women can still learn at this age and we can still benefit from what they have to teach us as well.

The dynamic Cairene writer claimed to speak from her experience, explaining,

I am sixty years old now. In the past, when a woman was sixty she was supposed to sit at home waiting to die, having already married off her children. I now have four children and eight grandchildren, but because I have my own concerns and ambitions as a writer and a politician I do not feel that I am getting older. I wanted to communicate this in a serial.

Al-ʿAssal's socialist feminist message: advocating socially useful roles for women, skills and activities that could take them beyond their place in the family and home, and economic independence that would alleviate the worst effects of male domination, is impressive. This politically motivated position is underwritten by al-ʿAssal's anger. Her father was a wealthy businessman who married twenty women after marrying (and eventually divorcing) her mother. Al-ʿAssal was determined to become educated herself and still believes in education as the key for women — and to social progress. She began her career as a serial writer when she found that the students she was teaching to read and write deserted the classroom to listen, with the janitor, to radio melodramas.

She works the importance of literacy into many of her plots. She proudly told me about one called "Moment of Choice," about a woman of fifty whose husband ran off with another woman, leaving her with no skills or identity. As al-ʿAssal described it,

It was about how she was able to deal with life, how she refused to ever return to being the wife of so-and-so, how she had to become a person in her own right, how she worked in a publishing house and read and expanded her horizons, and finally how she wrote stories and won a prize for them. The serial ended up on that note, in order to show how she was able to win the prize herself; she was the sole master of the victory.

How might a theme like becoming literate affect Zaynab? Just the year before *Mothers in the House of Love* was broadcast, government-sponsored literacy classes for women had been set up in and around the village. Attending was out of the question for someone as busy as Zaynab. Women went for a variety of reasons but all those who attended had one thing in common: they had no children, or very few that someone else could watch for a while, and their family situations were such that they could be released from work for a few hours in the afternoon.

In January, when I went to pay a call on Umm Ahmad, another woman I knew and liked, I asked if she was going to the classes. With her eyes bright and a big smile she said she really wanted to; she was dying to learn to read and had been trying to collect her father's pension (the octogenarian had recently died) and hated it that she couldn't even sign her own name. "Can I learn?" she asked me dubiously. "No, I'm too old. I've got no brain," she laughed. Then she added, "An old woman — why they'll talk. They'll say, 'Why does she need to go and learn?' " I asked who would talk and she said, "The men. The men will talk."

She told me that classes were being held in three places nearby. I suggested she could accompany two women from the hamlet that I (and she) knew. One lived just opposite her. She said no. She'd go to a different one she could get to quickly, through the fields so people wouldn't see her going.

When her son, a young man in his early thirties and father of two young children, walked into the room, I teased, "Hey, you should let her go to the literacy classes." He replied, "Fine, that's fine. She can go." Turning to her with a smile he added, "In fact, I'll get you a book bag." This was an amusing idea since village women never carry satchels or handbags. If they go to market or visiting, they carry a basket on their heads. Otherwise, what they need is tucked inside their long black overdresses. Only schoolchildren and city people carry bags.

But Umm Ahmad was no downtrodden, superannuated old woman lacking any socially useful role or skills, as Al-'Assal might have feared. She was a grandmother, but a wiry and energetic one: working in the fields, caring for her water buffalo, and selling cheese and butter locally. Her situation was somewhat unusual, but in my experience everyone's story in the village was unique. She had had a bad marriage and returned to live in her father's household. She had only one son who, also unusually, lived with her and worked her father's fields, as well as holding a night job as a guard at a nearby Pharaonic temple. For years she had taken care of her father, who was in poor health and not always lucid. A founder of the hamlet in which they lived, he had been an important figure. Umm Ahmad had been in charge of running his household and the farming enterprise, especially the livestock, as her son was growing up, not to mention when he left, desperate for income, to work briefly for a chicken breeding factory near Alexandria.

What significance could a group of wealthy or formerly wealthy women, sitting around a comfortable retirement home and suddenly putting aside their individual troubles and overcoming their sense of helplessness and uselessness, have for Umm Ahmad? What about the modernist feminist ideal of women's rights to education and a meaningful career, or at least socially useful work? What about the idea of winning a prize for writing? Umm Ahmad had to contend with a gender system that constrained women, but this was hardly the main impediment to securing a decent life. Other concerns were more pressing: the cost of farming with more expensive fertilizer, the depressed prices the government paid for crops, the IMF-enforced lifting of subsidies for wheat that made provisioning households with bread a strain for most local families, the higher cost of living in an area where hotels catering to tourists drove up prices, the felt need to get children educated so they might find employment, and the vast inequalities between large landlords and the majority of households.

What possibilities did Umm Ahmad or other women have for meaningful careers that would provide personal fulfillment and the financial independence necessary for marriage based on equality when even the finest local men who had become educated might have to content themselves with being foremen of laborers at archaeological sites? Or perhaps waiting for five or six years after teacher's college for a government job as a librarian in the local high school, working a couple of hours a day and making barely enough to pay for cigarettes?

## Critical Interventions

The problem is not just that cultural producers like al-ʿAssal come from a different social class than these village women who watch her programs, though this is significant. Nor is it a matter of the difference between urban and rural experiences, however considerable.[3] Al-ʿAssal has actually tried to bridge this kind of difference by writing a serial, broadcast in 1993, about rural Upper Egypt. The serial showed the cruelty and power of large land-lords and the powerlessness of peasants who don't seek common cause. But the main theme was revenge (the feud), the metonym by which Upper Egypt has been known to generations of northern Egyptian writers (the violence it signifies now transferred neatly onto Muslim militants and terrorists).[4]

Al-ʿAssal wrote this serial out of genuine concern. She even spent three months living with a rural family to prepare herself to write the script, just as she had studied a retirement home to write *Mothers in the House of Love*. As a radical politician, she was deeply concerned with social conditions and the terrible poverty of the region. But her focus on vengeance and the solution she offered reproduced the discourse of enlightened modernity against back-ward customs that continue to denigrate Upper Egyptian men and women. The hero and heroine of the program were a young couple, a latter day Romeo and Juliet, whose modern education and enlightened ideas led them to reject the feud (a "backward" tradition still nurtured by older women) and to attempt to break the hold of the feudal lords, and their wives, by supporting peasants' efforts to set up a collectively owned factory.

Al-ʿAssal's feminism, like her progressive politics, is part of a public discourse of reform and uplift, in the name of modernist ideals, whose con-tours can be traced to the colonial and anticolonial nationalist efforts to make Egypt modern. Tempered by ethnography and broad sympathy in al-ʿAssal's case, this general attitude of knowing what is good for "society" (seen as an object to be manipulated by using one's expertise), underlies the work of many of the writers of television serials, just as it shapes the myriad projects of reform from schooling to public health plans in which villagers find themselves involved. Because of television, this bureaucratic national discourse on modernity is widely disseminated.

Such discourses of enlightenment must be looked at critically. Had Umm Ahmad been able to attend her local literacy classes, she would have learned to read and write using textbooks of didactic stories about the value of small families, neighborly cooperation, and national responsibility.[5] Until she gets her book bag, she is subjected to this pedagogic discourse mostly by watching television, which she does. How does this discourse help her place herself? As someone who could carry a book bag? As someone whose life is different from the ones portrayed? Or as someone whose life is hopelessly inferior?

If through fieldwork in rural and regional peripheries one can begin to tease apart the structures of power within which women like Zaynab and Umm Ahmad live their lives, and the ways television is a new part of that, in households, in communities, and in imaginations, can one enter into debate with concerned writers one admires, like al-'Assal, regarding how to think about their audiences and their political projects?

I am interested in using my experiences of village life this way because I respect such writers' social concern but also know that from the vantage of Upper Egyptian villagers, for example, the answers these writers offer for social problems facing ordinary people often appear unrealistic, and almost as foreign and forced as the colonial, neocolonial, or commercial alternatives. Television intersects with and extends the discourses of experts. It is directed at stereotyped audiences, the same generalized objects targeted by social reformers. Is there a way to complicate urban intellectuals' understandings of Egyptian villagers? Is there a way to use ethnography to make feminist writers like al-'Assal see uneducated Upper Egyptian villagers as something other than "backward": to complicate their visions of the forms of power at work, and the layered sources of village women's personal pains and satisfactions? Can they take more seriously the complexity of the forms of cosmopolitanism found across Egypt? Zaynab and Umm Ahmad are, after all, women who know about other ways of life, even about dissertations, fellowships, and development films. Many have been to Cairo, all have watched countless Egyptian films set in Cairo, and American soap operas set in Colorado. Can there be a way to see the forms of power Zaynab exerts because of her hard work and, like the wives of many migrants, because of her absentee husband? Or the power other village women, more privileged than Zaynab, derive from appealing to their wealthy landowning fathers?

Western feminists have been accused of rendering Third World, or Middle Eastern women, silent victims.[6] But Arab feminists, usually privileged and educated, and usually modernists, can find themselves similarly patronizing.[7] Al-ʿAssal distinguishes her brand of feminism from that of a Nawal El-Saadawi (the much translated Egyptian feminist physician and writer) by its insistent linkage of women's issues to larger issues of socioeconomic and political injustice. And to her credit, one of her aims in writing the serial on Upper Egypt was to show, as she put it, "that the real vengeance would be to lash out [through development] against the circumstances that have led them to be attached to the vendetta in the first place." But by continuing to subsume much more complex stories of rural life under the familiar modernizing trope of a negative "tradition" and "backwardness,"and by offering, as have Egyptian feminists since the turn of the century, education and companionate marriage as panaceas, this impressive writer and politician risks reaffirming the marginality of such women as Zaynab and alienating herself from those whose cause she has taken up, even though she genuinely cares about their predicament.[8]

I am grateful to Fathiyya al-ʿAssal, Omnia El Shakry, Siona Jenkins, Hasna Mekdashi, Boutros Wadiʿ, and the women in the village, for their contributions to the research on which this article is based. I received very helpful comments on an earlier version of the paper from Faye Ginsburg, Brian Larkin, Tim Mitchell, and Sherry Ortner.

# Sudanese Women and the Islamist State

Ellen Gruenbaum

In the twenty-six years since I first began my association with Sudan, starting with five years residence during the Nimeiri government in the 1970s, its struggling economy, the Islamist movement, and its civil war have each produced strains and pressures on the Sudanese people. But following the accession to power of General Omar al-Bashir in a coup d'état in 1989, the development of an expressedly Islamist state under the National Islamic Front (NIF) has intensified the pressures for the Sudanese people, especially its women.

The mid-1980s, after Nimeiri was ousted in 1985 and an elected government took over in 1987, were a period of optimism and democratic flowering, when newspapers in several languages and of various political views flourished and trade unions and a broad spectrum of political groupings exercised freedom of speech. Many felt that the multi-ethnic, multi-faith country, where only about two-thirds of the citizens are Muslim, was on the eve of a major, negotiated break-through that could end the civil war with the Sudan People's Liberation Movement and provide a workable framework to allow non-Muslims more freedom from the Islamic laws Nimeiri had instituted. But those hopes were dashed when, in June 1989, the NIF took power to prevent those developments.

At that time no one imagined that the regime could last long. El Bashir's government fired dozens of civil servants, judges, and military officers who were "too secular" or otherwise opposed to the declared program of Islamicization of government. These sackings resulted in major problems with the delivery of basic government services. The government's draconian price reductions of commodities, initially welcomed by the people burdened by inflation and black marketeering, led to a disappearance of meat from the Khartoum market as butchers could not afford to slaughter. Sugar, flour, bread, tea, coffee, and batteries were all hard to find in 1989, and merchants were forced to open their shops at military gun-point in some cases, to sell at the lowered prices or be arrested for hoarding. Despite initial public support, the new government's attempts to suppress the black market and the hardships resulting from the disappearance of so many commodities eventually led to criticism of the government's incompetence at managing the economy.

Yet in spite of many protests and plots to undermine the regime, it has hung on for more than a decade, and the civil war has escalated, both in the South and on new fronts. This tenacity reflects not only the government's willingness to use repressive means, but also its determined ideological use of Islamism together with other symbols of wealth and power.

As one example of such symbolism, in 1992 the Islamist government celebrated the third anniversary of the military coup that brought it to power by building a huge new public park south of the Khartoum airport, featuring hundreds of hurriedly transplanted trees, bushes, and flowers. The impressive determination and efficiency the project commanded seemed calculated to prove to Khartoum's urban masses that this is a can-do government. But at the same time, cynicism was rife. Although urban shops were well stocked with the commodities consumers wanted — stacks of the favored white wheat bread were available all day, and any government employee who wanted one could get a sack of sorghum to keep at home as insurance against future bread shortages — the full shops and bright flowers represented a superficial improvement, one that masked a deep and very painful erosion in the quality of life in Sudan. The pressure for Islamicization of the state and the culture has entailed not only political repression, but also economic mismanagement, which has hurt almost everyone but those in power, and cultural shifts that are having a particularly pronounced effect on women's lives.

In 1992, one did not have to look far to see the stress of living in Khartoum. Basic services were faltering; power cuts were scheduled for eight hours every work day in the heat of May, when temperatures soar over 110 degrees Fahrenheit. Rampant inflation, coupled with the outlawing of trade unions that might have helped wages keep pace, meant that middle class and poor alike suffered tremendously. Many middle class people in Khartoum had cut back on protein consumption and were even skipping meals. Working two jobs or undertaking petty trade on the side were not uncommon. For refugees from the civil war and for the urban poor, the situation was far worse.

Under conditions like these, employed women are desperate to keep their jobs. But there is ideological pressure from the government and state-sponsored Islamic organizations to stay at home and follow the movement-defined Islamic roles for women. The Islamists argue that women's true cultural heritage is to be found in their interpretations of Islamic law, and they criticize even the traditional modest dress of northern Sudanese women, the *tobe,* as too revealing. This head to foot wrap-around veil, which does not conceal the face, is usually of a light fabric worn over other clothes. According to Islamists, clothes that do not adequately cover hair, the forearms, and the neck lead to public disorder and should be replaced by hijab "Islamic dress." Their goal is to have all women who appear in public wear opaque clothing which conceals all hair, covers the neck under the chin, and is long-sleeved, loose, and floor-length, preferably of a plain dark color. Face veils are optional and rarely seen in Khartoum. While the Qur'an does not explicitly require such garments, influential Islamic scholars allied with the National Islamic Front argue for this interpretation, which apparently is also favored by the Iranians who have at times aided Sudan's government.

The vast majority of women, whether urban or rural, have not adopted Islamic dress as yet, but many are worried about the issue, since it is difficult to know when one might be criticized, taunted, or even apprehended. For example, people in Khartoum were outraged by a case in October 1991, in which a woman was arrested on the street and taken to a "public order" court for being in violation of the unwritten dress code. Although she was dressed in a manner that has gained acceptance in the cities, a modestly long skirt, loose shirt with mid-length sleeves, and a light scarf which many women allow to fall to the shoulders but have available as a head covering when needed, she was found guilty of creating public disorder and sentenced to receive lashes and a fine. The woman had no way to defend herself since she had violated no specific statute. Her father paid the fine and successfully begged the judge to suspend the lashing.

In response to the public anger over this case, the government slowed the pace of enforcement of "Islamic dress," but its determination persisted. Articles in the press offer fashion advice for Muslims: women are to avoid looking "like a man" or wearing tight or clearly European clothing. In the past, women objected to Islamist pressure to wear hijab, claiming that they had no money to purchase such clothes. So in 1992 loans equivalent to about

$30.00 were paid to women government employees, to be repaid through payroll deductions, and employed women and students were given a deadline by which time they would have to wear "Islamic dress" on the job or risk being fired or arrested. Some Sudanese viewed this as an attempt to displace women from skilled and professional public employment. Many women were furious, but most felt they must conform, since their jobs are vital to family survival.

In the universities, women had already experienced strong social pressure from Islamists to wear the hijab, and a significant minority were already wearing the strictest type before these rules. Among students, a wide variety of less than strict clothing styles is common — especially long skirts, loose shirts, and scarves that do not conceal all hair completely. But in 1996 female security guards were regularly posted at the gates of the University of Khartoum to prevent entry if a woman's sleeves were too short or the clothes judged inappropriate. The same standards did not apply to women who appear to be of Christian background.

Among the poor and working classes, the Islamist movement has had less evident impact. Women still sit on streetcorners or in the market selling tea or crafts, and they travel, dress, and work according to their former patterns. But here and there women wear more concealing clothing, and one hears of some having to conform to greater restrictions on their movements. A former neighbor, who had managed her household of younger brothers and sisters in 1989, had by 1992 married a day laborer who was a strict Islamist. Her husband rarely allows her to leave the house and has ordered her to wear a black face veil, *abaya,* and gloves when she does.

The government's desire to implement shari'a and an Islamic constitution does not seem to represent a public consensus. The fact that it has been as successful as it has can be attributed to the skillful political use of real social change occurring in the region. A backlash against the colonial past, and a response to the dramatic, destabilizing change of the contemporary global relations, has allowed Islamists to foster a struggle over Sudan's authentic identity and culture.

The fact that many women are voluntarily wearing — and advocating — Islamic dress does not mean that they necessarily view women's rights and opportunities as a "Western"-inspired diversion from their cultural and religious roots in Islam. But the struggle does pose the risk that women's rights (labeled Western or feminist) and Sudanese traditions might both be buried in the version of Islamic society being advocated by the National Islamic Front.

The situation of non-Muslim women in Sudan is also potentially explosive, despite NIF claims that non-Muslims will not be coerced. The government has declared its civil war with the factionalized Sudanese People's Liberation Army, which advocates a secular government, a sacred struggle, a jihad against the enemies of Islam. Many interpret this to mean that land, cattle, and women in conquered areas can be claimed by the conquerors. One influential woman leader in the Islamist movement suggested that a solution to the "southern problem" was for Muslim men to take non-Muslim Dinka women as second wives or concubines, assuming their children would be raised as Muslims. Raiding of Dinka areas by armed militias has indeed resulted in alleged abuses of captured women and children. Ironically, pro-government propaganda has urged support for the war in order to protect Muslim women from southerners portrayed as wanting to invade the Sudanese heartland.

## Rural Influence

Although some have said that this regime holds power only in Khartoum, the Islamist impact on the two rural areas where I have done long-term research, one in the Gezira Irrigated Scheme and one east of the Blue Nile, is stronger than I had expected. Some of this comes from a genuinely religious inspiration. Many people in the villages feel that what they or their children have learned about Islam working in Saudi Arabia, for example, is a more correct or complete practice than Sudanese traditional practices have taught them. As one highly educated woman said in reference to her conservative Islamist views, "Before, people assumed I just said those things because I went to the university, so they ignored me, but now they are starting to listen." Some also mentioned Islamist missionaries — whether teachers who take up residence for a time or those who organize youth rallies to chant "Allahu akbar!" — as being influential.

One of the villages in the Gezira has for decades had close ties with the urban areas through schools, migration for employment, and trade. Since it has had electricity for years, and many of its educated young people found employment in the Gulf countries and Libya and sent home expensive goods, this village has been saturated with televisions. Nightly during my research visit in April 1992 large groups gathered to watch government reports of bumper wheat harvests, Egyptian soap operas, religious programs, and war scenes with marital music glorifying the government's role in the civil war. Improvements in mass communications — rumored to be a special beneficiary of Iranian aid — appear to have given the state an increasingly effective tool with which to influence public opinion.

The tenor of political discussions had definitely changed since my 1989 research. Although people still complained about the economy and expressed fear of government repression, there was far more discussion of topics such as proper attire for women, the civil war, and relations with non-Muslims. Many women were listening seriously to one who had been an expatriate in Saudia Arabia, who claimed that the Qur'an specified that women must wear long sleeves. Both women and men debated whether the civil war was a jihad (some said the SPLA was trying "to take Sudan away from the Sudanese," meaning Arab Muslim Sudanese), echoing a government argument that practicing Islam freely necessitates an Islamic state, but expressing dismay at the bloodshed and economic costs of the war. And people discussed the rights of non-Muslims versus the desirability of converting them to Islam.

In the other rural area where I worked there were no televisions and there had been little labor migration. There, experience with formal education was so recent that urban culture had far less influence, but there, too, the Islamists had made some inroads into women's cultural traditions. In neither area were the men tolerating the spirit-possession rituals of the zar. Some claimed it was merely dying out, rather than being forbidden, but some women said their husbands would not let them participate. Given the potential for zar practices to offer women mutual support and a form of resistance to subordination, its suppression is significant for women.[1] In the Gezira, health workers and educators exerted strong pressure to end pharaonic circumcision (the clitoridectomy and infibulation still widely practiced in northern and central Sudan), which was partially endorsed by the Islamists, who supported the modified Sunna circumcision. But in the other area (east of the Blue Nile) this was not yet an issue: "It hasn't reached us yet," women said, showing their awareness of the drift of social changes toward their area. They also were not yet concerned about Islamic dress.

## Group Weddings

Government sponsored group weddings were an innovation of the Islamist government which met with much praise, and some criticism, in both rural areas. Growing out of a sometimes-practiced tradition whereby two or more families might agree to hold weddings for their children on the same day to save on expenses, the government sponsored Islamic group weddings on a massive scale. Offering incentives such as plots of building land and cash grants (about $100 in 1992) for newlyweds, couples are encouraged to register at the Rural Council prior to presidential visits. The couples are brought in by bus and married en masse in the presence of President-General Omar al-Bashir. When Iran's former President Hashemi Rafsanjani visited a few years ago, he and al-Bashir attended a group wedding in Hasaheisa, where several hundred couples reportedly tied the knot.

For the poorly paid and struggling young people of the countryside, this took one of the most painful stings out of the inflation rate, by allowing them to avoid the usual high costs of marriage or the risk (for women) of becoming too old for marriage. Those more concerned about demographic issues and the costs of schools were less enthusiastic: "What will we do with all the babies when they get to school age?" asked one teacher. Although group weddings have now decreased (there has been some criticism from the Muslim Brothers about the immodesty of bringing all these unmarried women and men together), the government bought a great deal of political good will from many couples and their families. "It's just plain sugar," was one rural man's opinion.


## Obstacles to Resistance

Individual acts and expressions of resistance are not uncommon. One Khartoum woman I know cut her hair short, defiantly waiting for anyone to tell her she looks like a man, and wears short-sleeved shirts with her long skirts. But organized resistance has been difficult. Pressure to conform is felt by many who do not like the changes, resulting from the individual choices made by others out of a sense of duty and desire to live up to Islamic ideals in a way they have come to believe is more correct. Here the ideological use of mass media and missionary work is difficult to distinguish from a social process based in people's real experiences with migration, religious revitalization, and resulting cultural debates.

When the banner of Islam is claimed by the state, the state's policies become difficult to counter. Even the long-accepted democratic argument that people should be free in their practice of religion, allowing tolerance of Christians as well as variations in Islamic observances, is difficult to sustain as some are increasingly convinced that they know what God wants. Those who argue for democratic freedoms and human rights have been branded as Westernized elite intellectuals, who are undermining the "true" Islamic heritage with secular ideas. But there is recognition that arguments against pluralism, tolerance, and traditions unrelated to Islam can also be read as arguments against Sudanese, as well as European, cultural themes, offering a basis for nationalist opposition to some of the Islamist extremes.[2]

For example, some women who had previously given up the tobe for western clothes are wearing the tobe again, to emphasize their national/ ethnic pride and rejection of the hijab, which they consider a manifestation of cultural imperialism. But even such national/ethnic pride is ultimately vulnerable to the ideological hegemony of the Islamists, who argue that Sudanese customs — particularly northern and central Sudanese women's customs such as wailing at funerals, *zar* spirit possession, pharaonic circumcision, and dancing unveiled in mixed company at weddings — are backward holdovers from a pre-Islamic past.

More organized protest has been prevented by strong political repression, including the effective suppression of the trade unions and women's organizations other than those sanctioned by the regime. Organized opposition is considered extremely dangerous; both in Khartoum and in the rural areas people worry about spies and arrest. Mohamed (a pseudonym), a professional in his mid-thirties, was arrested and held extra-judicially for two months with other prisoners on a rooftop, unable to contact his wife and children. The security police investigated him for having collected money to aid the families of men who had been arrested as trade union leaders and political activists. Such humanitarian work, he was told upon his release, is itself subversive. Although he was freed, he later lost his job and now lives in exile. "We are waiting for a new generation of leaders to emerge," he says sadly.

Many university faculty were purged from the Universities of Gezira and Khartoum in March 1992, many of them trade union leaders or political opponents of the government. Ironically, since their salaries have been so severely eroded by inflation, most faculty cannot support themselves with university employment anyway, earning the equivalent of only about $200 per month. In May 1992, Amira, a teaching assistant in her twenties who seldom covered her hair but wore a transparent scarf around her shoulders or well back on her head, told me she was worried that she might sometime be arrested for the way she dressed. By the end of the month she had been fired. Within a few months she left the country, one of the few lucky ones who found a way to pursue her studies abroad. Since then, she has been able to make visits to family in Khartoum, but while there needed to borrow clothes with longer sleeves to avoid harassment.

An exodus of Sudanese intellectuals has been going on for some time because of Sudan's poverty and political problems, but now there are more women lining up at the airport. Yet many stay, struggling to keep food on the table while attempting to improve the situation of women. Some work to get more of a role for women in development projects, to improve women's health and end female circumcision, or to expand educational opportunities for women and girls. Ahfad College has long been a leading institution in education for women and in the early 1990s another new private women's college was started, Sudan University College for Girls, to provide training in journalism, computers, business, and other professions. Many of the students come from families who left for work in Saudi Arabia and the Gulf countries; their parents therefore have much more money than those who stayed in Sudan. Women's Studies has an important place in the curriculum of both of these institutions. Some critics hope that the educational system, by encouraging inquiry, comparative studies of other third world countries, and discussions of human rights and family welfare issues, etc., will keep critical thinking alive, despite the strong impact of well-financed ideological work by Islamist organizations. Just helping people to survive is an important service: the Babikr Bedri Scientific Association for Women's Studies publishes a magazine with practical information for women on such topics as coping with inflation, recycling, and preserving the environment.

Hearing so many stories of personal hardship, I often asked, incredulously, how they could manage. I was usually greeted with laughter, "We don't know, but we are surviving." After all, these friends have grown up with the loving appreciation of Sudan's hard circumstances, which no foreigner understands completely, expressed in sayings such as "When God made Sudan, God cried." Or as others tell it, God laughed: poor Sudan, the big joke. But as Amira said, bouncing back emotionally from the loss of her job, "We are something that sticks," she says. "We'll never give in, never give up."

## Emigres, Dissidents, Adaptors, and Proponents

As Sondra Hale concludes in her analysis of gender politics in Sudan, it would be a mistake to assume that women have been merely victims in the Islamist movement. Women inside the movement of the NIF have been actively creating the definitions of what proper Muslim women ought to be. This was evident from the large and vocal group of Sudanese women who attended the Non-Governmental Forum of the Fourth World Conference on Women in Beijing in the late summer of 1995. Many of the Sudanese women who attended were allied with the government: as members of Parliament, leaders of the government-affiliated Women's Union (an Islamist replacement for the Sudan Women's Union, whose leader Fatima Ahmed Ibrahim is now living abroad), or of the so-called Popular Defense Forces, or family members of political and ideological leaders. Others were non-Islamist scholars who are trying to coexist and preserve "critical thinking" (as one termed it) in educational and research institutions. Others were more outspoken leftist dissidents, some attending from exile, others from their careful internal positions. A very local group were the southern women who are now living in exile in East Africa.

The Islamist women, as one might expect, denied that oppression of religious or ethnic minorities was occurring. Even one northern Sudanese Christian woman (who therefore was not wearing hijab) argued that the fact that she herself was serving in Parliament offered evidence of greater openness and equality than is reported in the Western press. Others confidently denied the reports of raiding and enslavement by government-funded militias, again certain that this is due to an anti-Islamic bias of the United States and Europe. Women members of the pro-government Popular Defense Forces portrayed their work as beneficial to the rual areas of the south, where women work with men, they said, to provide conditions that would allow rebel soldiers of the SPLA to lay down their arms and return to peaceful economic pursuits. A researcher critical of the Defense Forces was scheduled to give a presentation at the conference, but when, the day prior, one of the members of the Defense Forces asked to join in the session, the original researcher decided it was too risky to show up, leaving the platform to the young women dressed in khaki tunics and white scarves sporting hand-lettered "Peace Maker" signs.

While the counterinsurgency element of their work was clear from the Defense Forces presentations and posters, they spoke with the confidence of firm belief that they were doing the right thing. One Islamist professor, active in the government's women's organization, shared the publication that she and others had prepared prior to the conference; they had brought together in Khartoum most of the women who were going to be attending the Beijing conference to share their research papers and discuss the issues, explicitly hoping to reach out to those who were not in sympathy with the government. And some of those who are not supporters of the Islamist regime regarded this as a serious, though perhaps propagandistic, attempt at conciliation. A large group of women representing the various perspectives — pro-government, exiles from Sudan Women's Voice for Peace, internal dissidents, and northern professionals living abroad — even came together in Beijing for two long meetings to discuss what they could do, as women, to help to end the civil war. While they were unable to forge an agreement in the two meetings, not surprising given the length of this painful conflict and the complexity of the issues, the discussion exhibited some of the linkages among Sudanese women that may yet play a role in transcending the conflict. It remains to be seen whether the fact that these women could, despite their angry differences, refer to one another as "my sister," will contribute to more successful negotiations than the official party and faction leaders have been able to offer.

Despite this active involvement of Islamist women in shaping, as well as being shaped by, the course of the movement, it remains that women's roles are most strenuously influenced by the Islamist state, whether it be dress, employment, health practices, or the suppression of Sudanese traditions in favor of some more "authentic culture" of Islam.

# For the Common Good?
## Gender and Social Citizenship in Palestine

Rita Giacaman, Islah Jad, and Penny Johnson

For over half a century, to be a Palestinian has meant the absence of formal citizenship and the rights and duties it confers. While important elements of citizenship previously resided in membership in the Palestinian community and its institutions, the coming of the Palestinian National Authority (PNA) to Palestinian territory in the West Bank and Gaza, with its limited powers, patchwork jurisdiction, and dependence on Israeli and international goodwill, opens a new era where the contours of Palestinian citizenship are being shaped and contested.

Citizenship in Palestine is still fundamentally at question, with deep implications for women, as well as other social groups and society as a whole. While the draft Basic Law (Article 9) prepared by the Legislative Council affirms that "Palestinians are equal before the law without discrimination on the basis of disability, sex, religion or political opinion," citizenship itself will be organized by a Nationality Law, which, in the current draft, confers citizenship through an "Arab father."[1] On the ground, one emerging conflict with serious implications for women is between individualized and clan-based entitlements, whether in terms of political representation or social allocations. President Arafat's determined revival of traditional and often discredited forms of clan-based leadership and mediation excludes women from participation, as surely as it undermines political parties and the development of the institutions of civil society.[2]

Despite political polarization, the Palestinian women's movement, along with other social and political groups, is actively engaged in negotiating claims and rights with the new authority and, to a lesser extent, in the public arena. A main focus has been governmental representation: to date, despite a few high-level appointments (most notably Um Jihad as the Minister of Social Welfare and Hanan Ashrawi as Minister of Higher Education), women are poorly represented in ministries, commissions, and, of great importance, almost all policy-making bodies. The 1996 creation of a gender planning unit in the Ministry of Planning is a positive exception. Four of the 88-member Legislative Council, elected in January 1996 are women, a minority but by no means exceptional showing (neighboring Jordan has one female parliamentarian).

If we examine aspects of citizenship other than political representation, we find contradictory terrain. The social contract between citizen and state is still unwritten and unrealized. In the wake of the harsh effects of decades of occupation and underdevelopment on the well-being of the population, and the current severe crisis in unemployment and increasing poverty, core social entitlements, such as social and income security, old age benefits, social services, public housing, unemployment, and occupational welfare, are just beginning to be a subject of analysis, debate or policy-making.

The dominant trend that can be detected in recent policy documents, among them the important series of reports by the World Bank entitled "Developing the Occupied Territories: An Investment in Peace," is to place relatively short-term economic development as the urgent priority, both in response to the serious crisis in (male) employment, and as the most effective means to secure support for the peace process and stability and legitimacy for the new Palestinian authority. Here, economic improvement, primarily through stimulating private investment and creating new sometimes temporary labor markets, primarily for unskilled male labor, is seen as the key to political progress. This strategy has been only partly implemented: the Authority itself has an erratic policy toward private investment, and most notably has greatly expanded public sector jobs through the rapid growth of the police and security services, and through multiple appointments to the ministries as a form of political favoritism.

Economic strategies related to jobs and investment that complement the political agenda may well be of great importance. However, such market-oriented strategies are not a universal panacea; they also create new problems and divisions in society and have serious implications for women. Without social support to address those disadvantaged by, or excluded from, the market economy, security and well-being, whether individual, societal, or state, is unlikely to be achieved. This is particularly true of Palestine in the present period, as Palestinian society emerges from a prolonged and debilitating period of conflict, occupation, and "low-intensity warfare," where the population's political, economic, and social welfare has suffered sustained harm.

## Forms of Social Support

Existing social support in Palestine functions on multiple levels, and is generally characterized by fragmentation, inadequate provision, and a focus on emergency assistance, rather than stable social provisions. The two main providers of formal social assistance, the PNA Ministry of Social Affairs and the United Nations Relief and Works Agency, currently serve an almost equal number of recipients, with small monthly stipends in cash, food relief, or health insurance benefitting a total of 175–180,000 individuals, or roughly 8 percent of the population. As families with able-bodied men are excluded from both programs, women have an obvious distinct position as recipients of social welfare.[3] Widows, women with disabled, ill or absent husbands, and divorcees constitute major categories for assistance.

Aside from these formal social assistance programs, a nonstandardized and politicized system of claims and favors, characteristic of PLO political culture, continues to be an important modus operandi within the new authority and political factions, alongside the development of bureaucratic structures. This system reflects the wider informal networks of social support and mutual claims that have sustained Palestinians (although not equally) and helped them manage daily life under occupation.[4] These networks can and do extend beyond family and kin, although family and kin continue to be central to individual and communal social support.

In order to construct equitable and effective public social policies in Palestine, it is important to look more carefully at these family-based networks, rather than to assume their continuous and unproblematic presence in Palestinian society. This assumption obviously guides the World Bank's characterization of the Palestinian household as a "shock absorber" that will continue to absorb economic shocks in the future, including a possible decline in real wages.[5] There are several important points to consider here. First, Palestinian households have already had to absorb a series of severe economic shocks, including the effects of the intifada, the Gulf War, and the persistent Israeli closures of the Occupied Territories in the 1990s. It should neither be assumed that their absorptive capacity is "infinitely elastic,"[6] nor that such crisis and strain on households and their individual members constitute a desirable and normative state of affairs. Second, as a 1993 ILO Mission to Palestine pointed out, "women bear the brunt of this situation [increased poverty and unemployment] and in many cases have to be the breadwinners of the household through difficult subcontracting and home-based work,"[7] in addition to the increased burden of care within the household. Third, these networks are not equally accessible to all households or members of society. In a 1993 study, Geir Ovensen analyzes how Palestinian households have coped with the dramatic decline in male labor force participation by income-pooling within families and remarks that "because of their small size and low labor activity, most female-headed households fall outside this private 'social security system.' "[8] Within the household, women may also have less access to social support networks than male family members.

Given these realities, it is perhaps more appropriate to view family-based social support as in crisis, rather than a stable status quo. Clearly, public policies are urgently required that relieve some of the pressure on households.

## Toward National Social Policies

The World Bank's 1993 assessment of social security provisions for Palestinians as "patchy, inequitable and inadequate" is still very much the case.[9] But the question remains whether the resource-restrained Palestinian Authority will take upon itself the formulation and execution of national-level social policies. Will the Palestinian Authority focus primarily on the coercive and policing functions of a state, as has happened in postcolonial societies elsewhere in the developing world, leaving the development of social policies and services to international aid and nongovernmental organizations?[10] Or will the PNA play a central and active role in determining the social rights of individuals and groups? Will social policies and programs be constructed through concepts of citizens' rights and universal entitlements, or through notions of charity? And finally, will these policies take into consideration gender and other social divisions in society, in terms of rights, allocations, and claims on the social product? A recent trend among a number of ministries to focus on the problem of increasing poverty in Palestine is both hopeful and limiting, in that it does not include an underlying social philosophy of the social rights and claims of each citizen on the social product; it is also somewhat influenced by donor frameworks.

Given the absence of a clear social vision to date, one early attempt deserves critical scrutiny: the PLO's General Program for National Economic Development, 1994–2000, contains in its chapter "Social Welfare and Recreation," a rare attempt to offer national policy on social welfare.[11] In the introduction to the section, the author does define a priority for social welfare:

As for the Palestinian state, all efforts need to be doubled to reach the minimal accepted standard to deal seriously with the problems of health, education, social welfare, occupational welfare, and local community and family services . . . the state should consider this a priority because developing this aspect will reflect positively in other social, economic and political sectors in Palestine.

However, in the preceding paragraph, the following rather bleak view of fiscal realizability is given:

Ensuring social equity to all and the welfare of the individual and society is impossible in the prevailing conditions. Thus, it is the state's responsibility in the interim period to achieve a substantial degree of care and social welfare, especially to the low-income and poor classes.

This contradiction between two adjacent paragraphs is not resolved by any clear statement of priorities in resource allocation within the authority, or by any conceptual framework of citizen's social rights and entitlements. The recommendations on social welfare are essentially eclectic. However, a careful reading yields serious omissions in meeting the needs and rights of groups within the population, especially women, and also draws out an implicit structure for social entitlements that is gendered and discriminatory.

## A Two Track System: Rights and Needs

In brief, secure entitlements (social security, retirement, and unemployment) are derived primarily from market productivity and are seen as the deserved benefits of the individual's economic contribution to society. A second tier of social care deals with vulnerable groups, defined variously in the document as orphans, the poor, "women in special circumstances," prisoners, families of martyrs, refugees, and the disabled. The elderly are placed in both categories. Vulnerable groups are defined by need, cited sometimes as "extreme poverty" or "special hardship": the elasticity of the definition of destitution and the fact that the list of vulnerable groups varies in different parts of the document reflect the instability of the entitlement.

This broad division between entitlements by right and welfare allocations by need has been identified in a variety of social welfare systems.[12] The
division is fundamentally gendered in that women's non-market contributions to society, whether in the informal economy and household, in care-
giving, or in the broad processes of reproduction and socialization, are not
acknowledged.

In the Palestinian context, however, this division needs further examination. Emerging from an entirely different context than the existing welfare
states, the social role of the Palestinian authority cannot be assumed. Is the
role of the authority based on providing services to all citizens — given that
the majority of Palestinians have suffered serious consequences of occupation, and, consequently, deserve wide and comprehensive social support?
Here, in fact, another definition of contribution to society is utilized, that of
struggle and sacrifice for the national cause. This definition could be used
negatively (political favoritism) or positively (recognition that all have contributed and should be equal citizens).

## Basis of Equality

While the document begins by reiterating the importance of achieving equality among citizens, a later elaboration reveals that what is meant is political
and regional equality, without regard to the serious inequalities existing in
Palestinian society, such as class and gender. When the theme of entitlement
or the right of citizens arises, it is linked primarily to paid labor. A clear
example of this approach is found in the examination of the entitlements of
retirement, where the document states:

There is no law that gives the family of the deceased the right to acquire his salary
upon retirement, or in the case of death before retirement. Retirement salary differs
from old age salaries, as the worker spent long years in work, and has the right to live
the rest of his life secure and content.

On the one hand, the policy clearly bases its retirement/social security
model on the right of workers to live in security and dignity for the rest of
their lives, identifying older people as a social category that has specific
rights. On the other hand, the family of the deceased worker has no right or
claim to this social support, and old age benefits are a lesser entitlement than
retirement funds. That is, the right for service provision, security, and dignity
is primarily based on paid work, omitting most women in their old age, and

negating their important and complex non-market contribution to socio-economic development. Given that most women in Palestine do not currently participate in the formal labor force (1995–96 female labor force participation stood at roughly 11 percent),[13] the policy's old age pension model, which has elements of citizens' rights, is undermined because of its unequal treatment of different social groups.

## Women in "Special" Circumstances

If and when women are considered in this document, they are reduced to the category of "destitute," requiring assistance in order to alleviate severe life conditions, or in relation to male "workers," "martyrs," and "prisoners." Under the sole section on "Care of Women in Special Circumstances," the document reads:

Women play a crucial role in Palestinian society, especially among the poor classes that suffer from extreme poverty. Many women support their families, in some cases women are partial supporters of a disabled son, and in other cases they support their families completely in the case of a martyred husband.

While ignoring the complex and varying life circumstances of women (no women, it is assumed, are divorced, abandoned, or even single), it reenforces the assumed status quo, where women's needs and existence are viewed solely in terms of their linkage to men, family, and kin. It is assumed that women do not work in normal circumstances, only when a male provider is absent. Even within the limited framework of "poor classes," such work is viewed as exceptional (when a husband is martyred or a son disabled), although the document states elsewhere that 44 percent of all families in extreme poverty are headed by females. The latter figure is probably not exaggerated: for example, the World Food Programme reported in September 1996 that 65 percent of the targeted beneficiaries of its food distribution in Gaza were female-headed households.[14]

When women are highlighted, it is in the context of their family responsibilities. The document fails to examine the needs of women at different stages in their lives, such as girls and teenagers, who are not really integrated into the extensive recreational program that constitutes a sizable part of the proposed budget allocations; this seems designed to deal with "idle youth" and "juvenile delinquents," categories that are clearly male, and, it might be surmised, categories that pose a threat to social and political stability.

Conflating the needs of women with the needs of children, one of the few special provisions is birth allowances, given in the budget at $90 per child. In the absence of other social support for children and families, this implies a pro-natalist policy which needs examination, not only for its impact on women, but on overall future economic development. Persistent, if slightly declining, high fertility is a major determinant of women's lives in Palestine: in 1995, the total fertility rate stood at 6.24 (representing the average number of children born alive to a woman in her lifetime), with the rate in Gaza an exceptionally high 7.44.[15] The population in already-congested Gaza is projected to double within the next seventeen years.

In general, the fulfillment of women's needs is relegated to charitable societies and women's groups, as if women's groups have defined their role as restricted to caring for other women in situations of dire poverty. Women's groups are matched with the care of "women in special circumstances," and women's organizations are urged to establish centers for the counter-innovative task of craft production, as well as other small-scale income-generating projects. This recommendation does not take into account the considerable experience of the women's movement in this area, including the economic failure of many of these projects. The failure of many such micro-projects has emphasized the need for more innovative and mainstream economic strategies for training and integration of women into labor markets.

## Control or Participation?

What the document emphasizes is the central role of the authority in controlling the policy making and planning process. Planning here is seen as a mechanical, technical procedure rather than a continuous process requiring the participation of different social actors, including women. The author envisages the authority as the planner and the executor, with the nongovernmental organizations assigned varying responsibilities in provision, neglecting the lessons learned in other developing countries, especially the Arab World, where policies failed precisely because they were imposed from above.

The document's assessment of Palestinian NGO social service provision under occupation, where women have been principal actors, as primarily faction based, unprofessional, and requiring state control is disturbing, and was reflected in the Authority's initial posture toward the NGO movement. While political factionalism exists (and has multiple effects that need analysis), this assessment homogenizes a very rich experience and fails to understand the importance of the local NGO process in creating a key infrastructure of service provision as resistance to occupation. More important, it fails to realize the significance of NGOs in not only developing innovative and effective programs of service provision, but also in developing the experience of democratization and community action essential for the growth of civil society, two aspects in which women's NGOs and women in NGOs have been central. In particular, the women's movement has been a leading force in widening and redefining what are social, rather than private, issues and needs, a perspective that can greatly contribute to the development of social citizenship.

In Palestine, the objective constraints of the transitional stage, the sheer newness of the authority, and the limited state and national resources are objective limiting factors. For almost the same reasons, however, this is a critical time for setting foundations: specifically for equitable social policies, and more broadly for social citizenship and a democratic vision of Palestinian society.

While most actors involved in policy formulation give at least lip service to building democracy and citizenship in Palestine, few to date have focused on the development of the constituents of citizenship, in particular a system of universal social entitlements that recognizes the social rights of citizens and state responsibility for provisions and protection, and addresses the inequities in society. Gender relations are deeply entwined in all these aspects; indeed, the quest for a democratic relation between state and citizenry cannot be divorced from the search for more equitable gender relations.

# Women and the Palestinian Movement: No Going Back?

Julie Peteet

The era described in this chapter is precisely that — an era, one that has now ended. Thus it can now be approached from a more or less historical fashion, with the critical hindsight afforded by the passage of time and reflection. During the period 1968–82, Lebanon was a space in which the Palestinian resistance movement achieved a significant degree of autonomy; it was a space in which, loosely speaking, a project in social experimentation unfolded. The issue of gender was located at the forefront of this project and the trajectory of the Palestinian women's movement, and the particular issues and policies it did or did not pursue, must be closely indexed to that of the larger national movement and the specificity of its experience in Lebanon. While this chapter focuses on the era of Palestinian autonomy in Lebanon, it tracks the rather dramatic changes that have occurred in the wake of the abrupt end of this period, and their impact on women.

The Palestinian women's movement began in the national ferment of the 1920s. Upper class urban women, usually kinswomen of prominent political personalities, organized charitable associations and women's organizations to assist in the national endeavor. Their goals and activities were oriented toward achieving national independence and social development. Demands for improvements or reforms in women's positions were negligible, largely overshadowed by the pressing immediacy of the national struggle. There was little discussion of changes in women's predominantly domestic roles or subordinate legal status. Palestinian women were aware of the organic links binding their movement to the national movement and made little attempt to separate their own problems and prospects from those of the larger social body. The absence of an independent Palestinian state structure in which to agitate for and materialize women's demands seemed to inhibit any such movement.

The year 1948 marked a major turning point in the history of the women's movement. Denied the right to return, the vast number of Palestinians who had fled or been expelled from their homes and villages in the 1948–49 Arab-Israeli war became refugees and an integral component in an emerging diasporic society. Over the course of the next decade and a half, the women's movement was dispirited and fragmented between those remaining inside Israel and those scattered in the various countries of exile.

With the establishment of the Palestine Liberation Organization (PLO) in the 1960s, the women's movement was reformed as the General Union of Palestinian Women (GUPW) and officially made a component part of the larger national body. This major transition, formally linking the women's movement and the national movement, was accompanied by another: the movement's attempts to transform itself into a mass-based organization that would represent the bulk of Palestinian women. Whether this class transformation in leadership and mass base was successful is highly debatable. The leadership, though, was clearly no longer composed of women from the elite, sharifian, landed or mercantile families. Women of the new middle class that emerged more forcefully in the wake of 1948 prevailed in the leadership, although a corps of camp women cadres, usually from a peasant background, entered the resistance bureaucracy and middle level leadership positions in the women's movement over the next decade.

During the 1950s in the refugee camps, the Palestinians were dispirited and unable to develop a leadership and organizational format capable of addressing their concerns. This state of affairs changed dramatically after November 1969 following a series of clashes with the Lebanese Army. The government accepted an open, armed Palestinian presence in an agreement known as the Cairo Accords. Thereafter, in an increasingly weak Lebanese state and fragmented polity and society, the Palestinian resistance movement assumed daily control of the refugee camps, providing security as well as a wide variety of health, educational, and social services.

From the late 1960s until 1982, the Palestinian national movement in Lebanon recruited women and instituted a variety of social services geared to their needs, such as day care centers, after-school activities, clinics and health education programs, literacy classes, vocational training projects, and home industries. Though still a minority in the political organizations, women joined all spheres of the resistance. Few attained leadership positions, and most were concentrated in the social services sector. Nevertheless, women were now more than wives and mothers; they were fighters, leaders, workers, students, activists, cadres, and martyrs. The social practices associated with these categories of activism were accompanied by a new sense of identity and extra-domestic aspirations.

Women's entry into the domain of formal, national politics did not necessarily marginalize the women's movement. But the process of formal integration into the national political body diluted their movement's potential commitment to women's issues and autonomy over their policies, positions, and development. Ostensibly for the sake of national unity and the allegiance of a perceived conservative mass base, the resistance leadership was careful to avoid any actions by the women's movement that might cast the resistance in a role challenging extant gender structures and arrangements of authority. At the same time, and more important, the leadership itself with its na-tionalistic focus remained ambivalent on the issue of gender equality.

## Activating the Domestic Sphere

Integration into the national movement did not diminish women's participa-tion in informal popular community level politics. If anything, it gave these actions a new impetus and made them more meaningful by couching them in an idiom of nationalism and militancy. Women's activism was grounded in domesticity on two levels: politically unaffiliated camp women incorporated political actions into their domestic routine and interpreted domesticity as a form of political activism, and activist women's political tasks were fre-quently an extension of traditional domestic duties and visiting patterns.

Peasant women's tradition of spontaneous village level activism now assumed a national context. However, this was not entirely without historical precedence. Elderly women vividly recalled their actions during the 1936 Palestinian revolt. Um Yassir, the 85-year-old mother of a political leader, told me that she hid fighters in her house and kept the horses they had stolen from the British. Her guerrilla husband was often holed up in a cave for days at a time, where she would carry provisions to him. When the British attacked their village, the women ululated and danced to "encourage these brave men to be even stronger." Such women did not escape the attention of foreign observers and colonial officers. Women were reportedly involved in attacks on Zionist settlements and victims of the spiraling cycle of violence. Stirling mentions that "some Arab women lying wounded in the fields were seen to have their breasts scythed off by Jewish colonialists."[1]

Palestinian camp women in Lebanon, descendants of these peasant women, were continuing a pattern of women as active participants in struggles to defend their homes and communities. During the 1976 siege of Tel al-Zaatar refugee camp by the Maronitist Lebanese Forces, women nursed the wounded and organized relief activities and the sustenance of the fighters, and substantial numbers fought alongside men. They were not spared from intentional harm; many died from snipers' bullets while fetching water from wells during the siege, and untold numbers were killed after the camp fell to its besiegers and the population was evacuated.

The mobilization of the domestic sector during protracted crisis disputes any facile dichotomy between formal and informal spheres, and private and public domains. When the community was under attack, as in the massacres of Sabra/Shatila and Tel al-Zaatar, domestic boundaries were shattered, revealing the illusory character of domesticity as the realm of private, familial relations distant from the spheres of formal politics. Nor have women necessarily retreated to the domestic sector in the brief interludes between crises. In the camps and surrounding poor neighborhoods, it became an accepted part of domesticity for women to attend militants' funerals, demonstrations, national events, political lectures, and films. When a lecture or women's gathering was to take place in the camps, women went from house to house to pass the word and collect their friends and neighbors to attend. Women arrived in groups of kin and friends, with children in tow. Domestic functions were mobilized for service to the larger community and accorded a national context, and domestic duties were expanded to include popular political activities. Domesticity came to be associated with struggle and militancy.

## Affiliation

A sector of Palestinian women did formally affiliate with the national movement. Largely young, middle class, and educated, these were the women members, militants, and cadres attached to the various political organizations. These affiliations clearly had repercussions for their management of domesticity and often situated women within a conflicting set of loyalties and demands. To the activists, the popular, community-level actions of camp women were more in the nature of the "prepolitical," insofar as for them the hallmark of political awareness and commitment was membership in an organization. The educational requirements of organizational and administrative positions made it nearly inevitable that middle class women rather than poorer, less educated camp women would initially staff the emerging movement bureaucracy. Women were highly visible in administrative work and in the movement's social infrastructure.

There was one area of organizational work, however, where women formed a majority: mass work (*amal jamahiri*) carried out in the camps and surrounding poor urban neighborhoods. The aim of mass work was to mobilize the community to support the resistance, to raise their level of political awareness, and at the same time to keep abreast of and provide for their needs. Informed by a political ideology that stressed the cultivation of popular support, mass work was intended to maintain and extend genial relations between the resistance and the bulk of camp Palestinians. Its purpose was to let them know they were part of the resistance. Miriam, a 30-year-old married activist and one of the small but growing number of camp women to occupy a middle level leadership position, described her full-time mass work in Shatila camp:

Mass work is political work; it is social care, health care, and home visits to recognize the problems of poor people and help them. We conduct political education meetings in homes and we try to deal with women's everyday problems and activities. Mass work also includes mobilizing people into organizations.

Mass work was carried out in ways that did not fundamentally deviate from women's traditional visiting patterns. Mass workers visited camp homes in an informal fashion, but with a clear political intent. Traditional visiting and mass work visiting served similar purposes: to promote community integration and harmony. Women's traditional domestic functions were being put to the service of the national cause.

## Stirring Consciousness

Women's activism may have awakened the stirrings of a feminist consciousness. As women yearned to join political organizations and contribute to the national struggle, they confronted familial and societal obstacles. The implications of their subordinate position were made clear to them. Yet this newly awakened consciousness did not prompt the formation of a women's movement ready to confront all aspects of gender inequality. The level of crises, the protracted nature of the national struggle, and the communal bases of resistance clearly militated against such a trend. This coincided with a regional and historical pattern of national movements incorporating women's movements. Nor did women wish to extract themselves or their problems from the social fabric and the ongoing process of national resistance.

Women were vitally aware that their political consciousness and activism affected them as individuals and as members of families. Munifa, a 23-year-old, middle class university student, used to say, "For a girl like me there is no going back." She meant she had shattered certain culturally accepted boundaries of female behavior. Community consensus held that unmarried activists were likely to engage in disreputable behavior as a consequence of political involvement which gave them fairly free access to men. In Munifa's view, girls who had managed to remain active in spite of their families' opposition, and who had broken the reins of family control, could not return to a state of existence where others made decisions for them. For women, formal political participation, a traditionally non-female arena, implied a challenge to what was considered proper female comportment, tasks, and the social rules governing the use of space.

The seemingly radical impact of political activism must be weighed against the high female dropout rate that corresponded closely to major events in the female life cycle, such as marriage and childbirth. This usually indicated, if not a return to domesticity, at least a lessening of activism. Political activity had become an accepted part of "girlhood," the period just before marriage when women were active in the labor force and in politics. After marriage, commitment to and identification with domesticity tended to override political commitments. It was not always a simple matter of male opposition to a wife's activism. Domestic duties could be onerous and incompatible with sustained activism. Just as important, many women felt that housewifery and motherhood were women's primary roles. The seemingly radical nature of political activism must also be juxtaposed with the reshuffling of domestic labor among women rather than between men and women.

The PLO leadership did not deal with this transformation in women's intimate and personal lives in a consistent manner. On the one hand, it sometimes reacted positively and swiftly in instances where women faced a backlash from their families as a consequence of political involvement. Local resistance cadres occasionally intervened to prevent acts of male violence against women within the family. When eighteen-year-old Khadija was threatened with a beating by her brother, who opposed her growing association with the political organization that sponsored the sewing workshop where she was employed, Abu Tarik, the local responsible for this same political organization, went to her home to try to calm down the irate brother.

At the same time, with slight modifications, traditional forms and mechanisms of patriarchal control continued to govern women's behavior within the resistance. In the past, structural mechanisms such as separate quarters, veils, single-sex socializing, and complex sets of social rules governing male-female relations, buttressed by the threat of damaging gossip and violence, usually ensured female adherence to societal norms. The site may have expanded from the family to include the political arena, and the forms may differ, but contemporary political activism did not free women from these fetters. New mechanisms of control relied more on ridicule, censorship, and negative labeling than on the threat of violence or family dishonor. Men intimidated women by poking fun at women's concerns and implying that women's issues are not really "political" at all. Women suffered political censure for behavior that, if males had engaged in it, would have only raised a few eyebrows. For the most part, men were exempt from criticism if they were involved in premarital sexual relations. In contrast, women in a similar situation were the butt of jokes and lost respect.

One of the more potent but subtle ways of both silencing women and ensuring their adherence to modest demeanor was negative labeling. The sexual slur, calling women who interacted with men too easily and in a non-bashful way "loose women," made it difficult for them to sustain their political involvement and gain the respect of their fellow activists. Political slurs could be just as harmful. The epithet "bourgeois" was quite powerful in silencing women when they tried to raise women's issues in a movement that considered itself revolutionary.

The Palestinian leadership consistently failed to grasp, or perhaps grasped only too well, the long-term social implications of an autonomous women's movement. However closely linked it might have been to the national political body, it would have had the potential to challenge social structures and tenets; it would have gone far beyond the immediacy of national liberation to a form of social change that the resistance then considered secondary, or was not ready to consider at all. Palestinian women nevertheless argued adamantly that their struggle for equality was an inseparable component of the national movement. The women's movement did not have a wing, or individuals, agitating for a separate women's organization with a feminist agenda.

During this period in Lebanon, politically active Lebanese women faced many of the same issues. Both women's movements were operating in a context of political and military crisis. While the PLO operated without a state context, the Lebanese women's movement functioned in a weak, increasingly fragmented state where political organizations were highly fractured along ideological and sectarian lines. Lebanese women's organizations could not overcome the sectarian political divisions; women's organizations were components of each political group. Even more so than among Palestinians, for Lebanese women in these organizations, there was little space in which to promote women's issues or concerns.

## Deflecting Consciousness

That women's participation in national politics had a definite effect on their lives and relations is hardly debatable. What is debatable is the extent of change, its unevenness, and its inability to weather the tremendous transformations that were yet to take place in this community. Perhaps it is unfair to expect that real change was possible given the severity of the assaults and the concerted attempt to destroy the refugee camps and decimate a Palestinian leadership and political presence in Lebanon. Militant national liberation movements may inspire women's political movements; they do not necessarily ensure equal rights and opportunities, nor do they necessarily restructure asymmetrical gender relations. In participating in the formal political sphere, women did challenge societal norms of proper female behavior. But the impact on gender relations did not encompass a radical transformation in the division of labor or in the bases of patriarchal control. How did this process of deflecting and containing an emerging feminist consciousness proceed?

The emergence and consolidation of states can marginalize women's former spontaneous activism. With militant national liberation movements, a different process unfolds. Rather than distancing the domestic sector and women from the sphere of formal politics, the movements may recruit them as part of a strategy of mass mobilization. When formerly militant national liberation movements become states, and mass mobilization is no longer an imperative, the domestic sector and women can be pushed to the periphery.

In the Palestinian case, a number of questions need to be considered. Was participation in the national struggle challenging women's domestic roles and patriarchal structures of control, or had national struggle simply been grafted onto women's traditional roles in reproduction and production? Had the domestic sector itself taken on nationalist political meaning, in addition to its reproductive and productive functions? Had there been a transformation in relations between men and women and between women?

Palestinian women's political activism was often an extension of their domestic roles. Activists tended to be concentrated in social services such as nursing, teaching, and social work, or in clerical work or vocational training projects. In addition, politics had entered the domestic realm in full force, mobilizing domestic duties for political action and in the process politicizing their meaning. Women's activities during military crises crystallized around the home and the provision of sustenance to the fighters; women baked the bread, prepared the food, and tended to the wounded. They also made visits to the shelters to provide solace to the people and encouraged them to remain in the camps.

Women's reproductive roles were politicized as well, as they, and the community in general, conceptualized their childbearing capabilities as a direct contribution to the struggle. The "mother of the martyr" exemplified this: though she herself may not have been politically active, her maternal sacrifice was a supreme political act that translated into respect and prominent community stature. She was often invited to attend resistance events in the camp with the leadership, and they visited her. This newly-acquired stature served to cushion her loss. The "mothers of martyrs" became symbols in the camp community of the trauma of exile and resistance. They were presented to journalists and visitors as personifying a community in suffering, as living commentaries on resistance and sacrifice.[2] The reproduction of labor which took place in the domestic sector took on an added imperative in a society where young men were recruited into the ranks of fighters. The socialization of children to be nationalists was widely recognized as primarily the responsibility of women in the family, supplemented naturally by the schools and resistance institutions.

Women often justified their choice of domesticity over politics by imbuing child-raising with patriotic meaning. Jamila was a nurse by training, and mother of two children. Her husband did not mind if she worked as a nurse in a camp clinic. But she decided against the attempts of women cadres to mobilize her. She justified her decision by telling people, "If a woman raises children, she's contributing to the revolution one way or another." Rather than challenging domesticity, such redefinitions of women's roles expanded the tasks associated with it.

## Contradictory Relations

Women's discourse underscored the multidimensional and contradictory nature of their relations with the resistance. Reproduction and fertility took on an added imperative in a community engaged in protracted struggle. Raising children in a militant, nationalist environment was considered a primary contribution to the struggle. Women referred to themselves as the producers of fighters, and to their domestic chores and life as women in exile with the same terms — struggle (*nidal*) and steadfastness (*sumud*) — used to signify military struggle and political militancy. Frequent self-descriptive use of terms formerly the preserve of men attested to women's entrance into the realm of formal politics, and underscored their own sense of empowerment and expanded self-definition. Nonetheless, this transformation in the female lexicon did not indicate any lessened identification with domesticity.

Related to the deflected impact of politics on domesticity was a new pattern of relations between women along class and generation lines. Rather than repositioning men and women in the gender-based division of labor, political activism was reshuffling labor between women, or adapting prior patterns to new uses. In the case of poor camp women, domestic labor was shared between women members of extended families or between mothers and daughters, particularly the eldest daughter. Um Tarik used to leave her children next door with her mother-in-law while she pursued political activities. Um Khalid, who had no extended family in the camp, regularly left her eldest daughter Muna in charge of the younger ones while she was out of the house for political duties. Muna had little time for her homework and at age fourteen faced many of the duties associated with motherhood. Huda, active in mass work in the camp, could take her young daughter around with her while she worked. Her guerrilla husband, who was away most of the time, shared little housework even when he was home.

For middle class women with access to financial resources, poorer women often become their "shock absorbers," mediating the impact of political commitments on domesticity. Saada hired a maid, allowing her to work actively with a political organization. Families hired maids for the express purpose of freeing women, not men, from domestic work. This did not entail a redefining or restructuring of the sexual division of labor; it simply shifted the burden to other women.

Palestinian women, by becoming politically active in such a manner as to maintain their commitments to domesticity, did not pose a fundamental challenge to the asymmetrical division of labor between men and women.

Indeed, their activism engaged the domestic sector for political purposes and intensified existing labor-sharing relations between women of different generations and classes. Participation in militant national politics may initiate the process of challenging those patriarchal structures and ideologies that confirm and legitimize women's assignment to the domestic sector and men's exclusion from it, but it does not ensure any permanent and comprehensive sort of transformation. Indeed, community mobilization devoid of ideologies and prospects for gender equality may further institutionalize women's association with the domestic sector by infusing it now with national, patriotic meanings.

## The Aftermath

The period of Palestinian autonomy in Lebanon came to an abrupt and violent end in the summer of 1982. During the previous seven years the Palestinian community had come under attack from various Lebanese militias and faced continuous Israeli incursions into, and bombings of, the camps. In the summer of 1982 came the Israeli invasion and siege of Beirut, and the subsequent evacuation of the PLO's forces from Beirut which left the Palestinian community traumatized, vulnerable and impoverished. A Lebanese government and various militias intent on their containment, if not removal to another location in the region, meant that this community was the target of military and institutional attempts at marginalization.[3]

The post-1982 period witnessed the prolonged siege of the camps and their near destruction by the Syrian backed Amal militia and the further diminution of Palestinian autonomy and security. With the social services safety net that the PLO had provided for refugees all but removed, the standard of living declined drastically. Once thriving and economically sustainable camps now were places of destitution and despair. The Palestinians in Lebanon provide an opportunity to examine what transpires for a women's movement, and in women's daily lives, in the aftermath of political and military defeat, and in the absence of a national structure within which the women's movement operated.

At the same time, the intifada in the occupied territories and the ensuing peace process shifted the space of Palestinian political focus to the Occupied Territories. In the climate of military occupation, women in the Occupied Territories had been forming grass-roots organizations during the 1980s. These organizations took root in the specificities of a political climate quite different from the political openness of Palestinian activism in Lebanon. More decentralized than the General Union of Palestinian Women (GUPW) had been in the diasporic communities, these committees, as they were known, were less organized from the top down and, while affiliated with political organizations, the more underground nature of political activism under occupation gave them space in which to develop somewhat more independently than women's organization in the Lebanon era.

As the peace process unfolded, and with the emergence of an embryonic state structure, a notable shift could be discerned in women's priorities and organizing strategies. Legal issues have come to the fore in ways that they simply could not in the Lebanese arena. Women have formed lobbies to make their voices and concerns heard as the Palestinian Authority begins the laborious and contentious process of drawing up legislation in areas under its nominal control.

A new discourse for framing women's issues and demands has surfaced: that of human rights and democracy. To some extent it has superceded the nationalist discourse which, when it came up against the specificity of women's demands, ended up as a polarized debate that pitted women's demands against those of the larger community; the former was seen as somehow diminishing the assumed primacy of national concerns. By the early 1990s, if not earlier, this was a debate that had little intellectual or practical steam left in it. And indeed, its demise had already been signaled by the rise of Islamist groups which brought new challenges to both women's situation and concerns, and the nationalist political agenda. The controversy and conflict over the often violent imposition of the headscarf in the Gaza Strip in the late 1980s and the failure of the secularist national forces to respond effectively to this Islamist-driven campaign was an unambiguous signal that women's status and issues would be easily conceded to the Islamists.[4]

Currently, women in the refugee community in Lebanon are highly focused on issues of sheer survival. There is only a skeletal organizational structure within which women can express their concerns or organize. The women's movement, once so prevalent here in a variety of organizational formats — the GUPW and the various women's sections of the major political components of the PLO — is nearly defunct. While the GUPW still has a presence in the camps, it is without funds and most of its cadre have left the country or dropped out of political activity. This observation leads one to pose the question: what are the meanings of and implications for a women's movement that has been hitched so closely to a nationalist movement?

I have argued above that nationalist movements inspire and give legitimacy to women's movements, but they do not necessarily promote gender equality or restructure gender relations. The defeat in Lebanon provides an opportunity to examine what happens to women's movements once the larger national movement framework is absent. It suggests that the hitching is still a necessary component but the terms of the marriage are what is critical. The women's movement was not able to withstand the withdrawal of the larger national movement and the events that transpired in its wake, essentially the attempted destruction of community. The women's movement, primarily the GUPW, the umbrella organization for women, may have been overly dependent on the PLO both financially and for a good deal of its legitimacy and its ability to recruit women. More importantly, it was dependent on an atmosphere or climate of social experimentation ushered in and endowed with legitimacy by the resistance movement. Comparatively speaking, this was not a grassroots movement, as were the women's committees in the Occupied Territories, and this accounts, in part, for the void left in the wake of the withdrawal of the larger national movement.

Currently in Lebanon, the handful of Palestinian political organizations opposed to the PLO's peace agreement with Israel constitute the few remaining sources of political organization. However, they are all but broke and have only a nominal presence in the camps. The refugees have turned to another source of organizing for self-help, one with more traditional roots. Village associations have sprung up in the wake of political defeat and social destitution. Unlike Palestinian refugees in Jordan, the Palestinians in Lebanon did not develop associations along village lines except in the first decade of exile. The impetus to do so may have been bypassed by the development of militant, fairly autonomous political organizations which were able to meet people's daily needs for economic well-being, security, and the provisioning of a social safety net.

The village associations which have emerged during the 1990s are designed to meet the needs of people in dire poverty. A common fund of money is used, for the most part, to assist families in the event of a funeral or unexpected medical expenses. Recalling a pre-1948 gendered village division of labor in which men prevailed in the public face of politics, women are not visibly active in these informal associations. They are neither leaders nor in the upper echelons. As members of families from specific villages, they partake of the benefits of village and family membership, but these are not political arenas in which women can make specifically women's demands or have their voices heard. Within these associations, the immediate and most pressing concerns of families are what is addressed. There has been a debate about the political nature of these associations. Many former resistance cadres find them a reactionary reversion to a traditional order when male village elders ran village affairs. Others find in them a promotion of pre-1948 identities and recognize them as a source of assistance and support in a time of unprecedented crisis.

The most pressing issues facing this community are ones of security, economic sustainability, and legal rights. During the 1980s, the refugee community faced attempts to annihilate them physically and eradicate their communities from the map of Lebanon. Having given up these attempts, the Lebanese authorities are now engaged in a process of marginalizing the refugees economically and politically. Palestinians are legally barred from employment in over fifty categories of employment and have no rights to medical care or education in the Lebanese state. The hoped-for result has been their emigration or transfer en masse to another state. The post-war reconstruction of Lebanon does pose a series of immediate concerns and problems for women. As I have argued elsewhere: "By slating the camp areas to be sites for sports arenas and shopping malls, places of leisure and consumption, it disrupts women's ability to run their families and forces women to once again contemplate packing up and moving to a new place."[5]

While refugee status and legalized discrimination are issues of concern to all Palestinians, women face additional burdens. With a large number of widows among the refugee community, there are many women who are trying to raise children in near destitution; PLO-paid indemnities are no longer sent to widows and orphans of martyrs. For women, this means stretching already meager resources even further. A pointedly woman's critique of the era of the resistance is intimately linked to the survival issue in the forefront for all refugees in Lebanon. In the post-resistance era, Palestinian refugee women have deployed the notion of maternal sacrifice as a point of departure for a scathing critique of the leadership. Rhetorically, women have situated the war-time losses of their children and often husbands as a betrayal of sorts.[6] While the mother of the martyr was often celebrated for her patriotism and national commitment through her sacrifice, maternal loss is more recently a source of critical agency and a way of asserting the specificity of identity as the Palestinians of Lebanon (in distinction from Palestinians elsewhere in the diaspora).

During research I conducted over the past several years in Shatila camp on the outskirts of Beirut, I made many visits to women who had experienced the loss of children and husbands during the years of war. Indeed, what one noticed immediately after the war was the prominence of women and children in the camp's population. These women readily offered a critique of the resistance and that era of autonomy that few men were willing to broach publicly. In their highly critical narratives, women astutely deployed metaphors of "blood and milk." These bodily substances associated with birth, nurturing, and death evoked maternal sacrifice and the conflation of life and death. "We gave our milk and blood," one woman stated angrily, "and look how we are living. We are barely able to feed ourselves." Women are deploying the idiom of maternal sacrifice as a point of departure in a virulent critique of the leadership. In this sense, they have indirectly challenged the hegemonic nationalist discourse that glorified maternal sacrifice by taking back, if you will, the meaning of their sacrifice. Their faith in the resistance movement to bring about a positive outcome for their sacrifice was betrayed. These women did not deny the potency of maternal sacrifice but shifted its meaning from celebration to critical agency.[7] Mention of the peace accords elicited a host of comments such as "We have been abandoned! We gave our children and they (the PLO) have left us!" Such sentiments underscore a sense of rupture with the larger community of Palestinians. There is a fairly popular consensus in the refugee community that Israel is neither going to allow the return of the refugees nor pay compensation for the loss of homes and livelihoods. The 1993 Palestinian/Israeli peace accords are seen as effectively abandoning the refugee community in Lebanon and legitimizing their refugee status.

The peace accords and the shift to nominal autonomy and control by the Palestinian Authority in the West Bank and the Gaza Strip have opened the way for discussions of legislation and lobbying. While the now global discourse of women's rights as human rights, and as a fundamental component of democracy, is echoed in those areas under nominal Palestinian control, it is not necessarily as prominent among Palestinians in Lebanon. The refugee community in Lebanon harbors a keen sense of abandonment and feels a distance from events in the larger Palestinian arena. In postwar Lebanon, the refugees are in a wait-and-see situation with all the uncertainties and stresses that involves. The primacy of survival tends to mute the specificity of gendered issues. The atmosphere of social experimentation is now only a memory. Yet the resistance years did leave behind a group of women who had experience as activists in their communities. Although they are without an openly active women's movement and the institutions and social services it furnished, such as vocational training, literacy course, day care, and health clinics, they do have a memory of another time that promised more than the future now seems to hold.

# Searching for Strategies
## The Palestinian Women's Movement in the New Era

Rita Giacaman and Penny Johnson

In a heated student election campaign at Birzeit University shortly after the signing of the first Oslo agreement in September 1993, the oppositional "Jerusalem First" coalition made a striking spectacle as hundreds of its supporters marched smartly across the university's hilltop campus. In a prominent position at the head of the march, female students from the Popular Front, clad in blue jeans, brandished red-splattered rocks, while young men held banners against self-government. At the end of the march, "sisters" from Hamas walked as a segregated bloc. To the surprise of some observers, several young women were not wearing the obligatory head scarf. One bare-headed woman waved a green Hamas banner high overhead. In the middle, young women partisans of the Democratic Front (Hawatmeh) in casual Western attire mixed uneasily with Hamas men.

This scene, this coalition, depicts the unstable mix of gender and politics in Palestine today. The era ushered in by the signing of the Declaration of Principles pushed women activists to unite in order to safeguard women's interests, while at the same time it pulled them apart in the most profound split Palestinian politics has encountered to date.

Inside the women's movement, the atmosphere after Oslo was steadily growing more tense as women struggled to maintain the gender-based coordination of the previous several years in the face of radical political polarization. PLO leaders from abroad are sometimes referred as the "abus" (fathers), underlining the one common and persistent fear of women activists: that any gains by women in general, or as political leaders, will be ignored by the patriarchal character of the Palestinian Authority. An atmosphere of diminished hopes and anxiety over the future deeply affects both activists and ordinary women: "Oh, at least we might be able to travel freely to Jordan to visit our relatives," remarked women in more than one overheard conversation. Travel plans are replacing dreams of nationhood.

## From Intifada to Independence?

Shortly before the Gulf War, in a conference in Jerusalem entitled "The Intifada and Social Issues," the Palestinian women's movement first publicly raised concern that political fundamentalism, sanctioned by conservative nationalist forces, was imposing new repressive conditions on women. Their concern was sparked by the campaign to force women to wear "modest" dress and scarves. Over the next few years, Palestinian women and men met to discuss issues that were hitherto taboo: domestic abuse, sexual harassment and personal status issues, among others.

Accompanying these positive initiatives was a mood of self-criticism that was almost painful. In some forums, women's movement activists, criticizing their previous lack of independence from male-dominated political factions, and their failure to address women's issues, struck a "mea culpa" note that starkly contrasts with the self-confidence and courage they evinced as they brought women into the streets during the first years of the intifada.

The crisis within the movement accelerated with the launching of the Madrid phase of the peace process. The impact was felt by women in terms of further marginalization. "Occupation destroyed the structural basis of the intifada, the neighborhood committees," says activist and academic Eileen Kuttab.[1]

Here, the women's movement began to go into its present crisis. Then came the peace process, shifting the struggle to diplomacy and away from grassroots mobilization. Women's skills, developed in informal settings, were not utilizable. The political conditions became confusing and women could not get back into action.

Kuttab also believes that the program of the women's committees in the 1980s did not constitute a radical departure from the social services approach favored by the older women's charitable associations. "The committee women were younger and more politicized," she says, but "during the intifada, we found out that there is a big gap between committee women in villages and refugee camps."

Islah Jad, a lecturer in Cultural Studies at Birzeit University, disagrees in part.[2] She believes the women's movement has a "strong foundation" for moving ahead, based on the living link between activists and grassroots women forged during the intifada. While she agrees with Kuttab that the women's committees were consumed, especially during the intifada, by "social service work with a political connotation," she believes that the new era will leave women space for other activities. "All the issues we used to postpone for the national struggle now have space to be addressed as women," she says.

Assessments of the current strength of the base of the women's movement vary substantially, since they rest mainly on personal experience. Data on membership or levels of participation and support are unreliable or nonexistent. The 1993 survey by Norwegian and Palestinian social scientists, however, provides an important new tool in analyzing women's conditions and attitudes.[3] It underlines the prevailing and overwhelming economic dependency of Palestinian women on the family, at the same time that women (and men to a lesser extent) may want or approve of work outside the home. The study also reveals a consistently more conservative attitude among young women aged 15 to 19 compared to women in their twenties.

## One Foot In

In examining the strategies currently being proposed by women activists for the new era, the mixed experience of the women's committees and the roller-coaster ride of the women's movement during the uprising are the immediate backdrop. But the overwhelming political question is the nature of the Palestinian Authority, its capacity and willingness to democratize, and how either to influence the emerging government effectively or to oppose it.

The maze of Palestinian "technical committees" operating out of East Jerusalem's Orient House, as the builders of infrastructure, bureaucracy and policy for Palestinian authority, has been the object of periodic media attention. A Women's Affairs Technical Committee, headed by leading activist Zahira Kamal, is among these quasi-governmental bodies. But it was established six months later than committees on matters such as transportation and education, and it does not receive funds from the regular budget: this committee resulted from a political struggle waged by women, and it is funded primarily by a foreign donor.

"We have a choice between investing our resources in a bureaucratic governmental structure — training ourselves to be administrators — or transferring these resources to the grassroots," argues Jad, a member of the committee. "The argument for the first choice required confidence in the future authority. We discussed the evidence and found that it was not enough to be sure that what we might build would be accepted. We decided to consolidate at the grassroots — as a pressure group really — while continuing to have a position in the emerging authority. It is a foot in/foot out strategy."[4]

The committee has formed subcommittees to examine issues such as legislation, education, and employment, with the aim of making policy recommendations. Its ability to influence political decisions remains in doubt: Yasir Arafat's appointment of an executive staff for the Palestinian Economic and Development and Reconstruction Agency (PEDRA), headed by himself, did not include any women. Among the committee's most ambitious projects is a draft Women's Bill of Rights, which is seen as a mobilizing tool to show the interests and strength of women prior to the introduction of key pieces of legislation, such as a constitution.

It is of course striking that the committee, once officially part of the emerging authority, sees itself as a "pressure group." In this it is allied with nongovernmental organizations, oppositional women's groups, and what can broadly be called "democratic forces." Most, although not all, members of the committee do not view themselves as "governmental," and are surprised when others do. But the introduction of a quasi-governmental link in the women's movement initially produced stresses and strains. Women opposed to the agreement at first affirmed that they cannot work under the sole banner of the technical committee. For them, the most urgent priorities are, as one activist noted, "to defeat Fatah, to make the interim period a failure, and to build a democratic society." The three aims are seen as inseparable: thus women deeply committed to the aim of democracy have suddenly found themselves allied with Hamas in order to accomplish the first two goals.[5]

## Two Feet Out

One Popular Front-allied woman from the opposition endorsed the political alliance with Hamas in these terms:

You must understand that we have calculated that this is a dangerous alliance. But such an alliance is only temporary. And it is legitimate because the main aim is to do away with self-government. It is bringing to us a very undemocratic, fascist regime. The alliance is, moreover, only political, and does not touch on our social program.[6]

There is a further twist to the justification:

This alliance with Hamas is the first test that our men will be subjected to. It will be very interesting to see how well our men will be able to defend our social agenda in front of Hamas. Such a confrontation will give women the chance to assess the situation internally for the first time.

Putting young women at the head of a march or running two women on the nine-person Birzeit Student Council slate did not sustain secular leftists in the volatile alliance with Hamas. In elections in the spring of 1997, leftist groups on campus ran as a united bloc against separate Fatah and Islamic lists (the Islamic Bloc had won the majority of seats in a previous election), and sharply disagreed on social issues with the Islamic bloc in election debates (the left was roundly defeated). Hamas's pact with the Popular Front to "agree to disagree" over social issues was short-lived. One careful feminist observer of Hamas in Gaza notes, "I've heard Birzeit people say, 'Hamas is no big deal.' I think it's a false assumption, borne because Fatah's power seems to be the main danger. But the day of a Fatah-Hamas alliance may well be coming."[7]

## Donor Discourse

The intifada left women's groups with a legacy of heightened consciousness and failed initiatives, exemplified by the closure of many of the small-scale women's production projects. In their urgent search for a viable strategy for the new era, Palestinian women activists have seized, perhaps too quickly, on concepts developed elsewhere. Much emphasis, for example, has been put on women's meetings and the need for "gender training." This clearly appeals for two reasons: cadre women are eager to advance their own abilities to understand and deal with gender issues, and they hope to influence their male colleagues. The fact that international agencies smile favorably on "gender training," and that it is a part of their fashionable discourse, is a third factor. The magic of "training" and the methodology of "workshops" can perhaps offer women useful tools — there are examples of useful community-based training workshops for women in Gaza, for example — but they are a poor substitute for a strategy or a program for change.

Another "new era" concept with positive and negative features is that of a "women's lobby." In the current stage of the U.S. women's movement, this reflects women's increasing economic integration, as well as the nature of the system itself. Palestinian women's groups uniting to pressure the emerging authority for policies favorable to women's interests would be, incontestably, a positive development. The notion of a lobby also addresses a pressing need for new forms of women's organization. In the past few years, a spate of women's research and training centers and a women's legal center were born in response to the same need. A lobby, however, emphasizes the exercise of influence, rather than a more public contest for equality.

In this regard, it is striking that the increase in feminist consciousness, often remarked on, has so far found little resonance in institutional struggles over women's issues, whether at schools and universities, factories, or hospitals, three sites where women's presence and gender inequities might reasonably engender women's demands. A continued focus on the national arena, even in gender issues, is a partial explanation. However, as the women's movement and other democratic forces stress the development of civil society, it will be important that civil institutions, as well as the new authority, become a focus for transformation.

Women leaders stress time and again that, in the words of Jad, "We cannot defend women's rights without defending democratic rights." The women's struggle is placed squarely within the task of building a democratic society. But this having been said, women activists find themselves facing troubling questions: does the greatest danger to democracy come from an unbridled and unaccountable Palestinian Authority and its gendarmerie, as opposition elements claim, or from "playing with fire" in an unprincipled alliance with the anti-democratic Hamas, as other critics assert? Or is it possible to pose a third question, and to unite to counter these dangers, whatever their position on a sliding scale, and thus move the long struggle for the rights and equality of Palestinian women to a new stage?

## Postscript

Amid the myriad difficulties of the post-Oslo era, the women's movement has been seeking to navigate between the political poles of support for or opposition to the Oslo agreements (and the host of unresolved national and political issues therein) by using the rudder of "women's interests first." In part, this refocusing of the women's movement on women's, rather than national, interests stems from a lengthy and informed discussion and experience of pressing social problems in Palestinian society by the women's movement, as well as by its own experience of gender discrimination in the

national movement. It also clearly arises from the relentless institutionalization of the Oslo agreements, whereby on the positive side, the women's
movement is meeting the challenge of the process of state-building with a
gender agenda, and, on a less positive note, it is accommodating itself to the
fact that Oslo and its children are "the only game in town."

Thus, factional polarization in the women's movement subsided markedly as the first "shock" of the Oslo agreements gave way to accommodation, particularly in the wake of the implementation of the Interim Agreements (Oslo II) in late 1995 and the January 1996 elections for the Palestinian
Legislative Council. These elections, in which four female candidates were
elected to an 88-member Council, were intended and served to give popular
legitimacy to the Oslo process. Despite the inefficacy of the Council to date,
the elections marked a turning point in Palestinian political life, where new
oppositions within the framework of Oslo, such as between the executive and
the Council, and new constituencies, including a women's constituency, began to emerge. The implementation of the interim agreement, through the
takeover by the Palestinian National Authority of Palestinian cities in the
West Bank and the elections, marked a significant institutionalization of
the Oslo process on the ground that affected all political forces. By and large,
politics began to operate within the Oslo framework, despite the emergence
in Palestinian public life of specific issues relating to human rights violations,
patronage, and authoritarian behavior by the Palestinian Authority and its
officials, as well as to the continuation of the Israeli occupation.

In 1996, the Palestinian Women's Committee (PWC), an affiliate of the
Popular Front, joined the Women's Affairs Technical Committee (WATC),
which it had previously opposed. In part, the PWC was convinced by the
WATC's consistent policy of "women's interests first" and its nongovernmental character. In addition, the PWC, while holding real interest in developing women's issues, had been considerably weakened internally and
needed to become a "player" in the new terrain of women's advocacy and
lobbying to reconstitute itself and have access to resources, whether material
or political.

Whether the new strategy of women's advocacy and lobbying replaces
or complements grassroots mobilization is still an open question. The heart
of the women's movement — the women's committees — have retained a significant portion of their constituency, but there have been no new recruitment
drives or indeed, new members. The professionalization of Palestinian political life — through the Palestinian Authority on one hand, and professional

NGOs on the other — has been remarked elsewhere, and the women's movement is no exception. The return of the leadership and structures of the General Union of Palestinian Women so far has not served as a vehicle for membership and mobilization, but on occasion has mired the women's movement in additional bureaucratic conflicts. The women's movement has had an impressive record in responding to and abolishing a number of new discriminatory regulations (for example, the necessity of the approval of a male guardian for a passport), and has actively intervened in debates on new legislation (still in the draft stage, as such key instruments as the Basic Law have not yet been issued). It has also conducted impressive campaigns for women candidates and worked in sustained ways on legal awareness, early marriage, domestic violence, and other important issues. As one analyst observed: "Compared to other popular movements, women's groups are much more politically organized; they have obtained resources, and they see this transition period as a very crucial window of opportunity for women."[8]

The women's movement, however, has also made a considerable effort to define women's advocacy and lobbying as a tool to empower women at the grassroots. "The lesson from the January 1996 elections," noted Islah Jad, "is that the women's movement is weak in the rural areas." One new project seeks to establish local village networks which provide resources and training to groups of rural women so that they can target and advocate their own issues. Jad noted women activists' concern to link these practical issue with "strategic gender issues" that advance gender equality in Palestinian society, observing that women in gender training sessions she has coordinated are quick to link practical issues with strategic gender issues. Unlike men, women will add to a discussion of such practical issues as jobs and health-care that "Oh, but we must change people's attitudes" or "We must change the laws."

While the Palestinian women's movement, and women in many settings, have identified areas where change is imperative and possible, the role of international donor organizations is prominent in funding these campaigns, and, more debatably, in promoting frameworks for these activities. The international discourse, for example, of "legal literacy" and "violence against women" has been actively adopted and often shrewdly used by Palestinian women's organizations: but whether these frameworks are conceptually adequate or broad enough really to address the roots of legal discrimination and family and societal violence in Palestine is an important question.

The limited but important successes in women's advocacy are also framed by the larger political, economic, and social crisis facing Palestinian society. Here, the "national question" in its complex articulation, rather than in the rather tired slogans that at present are neither abandoned nor utilized for real mobilization, remains to be addressed by the women's movement, as well as by other democratic movements in Palestinian society.

# Gender and Citizenship
## Considerations on the Turkish Experience

Yeşim Arat

In the summer of 1993, the True Path Party (Doğru Yol Partisi) delegates — 99.8 percent of them male — selected Tansu Çiller as the Chairperson of their Party and thus their candidate for prime minister. For the first time since 1934, when women gained the right to vote and to be elected to parliament, a woman became Prime Minister of Turkey. If citizenship involves the rights and responsibilities of membership in a state, here was a woman who had exercised her right to head the government of her country.

Not all women were so successful. Only 12 of the 1169 party delegates were women and only 8 women were among the 450 member parliament of 1991. When Tansu Çiller campaigned, a party member claimed "a woman cannot be a prime minister, a woman cannot even lead a funeral prayer!" Others said that their party cannot "shoulder" a woman president; that they want a leader they can (literally) carry on their shoulders.[1] These and other remarks revealed the limits of tolerance of women's exercise of their citizenship rights in politics. There were other limits on other fronts.

Perhaps what throws more light on the gendered nature of citizenship rights in Turkey was Tansu Çiller's public pronouncement that Özer Çiller, her husband, is the head of their family at home. Despite Özer Çiller's objections and his insistence that decision-making is democratic in their home, Tansu Çiller insisted that he is the head. After her election as prime minister in 1993, True Path Party delegates argued that this was only a natural reflection of Islamic as well as Turkish and Anatolian tradition. She could be the prime minister, but at home he would be the head; after all, even the Civil Code declared the husband the head of the family.[2] Democracy at home is not considered to be compatible with, let alone a necessity for, democracy in the public realm. In a country where interpersonal relations are hierarchic and most women publicly accept this state of affairs, perhaps it follows that there are very few female party delegates and MPs, that men dominate the public realm, and that women have to campaign against sexist remarks.

Regardless of Özer Çiller's status in the home, Tansu Çiller, in the public realm, was keen to exhibit a Thatcher-like image of an "iron lady," unfettered by women's concerns and interests. Though she appealed to women when she needed their votes, she acted like a man in politics. The caricature by Turhan Selçuk in *Milliyet* (Figure 1) has Çiller sitting with legs crossed — improper behavior for a Turkish woman — before President Demirel. Popular discourse refers to Demirel as "baba" (father) and Tansu Çiller as his "daughter." In this cartoon, "baba" is telling his "daughter" not that she could not be prime minister but that she could not be a woman: the role of the prime minister is not considered compatible with being a woman in the Turkish context. The woman prime minister who has succeeded in exercising her right to head the government has to wage a political campaign against those who oppose her because of her sex, publicly affirm that in the private realm she plays the woman's role, and when she does win, play the role of a man in the public realm.

At the formal legal level, women have acquired many of the citizenship rights of men. They are thus exposed to problems of formal equality, as opposed to the problems of substantive equality of citizenship that women in Western democracies confront. Yet, women's experiences of citizenship vary over a wide spectrum involving differences of class, region or religiosity.

## Formal Status as Citizens

When Mustafa Kemal founded the Turkish Republic in 1920, he initiated what could be called "citizenship from above."[3] Citizens were expected to be passive agents and accept those civil, political, and social rights granted to them. Women soon gained access to these rights, with some limits, along with men. The 1926 Civil Code, which replaced the shari'a, gave women equal rights to divorce and inheritance, abolished polygamy, and made civil marriage a state requirement. In 1934, suffrage was granted. The 1961 and

BABA - KIZIM, BEN SANA BAŞBAKAN OLAMAZSIN DEMEDİM, KADIN OLAMAZSIN DEDİM...

Figure 1. Turhan Selçuk, "Söz Çizginin" (The cartoon has the last word), *Milliyet*, 28 July 1995. "Baba" (Suleyman Demirel, standing) says to "Kizim" (Tansu Çiller, seated), "I didn't tell you you couldn't be prime minister; I told you you couldn't be a woman."

1982 constitutions elaborated civil and social liberties that men and women could possess without gender discrimination.

Feminists today are critical of the shortcomings of the present legal framework, especially the Civil and Penal Codes. As mentioned, the Civil Code still maintains the husband as the head of the family (Article 152); it also allows the husband to choose the place of family residence (Article 152/2), expects the wife to be under the surveillance of the husband (Article 153), and requires the woman to use her husband's surname (Article 153).

The legal framework, even if it were more egalitarian, exposes women in Turkey to the same problems and biases to which women in liberal Western societies are exposed. To the extent that Turkey formally aspires to be a liberal Western democracy, its female citizens are assumed to have signed their "social contract" to become individual bearers of rights with constitutionally guaranteed gender equality. The exclusionary nature of the liberal concept of citizenship remains. Women are treated as ahistorical beings who assume neutral gender roles inconsequential in the exercise of their citizenship rights. Yet, as feminist critics have shown us, it matters how gender roles are played.[4] Women are citizens who can benefit from these formal egali-

tarian rights to the extent that they can ignore, suppress or deny their traditional roles as mothers or wives: it is because mothers or wives have the
responsibility to care for children, cook, and clean twelve hours a day that
before the 1999 elections there were only eight women in the 450-member
parliament that decides policy. (In 1999 23 women were elected to the 550-
member parliament.) If fathers shared domestic chores, mothers could at
least be more informed and active citizens and set different role models for
their daughters. Maternal roles and how they are defined are intimately related to how citizenship rights are exercised in Turkey, as in other places.
Similarly, where 73.13 percent of inter-household property belongs to men
and 8.71 percent belongs to women, having equal rights to inheritance as
equal citizens means little.[5]

## Womens's Experience of Citizenship

As a starting point to observe women's experiences of citizenship, official
statistics can tell us how women benefit from their civil and social rights as
citizens. According to 1990 figures, 31 percent of women are illiterate. Some
46 percent of elementary school graduates and 41 percent of secondary
school graduates are women. Of those with higher education diplomas, 35
percent are women.[6] Where they live, their age, and their income all shape
women's access to education. Illiteracy of women is twice as high in rural
areas and for older women.

Labor force participation rates give some idea of how women use their
rights to employment in relation to male citizens. In 1992 women constituted
32 percent of the labor force; 50 percent of women's labor force participation
is in rural areas. Women are 65 percent of the unpaid family workers. Wom-
en's activism in the public realm shows a stark difference from that of men. In
1990 women constituted 30 percent of those employed in central government
and only 18 percent of civil servants employed in local administrations.[7]

Male and female citizens perhaps have the sharpest difference in their
political participation through formal institutions. As mentioned above, less
than 2 percent of the 450 MPs in the 1991 elections were women. The 1995
elections brought 13 women to the 550 member parliament. The figures have
never been higher than 2 percent since 1946, when the first multi-party
elections were held in Turkey. In provincial and municipal councils the figures have shown little improvement.

These statistics and ratios present an inadequate picture of women's experiences of their citizenship. Women relate to the state in diverse ways: on the one hand, indigenous forces undermine women's recognition of their citizenship rights; on the other hand, women actively seek to restructure their relationship to the state. The following examples reflect a range of women's experiences of citizenship.

## Carpet Weavers

Suad Joseph's observation that in Lebanon women experience their rights and obligations primarily with reference to their immediate communal group rather than with the state seems to reflect the experience of many women in Turkey as well.[8] Among the carpet weavers in Central Anatolia, we are told that when girls are born, the fathers exclaim "it's a factory," which they can exchange and from which they profit.[9] The few "rights" these women have emerge from the context of kinship. It is in the context of family relations that women engage in what Deniz Kandiyoti calls the "patriarchal bargain" and work in arduous conditions weaving carpets.[10] The state might be considered responsible for the unfair deal these women are getting or for their lack of social security. For the women involved, though, rights, interests, advantages, and obligations originate in the context of kinship, which organizes and regulates carpet weaving. Mothers-in-law rather than civil servants help regulate and ensure sons' and fathers' control over the labor of women weavers.

## Islamists

For many Islamist women who are politically active in the public realm, citizenship rights are a means to promote their Islamic worldview. These women engage in protest activities to be permitted to cover their heads in public institutions, especially universities, or they work as activists in the ranks of the Welfare Party, the main Islamist political force in Turkey. Their "contract" is with God. They are the citizens of a holy community where rights and obligations are defined by God. Since the sacred community they endorse does not have a political state, and since they have to function in an allegedly secular and liberal republic, many appeal to the constitutional framework and the citizens' rights asserted by the republic. These women proclaim their need to cover their heads with reference to their civil right to practice religion without the hindrance of the state.[11] Paradoxically, in doing so they propagate a belief system where civil rights as such have no relevance.

Women's claim to citizenship rights to cover their head has had repercussions in party politics. The Islamist Welfare Party, the major coalition partner of the government formed with the True Path Party in the summer of 1996, has kept the issue on the public agenda. The Welfare Party promised to amend the legal framework to give women the formal right to cover their heads in public institutions, including universities. While the promise is yet to be fulfilled, the party uses the issue as a bargaining chip against its opponents and threatens to pursue the issue when it deems appropriate.[12] In the process, women become pawns in the politics of citizenship rights.

*Feminists*

As a final example of how women experience their citizenship in Turkey, the demands of contemporary feminists can be cited. Since the early 1980s, women calling themselves feminists have been politically active in civil society. Unlike carpet weavers or Islamists, feminists seek to expand their citizenship rights politically in pursuit of personal liberation in a secular context. Unlike some other Middle Eastern countries like Egypt, women's protest against the state has not been a republican tradition in Turkey.[13] It was only from the 1980s that feminists sought liberation beyond emancipation, and women began to criticize the state in defense of their civil and social rights.

Feminist activism in the form of public demonstrations, petitions, and journals, though humble in its scope, has radically challenged the prevailing conception of egalitarian citizenship. Feminists not only have criticized the legal framework of the state, its civil, penal, and various other codes, but also have sought a new, gendered definition of the relationship of citizens to the state as they insisted that the private is political in the Turkish context as well. Women's subordination in private, they argue, has to be politically recognized. A neutral concept of citizenship ignores the radical political implications of the private.

These arguments have been made elsewhere, and Turkish feminists were challenged for imitating Western feminism. In a private interview Ayşe

Düzkan responded to the criticism that their feminism was not indigenous: "Neither did socialism blossom in the plateaus of Konya [in Central Anatolia]." Unhampered by the influence of the West, and voicing similar concerns they share with feminists abroad, they have worked on reconstructing a gendered concept of citizenship.

Their concept of citizenship is new not merely because they advocate more egalitarian laws, or because they are active rather than passive citizens, but because they have politicized and brought to public attention problems women have as women, which cannot be accommodated within the allegedly neutral concept of citizenship. Their major campaign has been against domestic violence. They initiated the Purple Roof Women's Shelter Foundation to provide shelter for victims of domestic violence and led the state to open shelters against domestic violence. With most of the state-initiated shelters of 1990 and 1992 now closed, feminists secured financial support from the Minister of State responsible for women's affairs for their own shelter. Feminist journals have focused on issues of marital rape and sexual harassment.[14] They have proposed amendments to the existing laws to accommodate victims of domestic violence. Feminists argue that egalitarian laws are not enough: a fair concept of citizenship requires pushing for civil and social rights that recognize women's special needs.

## Conclusion

Women's experiences of citizenship in Turkey reveal that the seemingly neutral concept of citizenship is indeed gendered. Turkish women experience citizenship in many ways. Whereas citizenship is irrelevant for women whose rights and responsibilities are communally defined, others use it as a means to promote a religious worldview in which a secular concept of citizenship is irrelevant. For yet another group, citizenship is a gendered relationship that needs to be redefined in order to seek substantive equality in a politically fair community.

# Women in Saudi Arabia
## Between Breadwinner and Domestic Icon?

Eleanor Abdella Doumato

In September 1998 an official decree was issued in Saudi Arabia that would bar women from riding in taxicabs unless accompanied by a male guardian or by another woman. In this kingdom where women are not allowed to drive cars, the ban was an unwelcome and humiliating decision that called women's character into question and, if implemented, would immobilize women who depend on public transportation.[1] Remarkably, shortly after the ban was announced, rumors began to circulate that Saudi Arabia's consultative assembly, the Shura Council, was discussing allowing women to drive cars, though only during daylight hours and with the permission of their male guardians. The rumors could only have been initiated at the highest levels of government because reports of these discussions were published repeatedly in the self-censored Saudi press, even while council members were denying that the subject had ever been taken up at council meetings.[2]

However incongruous these two initiatives — banning women from taxis and also allowing them to drive cars — they reflect a long-standing polarity in Saudi society and illustrate how the regime manages to address two widely disparate constituencies at the same time. After twenty-five years of aggressive development, with women graduating from universities and entering nearly every field of employment, women remain at the center of a decades-old national contest over culture and the role of the state as its guardian: are women to be considered fully adult with equal rights as citizens, or are they to be perpetual dependents of men and standard-bearers of culture, with their minor status encoded in laws of the state? Is society frozen by a hard core of conservatism that will not yield to alternative voices, or will more liberal voices — buoyed by economic necessity — set the pace and turn the rest of society around?

What is clear is that developmental changes affecting women have been occurring all along, even as conservatives hold the discursive high ground and continually attempt to control women through decree or fatwa. Between the two sides is the state, cautiously putting its political weight behind both, but with never enough conviction to satisfy either.

## The State as Guardian: Saudi Arabia's Political Culture

There is virtually no way to voice an opinion publicly about culture or society in Saudi Arabia, if one wishes to be heard, except with reference to Islam. In the political culture of the kingdom, Islam is at once national identity, religious faith, and mode of governance. The burden placed on Islam to be all things to all people is cultivated by Saudi Arabia's rulers, who legitimize their rule over the kingdom by claiming to be committed to a seemingly fixed concept of "Islamic government," with the Qur'an as constitution. How they define Islamic government and the Islamic society they control can be flexible and adapt to changing circumstances. However, when it comes to women, any change begins from a uniquely conservative starting-point because of the historical combination of tribal culture and literalist Wahhabi Islam adopted by the ruling family and propagated throughout the peninsula.

The modernization of Saudi Arabia did not loosen the social controls women experienced in the past. Instead, as the influence of the state expanded, restrictions that once operated on the level of cultural understandings become institutionalized as rules enforceable by state agencies. At one time, for example, a woman didn't go outside her neighborhood without a male guardian, her *mahram,* but the introduction of the airplane turned a local custom into a bureaucratic procedure at airports, with women having to produce written permission from their closest male relative to travel. Based on the same moral premise, the opportunity for women to study abroad brought a rule that government scholarships would go only to women who had a male guardian to accompany them. Similarly, since townswomen customarily kept themselves separated from unrelated men, the opportunity to work in an office situation brought rules preventing women from working in a sex-integrated environment, and the introduction of restaurants brought rules designating separate "family" sections for women, and sometimes rules preventing them from eating in restaurants at all. When public education was introduced in 1961, the rule was that education was to be sex-segregated at all levels, dedicated to shaping girls into better wives and mothers, and, at the university level, women would not be offered courses that would lead to working with men. Other rules followed the increased interest of women in commercial enterprises. In 1995, for example, the Ministry of Commerce made it more difficult for women to operate a business by announcing that they would no longer be issued commercial licenses for businesses requiring them to supervise foreign workers, interact with male clients, or deal on a regular basis with government officials.[3] The decree to keep women out of taxis (alone with an unrelated man) and the ban on driving issued in 1990 (bereft of a man's protection) stem from the same moral logic.

Some of these rules are more rhetoric than rules to be enforced. For example, a rule exists in hospitals that women are not to receive medical treatment except with permission from their mahram, but in practice decisions about medical care are made in consultation among the patient, medical staff, and family members. In spite of a fatwa issued in 1995 forbidding women's attending conferences, women do go abroad where they are free to do what they like, and women cannot be prevented from having private gatherings in their own homes. Women university students have not been eligible for scholarship money to study abroad since 1982, but some still do receive scholarships if they pursue a subject not taught in Saudi universities, and others go on their own without government support. When Abd al-Aziz Bin Baz, Saudi Arabia's now-deceased Grand Mufti and head of the Council of Senior Ulama (Islamic Scholars), issued his 1996 fatwa, quoted below, condemning work outside the home for women, there was a brief period of consternation as to what the fatwa might signify, and then nothing happened.

Rules about women often serve as statements of principle, and standing behind the scholarly officials who issue them is but one way the regime displays its identity as an Islamic government. The state also funds mosques and Islamic higher education, in addition to hosting numerous international Islamic associations. The state has incorporated the traditional Islamic judicial system into its judicial apparatus, and maintains an official Islamic advisory council known as the Council of Senior Ulama to approve decisions taken by the government. A separate body with subdivisions throughout the country, known as the Committee for the Promotion of Virtue and Prevention of Vice (al-Hai'a lil amr bilma'ruf wa nahia 'an munkar) employs cadres of morals policemen to insure shop closings during prayer times and proper clothing for both men and women; the committeemen also run spot-checks to see that men and women together in cars or at restaurant tables are married or related, and search out drug and alcohol violations.

Even with all these additional displays of commitment to Islamic governance, however, rules about women are still of critical importance in asserting the Islamic identity of the regime: it is these rules that touch individuals most personally, impacting on their daily lives, their incomes, and on their family relationships, and reinforcing the dominance of men while offering assurance that family values are values worth affirming. Rules about women, then, are also a source of popularity for the regime.

## The Discursive High Ground

In the years just after the war with Iraq in 1991, the framework for formulating public policy regarding women's rights and women's roles in society shifted farther to the conservative right. Saudi Arabia had already experienced the religious revivalism that swept the region during the 1980s. But as a response to military intervention from the West, on top of widespread antipathy toward the Saudi regime for having to ask for it, a rise in nationalist sentiment occurred that came dressed as Islamic identity. The new militancy was reflected even within the state-funded, king-appointed Council of Senior Ulama, which exercised its growing political clout in September 1994 by forcing the Saudi government to withdraw its participation in the United Nations Population and Development Conference in Cairo. The Ulama objected to the conference's call for "freedom and equality between men and women. . . . Equality is against God's law (shari'a) they said, "and against the law of nature."[4] Their objections were really about men's fears of losing control over women: they objected to the use of contraceptives, to the availability of abortion advocated in the conference agenda, to recommendations for raising the minimum age for marriage, promoting coeducation, and distributing reproductive health care information. In the council's opinion, the conference was an insult to the values of Muslims, and promoted illicit sexual relations that would undermine family values.[5] (On this point the Vatican, the Christian Right, and conservative Muslims were in agreement.) When the United Nations Fourth World Conference on Women met in Beijing the following September, Saudi Arabia was the only country that did not send an official delegation.

A string of fatwas on women followed. In June 1996, for example,

Shaikh bin Baz, perennial advocate for women's divinely-ordained subordination, issued an opinion in the religious weekly, *Al Muslimun,* saying that women should not work outside the home at all. "Removing a woman from her home, which is her kingdom, means removing her from what her natural state and her character require. Women entering the realms of men is a danger for Islamic society in that it leads to mixing of the sexes, which is considered the main path to adultery, which splits society and wrecks morals."[6] In another fatwa, he wrote that women should stay home because they "are a temptation or trial for the living because the woman is *awrah* [sexually private] and by her going out and being visited by men she is not related to she becomes a trial and may lead to a great sin."[7]

Other powerful shaikhs in Saudi Arabia share these opinions: "Women are a place for fulfillment of desire," wrote Shaikh Abu Abdullah ibn Uthaimin at-Tamimi, who is also a member of the Council of Senior Ulama: even her voice can be a temptation for men, for although the voice is not awrah in itself, women should not mix with unrelated men except out of absolute necessity, and when doing so, they must avoid flirtatious speech.[8] For the same reasons, and because "men are the protectors and maintainers of women, because Allah has made the one of them to excel the other," women should not leave their home without their husbands' permission. For the sake of keeping a woman "safe" she should, furthermore, never be alone with a chauffeur, unless he is her guardian.[9]

Politically active groups opposed to the Saudi regime harbor similar views on keeping women safe. One of the most outspoken opposition groups, which began in 1993 as "The Committee for the Defense of Sharia Rights" (usually seen as "Legitimate Rights" in its English translation) aims at eliminating abuses of human rights by the Saudi government, but does not consider women's rights in Saudi Arabia abused. The CDLR's founder, Abdallah ibn Sulayman al-Mas'ari, living in exile in London, disseminates inflammatory information about members of the Saudi royal family and the state of repression in the country, and in a CDLR press bulletin issued in February 1996, wrote that equal rights for women is a violation of shari'a, and he specifically opposed women's inheriting equally with men and any diminution of male guardianship over women or failure to wear "Islamic dress."[10]

It is not only men who express the view that women belong under the control of men, as women who want to appear respectable often articulate similar views and are critical of women who work for slighting their "Islamic" duties in the home, where, as wives, daughters, and mothers, they are supposed to "have all their rights." These views are formulaic, appearing in the Saudi press year after year as if popped out of a mold. Often these views are defensive, addressing perceived attacks by western critics and Saudi feminists. An example is a 1999 article written by "a female correspondent" and published in the Saudi newspaper *Al-Jazirah*. The anonymous author presents the views of numerous prominent women, including college teachers and members of the royal family, on the "security" of the Saudi woman. In the article, Princess Nawrah Bin-Muhammad, wife of Prince Bandar Bin Faisal al-Saud, defends Saudi society against "onslaughts by the proponents of civilization and modernity leveling accusations at the security of the Saudi woman," who is without question chaste, and is therefore secure, she says, because her chastity assures her husband's position of respect among the members of his family. Dr. Muna Abdallah al-Damigh, a dean at one of the kingdom's teachers' colleges, says that those who attempt to

cast doubt on the security of the Saudi woman . . . aim at corrupting society and fighting religion and making the woman go out unveiled and shameless. Those who cast doubt on the status of the Muslim woman and deem that she is restricted and guarded, are backing the war that the enemies of Islam are waging with the aim of paving the way for moral corruption. . . . Moreover, our wise government, which rules in accordance with the laws of God, affirms the effective role of the woman in society.[11]

Saudi women are said to live their lives under restrictions, Dr. al-Damigh continues, but these restrictions are imaginary. "We do not need their alleged freedom but we need to adhere to the law of God and the teachings of our Prophet Muhammad, may God's peace and blessings be upon him. This is the real freedom and this is the pure and chaste life."

One commentator in the article connects religious faith with loyalty to the nation. "We must remember that the secret of the survival of our nation is in our religion," added Professor Siham Justinah, an assistant director of a medical supervision center in Riyadh. In her view, the woman's role is to service her family's needs: "The principle of obedience in the relationship between the husband and the wife leads to family security and the understanding by the woman of her rights and duties." One of the duties of women of which society can be proud, she says, is care of the elderly in the family.

Voices arguing for "tradition" are not the only voices heard in the Saudi media. Others advocate for women's expanded role and for equality as citizens. Some, like traditionalists, try to justify the changes they want with reference to Islam, but instead of referring to immutable principles from the Qur'an they refer to history, citing examples of activist Muslim women from the time of the Prophet as models of emulation. Feminists, however, must rely mainly on economic realities and information about women's educational preparedness to argue for greater access to jobs and social equality. Conservative arguments, on the other hand, can appeal on an emotional level to religious identity, and the shaikhs who support them possess a monopoly on interpreting God's words and speak from the high ground of religious authority. The shaikhs, furthermore, have at their disposal policing mechanisms (the morals police mentioned above) to put force behind their opinions when they choose to, or when the state chooses not to obstruct them. However, in spite of the moral and political high ground from which traditionalists speak, conservative views are under constant attack, not only by liberals in the media, but by virtue of the incompatibility between the life-style they try to defend and the realities of women's lives today. In fact, the actual day to day experience of women, their education, and their aspirations have already turned in other directions, and for many, home and husband are no longer enough.

## Women on the Job, and Needing One

Women are graduating from the kingdom's high schools, teachers' colleges, and universities in ever increasing numbers: a great many of these graduates want a job or need a job, and have almost no possibility of finding one. Between 1995 and 2000, almost 79,000 women have joined the labor market, where they have run into major obstacles preventing them from working outside their home: the requirement that workplaces be segregated by sex, the near exclusion of women from most of the ministries, the difficulties in obtaining a commercial license, the need for adequate and affordable transportation, and a dearth of new job openings as more graduates enter the market at a time when the state is retreating from the public sector. To find a teaching job, for example, a woman now would have to agree to teach in a remote region that may be a two-hour drive from her home. If she is single, she cannot stay in the town of her employment, but must drive back and forth to her home every day, and then she can only hold down the job if she can find the transportation.

A study conducted by the Riyadh Chamber of Commerce estimates the number of working Saudi women in the year 2000 at 272,000, which is a very low 6.6 percent of the 4.1 million women of working age.[12] The largest employer of women is the public sector, where the vast majority (82.2 percent) work as teachers in secondary education, while 2 percent are in higher education.[13] The Saudification process is gradually bringing more Saudi nationals into the system, but in 1993 the numbers were still quite small: about 1500 women in all of the higher education institutions combined, and less than half of the 13,500 women teachers in the high schools.[14] Health care, like education, is one of the few areas of employment considered "suitable to women's nature," and women who work as physicians and health-care administrators comprise 6.3 percent of women public sector employees.

As public sector opportunities for women shrink, there are other areas of work becoming available. The hotel industry, for example, now has permission from the Ministry of Commerce to recruit women to work in marketing banquet facilities and in coordinating women's functions.[15] Women are also working in shops that cater exclusively to women, and in "women only" malls. Branches of banks for women, first opened in 1980, have now spread throughout the kingdom, providing employment for only a few, but providing banking facilities to many. Previously, because respectable women could not enter an exclusively-male bank, women placed money in a husband's account and were dependent on him to make deposits and withdrawals.

Computer programming is another area that should open up to women, if schools and colleges had the resources for computer training, especially because computer-based jobs can be carried out in a sex-segregated environment. As of May 1999, however, computers had not even been introduced in the girls' schools.[16] Women also work as architects, journalists, investors, and business managers: one source counts 500 businesswomen in the cities of Dammam and Al Khobar, 2,480 in Riyadh, and 1,246 in Jeddah for a total of about 3,300, while another source counts only 2,000 businesswomen in the whole country.[17] Whichever is correct, the numbers are still small, and reflect ownership of commercial licenses, not active involvement in managing a business.

The search for new sexually-segregatable areas of employment for women continues. Some have suggested, for example, that women lawyers (who, being women, can't be judges) be allowed to act as advocates for women in court, or that women be employed in the Ministry of Planning where they can have a voice in formulating national policies that affect women.[18] Another proposal is a women-only industrial zone, but potential investors have yet to obtain the necessary licenses.

Many jobs available for women continue to be filled by foreigners, including about 600,000 foreign women, whose employment costs the kingdom an estimated $11 billion a year.[19] The huge foreign work force hold jobs that Saudis cannot fill because they are not qualified, or don't want because the job is low-prestige, or cannot apply for because the job is considered unsuitable for women. The entire nursing staff at the Saudi Arabian National Guard Hospital in Riyadh, for example, consists of foreigners. Kingdom-wide, only 10 percent of nurses are Saudi nationals, even after twenty years of investment in local training programs in nursing.

One important explanation for the low number of women working is the strong social pressure fostered in the political culture that validates being a stay-at-home wife and mother. At the end of the twentieth century, however, this traditional role no longer fills the expressed aspirations of university graduates, and, more important, is no longer compatible with the economic needs of the family. With the decline in oil prices, the Kingdom's per capita gross domestic product fell by more than half, to $6,700 in 1995 from $18,800 in 1981, and with this came the end of guaranteed employment for every graduate who wanted a job.[20] Recent years have also seen a decline in subsidies for electricity, water, telephone, and gasoline, as well as subsidies for land and housing. By 1997 there was a temporary respite: the removal of Iraq from the oil markets boosted prices, increased Saudi oil exports by almost 50 percent, and earned for the Kingdom twice what it had spent to prosecute the war.[21] The embargo against Iraq will someday end, however, and there will be a price to pay for the luxury of having a stay-at-home wife, despite "Islamic family values." In the opinion of one Riyadh secretarial school administrator, it is the economy that will ultimately tear down sex-segregation barriers: when people are poor enough, she suggests, then the men of Saudi Arabia will be ready to let women drive themselves to work.

## What of the Future?

There is virtually no chance that the government will initiate changes that would liberalize the role of women without clear grassroots support. Prince Abdullah, acting as regent on behalf of his ailing brother, King Fahd, said as much in a speech in 1999 in which he seemed to encourage women's social advancement. "We will leave no door for giving closed to women," the Prince said, but with the condition that doors will be opened only "as long as it involves no violation of our religion and ethics."[22] Hinting at the possibility of a radical boost to women's empowerment, he added that "Issues like driving cars by women, and women [obtaining] ID cards, are comparatively simple. The most important thing is their full participation in the life of the society." However warmly the Prince's statement was received by Saudi progressives, his words must be taken with the caveat issued by a spokesperson for the prince: no action would be taken, he said, until religious scholars and others in society reach a consensus.[23]

Is there hope for a consensus? In recent years political challenges mounted against the regime tended to assure the continuing appeasement of conservative voices, and to mute the voices of liberals forced by the display of violence to consider the alternatives if the Saudi regime were to fall. At the beginning of the twenty-first century, however, these challenges have been suppressed and militant opponents have been exiled or imprisoned. That the regent himself is sending up trial-balloons for women's empowerment and responding to the real economic concerns of women and families is a radical departure from the past, when the state took the lead in promoting women's domesticity. On the other hand, while the social impact of the death of the regime-supporting, steadfastly conservative bin Baz has yet to be revealed, there are other opinion makers on the Supreme Council of Islamic Scholars who share his views, though none are as influential or powerful as he.

For the time being the political culture of Saudi Arabia, which emphasizes Islam as nation and domesticated women as the symbol of Islamic values, remains in a state of self-perpetuation. Saudi Arabia's holding pattern when it comes to women is reflected in a growing number of young Saudi expatriate women who live with one foot in America, making a life for themselves abroad while continually testing the social climate at home. These are people who, given the opportunity, would prefer to live as productive citizens in their own country, but as yet cannot. Only a radical change in public perceptions of women and the family, or a huge — and successful — political gamble on the part of the regime could make Saudi Arabia a hospitable home for women who want to be full participants in society.

# Women's Organizations in Kuwait

Haya al-Mughni

Women's groups, like all voluntary associations in Kuwait, are funded by the state. They have elected boards, written constitutions, and paid memberships. Law 24 of 1962 governing the activity of voluntary associations, partially amended in 1965 and still in force, gives the Ministry of Social Affairs and Labor full control over voluntary associations. The ministry has the power to license an association, to dissolve its elected board, or to terminate an association if it determines the group not to be beneficial to society as a whole or not to be abiding by its constitution.

As the only legitimate forum for Kuwaiti women to engage in public activity, women's organizations, by and large, have inhibited the development of a feminist movement, in part by giving elite women the power to control other women's access to the public sphere. Their activities have conformed to official policies, defining women's role in society, stressing traditional practices and *islah* (reform) rather than social change. This is evident from the rise and subsequent collapse of the women's movement for equal rights in the 1970s. The rise of Islamist women's organizations in the 1980s led to their alliance with the state in promoting its model of ideal womanhood. In the period following the Gulf War, the agenda of the women's movement has remained firmly under the control of elite and upper class women opposed to any radical change in the status of women.

Today there are five licensed women's organizations: the Women's Cultural and Social Society (WCSS), licensed in 1963; the Girls Club, 1975; Bayader al-Salam (the Threshing Fields of Peace), 1981; the Islamic Care Society (ICS), 1982, and the Volunteer Women's Association for Community Services, 1991. Membership is overlapping (some women may join more than one group) and the majority of members are middle-aged middle and upper class women. The low level of membership in women's organizations — 1,752 in 1988, about 3 percent of all women in Kuwait — is due to exclusivistic policies carefully practiced by organizational leaders to maintain control over their particular organization.[1]

## Early Women's Organizations

In the 1950s, the development of the oil economy and the rise of the modern state necessitated the integration of Kuwaiti women into the national economy to increase participation in the labor force and to reduce the country's dependency on foreign labor. The traditional practice of female seclusion was eroded, facilitated by the *nahda* movement, which advocated a departure from rigid traditions and customs in the name of *taqaddum* (progress) and civilization. This movement was led by young upper class men who had studied in Egypt.

In this climate of rapid modernization and state-building, women's associations were formed, giving Kuwaiti women access to a public sphere from which they had long been excluded and, more importantly, to the world of male politics. In 1963, the Women's Cultural and Social Society (WCSS) was established to provide a social gathering place for educated and comfortable merchant class women with the energy and wealth to indulge in charity work. This group extended women's traditional role of support and nurturing into the public sphere without challenging the position of women in society.

The same year saw the formation of the Arab Women's Development Society (AWDS), whose members were middle class women who focused on issues the WCSS avoided addressing, namely gender equality and women's citizenship rights. The AWDS challenged official policies on women's status, demanding the extension of political rights to women, equality in all fields of employment, the appointment of women as special attorneys to draft family law, the provision of child allowances to married women, and the restriction of polygamy. In 1973, 10 years later, the AWDS succeeded in forcing the all-male National Assembly to discuss an equal rights bill, provoking the stormiest debates in the history of the assembly. Opponents of the bill, who formed a majority, demanded the preservation of the patriarchal integrity of the society, claiming that Islam gave men and women different responsibilities and made men superior to women. The bill's supporters were the nationalists who also supported individual rights and democracy. The equal rights bill angered the male community and threatened political disarray. With support from the government, the assembly avoided voting on the bill by referring it to the assembly's Legal Affairs Committee for further "study."

The mid-1970s witnessed increasing state intervention to protect the traditional family arrangement and to reduce the influence of secular and feminist groups. The government urged the media to "combat all that threatens the existence of the family or distorts the character of solidarity between its members," and to propagate family values based on obedience to the male head of household.[2] The government also promoted the concept of *al-usra al-waheda* (the united family) as a way of reinforcing allegiance to the monarchic state.

In 1978, the government stressed its dedication to the Islamization of society. That same year saw the Personal Status Law enacted, legitimizing the control of men over women. Earlier clauses of the penal code relating to the crimes of *ird* (honor) and *sum'a* (reputation) were amended to bring tougher sentences to women offenders. The period of incarceration for women having sexual relations outside marriage, for instance, was increased from five to ten years.

The secular opposition and the women's rights movement responded with persistent demands for civil liberties and individual rights.[3] The Girls' Club, formed by a group of upper class women in 1975, sided with the AWDS to put further pressure on the government to include suffrage in the laws that benefited women. Together, the Girls' Club and the AWDS formed strong alliances with the vocal nationalist groups to give their campaign increased political weight and launched a series of conferences and seminars to increase interest in and support for what many others had begun to fear as a threatening movement likely to bring political chaos and social instability.

To reduce the influence of the secular opposition, the government closed the al-Istiqlal Club, the mouthpiece of the Arab nationalist movement in Kuwait, and dissolved the elected boards of most of the associations controlled by the left and nationalist groups and appointed new ones.[4]

In 1978, following accusations against AWDS leadership of financial fraud that were never adequately proven or investigated, a female government official was appointed president of AWDS. Two years later, after members continued to refuse to collaborate with the newly appointed leader, the government disbanded the AWDS, marking the end of a decade of women's rights movement in Kuwait.

## Women's Religious Groups and the Glorification of Motherhood

In 1981, the Islamic Heritage Society and two Islamic welfare societies were licensed. During the same year, a religious women's organization, Bayader al-Salam (the Threshing Fields of Peace), was also licensed. A year later, the Islamic Care Society (ICS) for women was established. Parallel to this expansion of religious groups was an explosion of writings and debates on "women's rights and duties in Islam." The Islamic veil made its appearance and a new model of womanhood emerged. Although there was no consensus as to what place women should occupy in society, most of the religious groups called for a return to traditional female virtues and morality. Women were defined as having moral duties to strengthen family ties, to raise good children, and to defend the traditions and customs of society. A body of discourse was generated to justify the importance of women's domestic role, emphasizing natural differences between men and women to rationalize asymmetrical gender relations in society.

The ICS, established by the wife of the Crown Prince and Prime Minister of Kuwait, Sheikha Latifa al-Fahad al-Salem al-Sabah, holds that the ideal women work for the interests of society and the family; she is religious but not fanatic. The ICS introduced classes in embroidery, dressmaking, oriental cookery, and *tajwid* (Qur'an reading).

Bayader al-Salam, a Sufi-like organization formed by upper class women, displaced women's interests from self-centeredness to God-centeredness, placing emphasis on *tazkiyat al-nafs* (self-purification) and on the acquisition of Islamic virtues. For Bayadar, the ideal woman fears and loves God and does *al-'amal al-salih* (virtuous deeds).

The WCSS and the Girls' Club silently observed the development of this anti-feminist movement, doing little to oppose or even resist the Islamic movement. On the contrary, they used their adherence to Islam to justify their attitude of complacency toward the patriarchal structure of the society. They supported the imposition of Islamic *adab* (female modesty and chastity) and perpetuated the myth that Kuwaiti women's achievements in education and paid employment were synonymous with female emancipation. Nevertheless, both the WCSS and the Girls' Club supported female suffrage and campaigned, albeit separately, to win the vote for women.

In 1980, the WCSS addressed a petition to the council of ministers demanding that Kuwaiti women be appointed to senior government posts. Positions such as those of undersecretary in various key ministries and college dean have been opened up to women. Involvement in key jobs serves the interests of both state and ruling classes. In her book *Kuwait: Anatomy of a Crisis Economy,* Dr. S. M. al-Sabah indicates that the integration of women into the labor force is central to maintaining social harmony and political stability, while "the absence of that stability, in the case of a nation such as Kuwait, threatens not only the prosperity of a country but also its very existence."[5] At the same time, throughout the 1980s women's groups worked closely with the government to teach women how to become better house-wifes and how to raise their children within the confines of Kuwaiti culture. Each group devised its own educational programs and worked independently under the umbrella of the ministry of social affairs and labor. Bayadar al-Salam focused on domestic consumption, while the ICS, the WCSS and the Girls' Club focused on mother-child relationships.

## Serving the Community

The period after the Gulf War saw two major developments. First, the ma-jority of women's organizations shifted their concern toward *khidmat al-mujtama*ʾ (serving the community). Second, in 1994, the Federation of Ku-waiti Women's Associations (FKWA) was licensed as the sole representative of Kuwaiti women outside Kuwait. All the women's organizations except the WCSS joined the FKWA. Sheikha Latifa, already acting chairwoman of the Islamic Care Society and the Volunteer Women's Association for Commu-nity Services, licensed in 1991, was elected president of the FKWA. This gave elite women full control over the activities and symbols of the women's groups, and the right to speak officially on behalf of Kuwaiti women.

The FKWA called on women to push for the implementation of shariʿa and to comply with "Arab and Islamic traditions," ignoring the many social and economic problems faced by Kuwaiti women in their everyday lives. After the Gulf War, the number of impoverished female heads of households increased, and the situation of Kuwaiti women married to non-Kuwaitis seriously deteriorated. Foreign husbands and children were denied all protec-tions to which Kuwaitis are otherwise entitled. The patrilinear character of citizenship in Kuwait allows the state to disavow any responsibility to sup-port them. Government housing, child allowances, and unconditional wel-fare assistance are provided directly to Kuwaiti men as heads of households. There are more than 7,000 Kuwaiti women married to foreigners, of whom 718 were on welfare assistance in 1993.

In 1993, when Kuwaiti women married to non-Kuwaitis sought refuge in the WCSS, the latter adopted their cause and demanded that Kuwaiti women be given the right to pass citizenship on to their children. For over a year, Kuwaiti women married to non-Kuwaitis used the premises of the Environmental Protection Society as their headquarters until they were told by the society's all-male board to look for a new meeting place.

The politics of female marginalization practiced by the state are supported by the FKWA. This group's leaders blamed women, not the state, for existing social problems, arguing that it is the fault of women if their marriages break down, if their husbands fail to support them, and if their children and foreign husbands are stateless and unemployed. They advised Kuwaiti women not to marry "outsiders" and to look after the stability of their family. The issue of women's citizenship rights has been cast aside as unimportant and incompatible with shari'a principles of differential gender responsibilities.

The WCSS, meanwhile, changed its former image of an organization devoted entirely to charity work. It elected a new president, Adela al-Sayer, and new members recruited from the middle and upper classes, most of whom are highly educated and hold managerial positions. The WCSS has reformulated its objectives "to raise the educational and cultural level of women, and to increase their awareness of both their rights and obligations as citizens and as family members." However, the formation of the FKWA reduced the authority of the WCSS, forcing it to look for new allies in the public sphere, notably the Graduates' Society and the Lawyers' Society. Although these societies are in favor of extending more rights to women, they are not in favor of conceding all men's privileges to women or changing gender relations. Nor was the WCSS interested in changing the traditional male-female relationship. During their first "Post-Liberation Conference on Women's Role in Cultural, Social and Economic Development," held in April 1994, Adela al-Sayer emphasized that the "women's role in social development should not be seen as merely a matter of achieving or seeking equality with men . . . but rather of participating with men in formulating new social models" that are congruent with Kuwaiti traditions and customs. In other words, men and women have different roles and responsibilities, and cooperation between them is essential for achieving harmony and social stability. Men are defined as husbands/brothers/partners with whom women share common interests and concerns.[6]

Family unity is essential for both the FKWA and the WCSS. The Fourth UN conference on women unleashed a furor never seen before in Kuwaiti society, with the Islamists denouncing the conference as subversive and a

Western ploy aimed at destroying the values of the Muslim community. During the conference, many members of the WCSS joined the FKWA and other anti-feminist groups to stage protests against abortion, gay rights, and sexual liberties that they feared would lead to the decline of the moral authority of the family and bring social disorder and instability. Aligning themselves with Kuwaiti officials, the FKWA made it clear publicly that they will not allow the implementation of "anything contradictory" to Islamic sharia and the tradition and culture of Kuwaiti society. The "headstrong attitude" displayed by the Kuwaiti women's groups in opposing resolutions contrary to religious morality and family values was praised by the Islamists and the government.

## Into the Future

Kuwaiti women's organizations, including the WCSS, have empowered those who are already empowered and reinforced women's subservience to patriarchal rule. There is strong resistance on the part of the state, the male community, and elite and upper class women to any changes in women's status. The closure of the AWDS, a vocal feminist group that advocated full citizenship rights for women, illustrates the anxiety of the patriarchal society over women's autonomy and independent status. This anxiety is shared by elite and upper class women; hence the contradictions in the WCSS's brand of feminism, which, on the one hand, advocates political and civil rights for women and, on the other, opposes the right of women to decide on matters affecting their reproductive health and sexuality. In addition, although the WCSS and the Girls' Club support suffrage for women and, since the early 1980s, have campaigned for political rights, they have made no effort to form a coalition. This lack of unity has undermined the women's political rights movement in Kuwait and has raised doubts about the commitment of women's groups to win the vote for women. It seems unlikely that the WCSS and the Girls' Club will join forces in the future; so deep is the divide between them that to bridge such division would require that the leaders begin to identify themselves with women's issues rather than with the groups they represent.[7]

# The Dialectics of Fashion
## Gender and Politics in Yemen

Sheila Carapico

The situation of Yemeni women is complicated and contradictory. On the one hand, compared with relatively fashion-forward Mediterranean Arabs, or even their affluent sisters in the Gulf, Yemeni women appear to be especially old-fashioned. One rarely sees a Yemeni woman outdoors bare-headed, and in the capital, Sana'a, most women cover their faces in public. Yet outward appearances can be misleading. While it is tempting to assume that women "still" veil because "tradition" tells them to, it is simply wrong to conclude that "traditionally" all women were secluded in their homes, or that how they dress now tells us much about their political and economic status. Clothes do not make the woman: lives are shaped by political currents and economic realities.

The public roles and civil rights of Yemeni women have been conditioned by the vicissitudes of national politics, with important differences between North and South.[1] Even in the more conservative North, by the 1970s permissive legislation afforded rights of pregnancy leave, voting, driving, travel, property ownership, and public office, and several women gained real national prominence as television broadcasters. Yet only the brightest daughters of educated parents could read. Through the 1980s, the overwhelming majority of urban females left school after a couple of years to become home-makers. Their country cousins, busy from dawn to dusk tending dairy cows, drawing water, collecting fuel and fodder, harvesting crops, and processing food, found respite only in the customary forty-day rest after childbirth or in old age.[2] Women's economic participation in the agrarian economy was substantial, and intensified due to massive male migration; but their participation in the modern sector was minuscule.[3]

After its 1962 republican revolution, North Yemen witnessed the popularization of veiling as the emerging bourgeoisie imitated the prim-and-proper "ladies" of the old gentry of the *sayyid* strata, symbolized by a particular style of full formal black veil called the *sharshaf*. Customarily, women dressed for the climate and for work, with wraps serving as pockets, sunscreen, and dust protection. In the steamy Tihama coast along the Red Sea, where Arabia meets Africa, women wore bright skirts and skimpy halter-tops, layered with a sheer, breezy caftan for going out; in the southern uplands, full, filmy shifts with a bright scarf loosely wrapped about the head, perhaps with a silk *abayia* for the city. In the cooler Zaydi highlands women wore wide *sirwal* pants beneath a fitted caftan, with a long scarf tied tightly in such a way that a *lithma* could be lowered beneath the chin or raised over the nose and mouth, all covered by the item Americans call an India-print bedspread. (Shafaʻi males typically wear a *futah* or sarong, whereas Zaydis prefer a white *thawb,* both with a sports jacket; most men cover their heads and, like the movie images of American cowboys, sometimes their faces.) The sharshaf, which rather resembles a nun's habit, traditionally signified elite women dressed up for afternoon tea. As society changed, however, many women thought in terms of the liberty to sharshaf, because wearing the veil symbolized relief from hard labor, dignity in the marketplace, freedom to study, and equality with the old elite. As they moved to the cities, or as their own communities urbanized, as they were exposed to an opulent Saudi style of hypermodesty, and as they entered school, the new generation of Northern girls adopted the sharshaf, even in Tihami cities where the heat makes them insufferable. Folk dresses became associated with old age and ignorance.

In South Yemen, by contrast, or at least in the formerly British colonial port city of Aden, where revolutionaries established the Arab world's only Marxist regime (the People's Democratic Republic or PDRY), women enjoyed rights unrivaled in the region. Females represented roughly a third of all Adeni students, teachers, medical personnel, civil servants, and factory workers and a visible minority among lawyers, judges, directors, administrators, middle-level party cadre, and parliamentarians. Courts granted mothers custody of children and the marital home in event of divorce.[4] As in the Northern hinterland, however, provincial dress and behavior varied considerably by region: for instance, the tribeswomen of the Mahra mountains were far more assertive and active than the demure housebound *sayyidat* of Hadrami towns.

Under the unity arrangements in effect between 1990 and 1994, Southern women, especially Adenis who moved to Sana'a, felt their freedoms slipping away. For instance, some husbands obtained "quickie" divorces or second-marriage licenses. Northern women, by contrast, experienced newfound political power. Ten female PDRY parliamentary delegates continued to serve in the first unity parliament. Over protests from some conservative jurists, a woman was appointed, albeit temporarily, to the fifteen-member Supreme Court. Others served in Aden courts. One woman was named to the seventeen-person Supreme Elections Committee. Fifty women, mostly independent urban intellectuals, ran amidst over 3,000 males in the 1993 parliamentary elections. Only two won seats in 1993, both in Southern constituencies, and some women candidates, like some male counterparts, experienced personal harassment during the campaign. Nonetheless widespread acceptance of universal adult suffrage was demonstrated by the fact that the neoconservative *Islah* party, standard-bearer for the religious right, conducted a special female voter-registration drive. Other women were named deputy minister of information, dean of education, and directors of various agencies. A survey found about two thousand professionally qualified women in education, health, communications, law, business, and other fields.

Unity brought some compromises in urban fashion. Adenis who came to Sana'a, whether in 1986 or 1990, almost inevitably donned a scarf and either an abayia or a European raincoat. It became fashionable for Sana'ani students to wear what they call hijab, a headscarf wrapped or tied under the chin with a modern long black silk coatdress over jeans, Paris fashions, or knock-offs. The appearance in cities of Egyptian-style "coiffure" shops reflected a trend toward hairstyling instead of wearing bright scarves for women's parties or evenings at home. The increasing politicization of sartorial issues was amplified by the stridence of emphatically sharshafed activists within the neo-Islamist movement, some of them effective public orators from beneath a full black face-veil. They contend that Muslim women and girls have rights to separate education, to financial support and legal mediation from male relatives, and to insert stipulations in the marriage contract.

Beneath their shabby polyester sharshafs, ordinary women worried about economics, not fashion. In the deep recession precipitated by the return of Yemeni migrants from Saudi Arabia and the loss of the bulk of its foreign aid due to the Gulf War, exacerbated by low oil prices and bad public management, the growing urban underclass and the increasingly impoverished rural majority's standards of living have declined. Among the burgeoning urban population, most women were uprooted from productive roles in their natal communities to nuclear households entirely dependent on spousal earning capacity and spending decisions. Alienated from both their families and the means of production, they are typically at the mercy of a matched-mate who is himself powerless except within the domestic domain. Their sisters and cousins who remain in farming villages bear the increased burden of maintaining cottage gardens, domestic livestock, and aging parents, all the more so if they send their daughters to school.

The majority of women neither vote nor want to talk politics, which they regard with justifiable skepticism as a violent male domain. Their conversation dwells on marriage, childbirth, and, increasingly, the loss of earnings, joblessness, high inflation, overburdened underfinanced social services, and diminishing returns from traditional agriculture and crafts. By the time parliamentary elections were held in April 1993, the most pressing issue among Southerners was the price of milk, which had quadrupled since unity. A year later, Sana'ani families who had always purchased bulk quantities of grain wholesale were reduced to purchasing flour by the kilo from the corner retailer. Meat, once a luncheon staple, was now reserved for special holidays.[5]

By 1994, the fiscal crisis of the state only exacerbated political competition between the military faction that had governed the former North Yemen and the Yemeni Socialist Party (YSP) that had ruled the PDRY. Eventually, the bipolar partisan competition erupted into a civil war wherein the former Northern army defeated what remained of PDRY forces. Socialist leaders went into exile. Although civilian casualties were relatively light, thousands of families were displaced to temporary shelters, and hundreds of thousands were terrorized by the sounds and sights of bombs, missiles, and gunfire, and by the suspension of electricity, water, and normal life. Women wept, and nowhere more bitterly than in Aden, site of so many episodes of urban warfare in the past generation.

The defeat of the separatist leadership of the Yemeni Socialist Party may have delighted freemarketeers, but it was bad news for advocates of female rights in Yemen, for a rightist coalition comprised of the military and neoconservatives triumphed. In the aftermath of the war progressive male journalists, professors, and party leaders were mugged or abducted by plainclothes security officers; newspapers were shut down or given new editors; socialist establishments, "coiffures," and even some southern saints' tombs were vandalized; and the constitution was amended to retract many of the rights and liberties granted after unification. One amendment specified that "women are the sisters of men," and new personal status and criminal statutes reduced women to legal wards of male kin. Although women were still guaranteed electoral suffrage and a token judicial and ministerial role, wives required their husbands' permission to work, to travel abroad, or to divorce, and in court a woman's testimony counted only half as much as a man's.

The Islamist dimension of these developments is distinctively modern and untraditional. Neofundamentalist ideologues identify themselves as Wahhabi or *salafi* (puritan), and they explicitly eschew popular Yemeni practices of Zaydi Islam in the northern highlands and the majority Shafaʿi Sunni sect in the rest of the country. This is why salafis attacked Shafaʿi mosques and shrines after the civil war and Wahhabis fought for control of Zaydi parochial schools. The neo-Islamists within and beyond Islah condemn many customs including sayyid privileges, traditional wedding celebrations, popular forms of feminine adornment, and the curricula of prerevolutionary Qurʾanic institutes. Their campaigns for feminine seclusion are one aspect of a broader, radical agenda that draws more inspiration from the schools of Islamic learning established in Pakistan to support the Afghan jihad than from Yemeni religious scholarship, practice, or belief. Within Yemen, this extremist group is known as "Afghan Arabs." One example of their absurd pronouncements (laughable to most Yemenis) is that it is *haram* (sinful) for females to milk cows because of the purportedly vulgar hand movement.

The plight of women and their families in the late 1990s was not unlike that of popular classes in many Latin American countries in a period of military-market fascism in the '70s and early '80s; there extrajudicial violence against men and threat of sexual censure against women were part of an apparatus of control in a system where officers helped themselves to both public and private sectors amidst inflation and economic reform imposed by foreign creditors. Privatization of the assets of a socialist state and of social services, including hospitals, utilities, and higher education, enriches the private holdings of a military class while impoverishing the masses drawn to the city by the false lure of civil service sinecures. Currency devaluation, investor incentives, and open markets satisfy foreign creditors that "reforms" are underway, and declining standards of living for the majority of the population are regarded as the necessary medicine. In Yemen, as elsewhere in the Arab world, the encouragement of neo-Islamic groups was one element of a decades long struggle by military leaders against all forms of socialism, communism, and left liberalism. The seemingly final repudiation of socialism in Yemen has been accompanied by a wave of radical neofundamentalism, albeit less violent than in Algeria, Afghanistan, the Occupied Territories, or Egypt. In the peninsula generally, neofundamentalist Islam — whether Wahhabi, Shiʾa, salafi, or another version — is now the main challenge to authoritarian states. Yemen is exceptional in that social conditions are much worse than elsewhere in the Arabian peninsula.

Nonviolent Islamist messages have considerable appeal among women. A physician from Aden recalled having partied in public on New Year's eve of 1986, which turned out to be the eve of a vicious bloodletting among the YSP elite. Concluding that "our lord was displeased," she said, university women began wearing hijab. As already noted, the Yemeni conservative party, Islah, conducted female voter registration and participation drives in both the 1993 and 1997 parliamentary elections. In the current environment of economic austerity, newly founded Islamic charities have offered a social safety net specifically designed to catch girls and young brides. To the typical Yemeni woman voter, who is a devoted mother, semiliterate, informally employed, overworked, highly vulnerable, and politically alienated, the Qur'an readings and paternalistic protections offered by some of the father figures in Islah (as distinct from the youthful militant "Afghan Arabs") have a certain appeal. Many seek solace and an "escape from freedom" in prayer, piety, and obedience. Moreover, the harassment of young men who hang out on the streets, typically unemployed migrant-returnees, who are more often rude than religious, has gotten so troublesome that many African and Western women wear the hijab, too.

Most women are more vulnerable than they have ever been. Whereas in the past bride-price provided some insurance of a wife's longterm material and physical wellbeing, nowadays more parents are tempted to "sell" their daughters to old men or military officers. Young brides who fall in love with their grooms may quickly squander their wedding gifts on day-to-day marital household expenses.[6] Health care personnel observe the greater frequency of still undocumented cases of spousal abuse among women too far from their parents to run home, although doctors realize that only the most egregious gunshot and knife wounds reach the hospital. Women who have never had their eyesight checked or their tooth-cavities filled are unlikely to practice gynecological birth control, but hospitalization for emergencies and widespread immunization against early childhood diseases have boosted live births while reducing infant mortality. The result by 1996 was the world's highest rate of natural population growth, 3.7 percent. Whereas when their mothers married they typically moved from one extended family to another nearby to raise five or six children among twenty cousins, sharing farm and nursery duties with mothers- and sisters-in-law, the typical woman of this generation is blessed with eight or nine children by her thirtieth birthday and struggles to raise them alone on whatever money her husband brings home.

Whereas her mother and grandmother were productive in agriculture, husbandry, and crafts, the modern Yemeni woman is a housewife, specialized in reproduction and struggling against rapid inflation in the costs of utilities, grain, and rent that leave precious little for meat, transport, medical care, or vocational training.

The combined pressures of antisocialist policies specifically including repudiation of women's rights, of economic austerity and recession, and of violence against critics of the regime certainly augur ill for women generally. And yet Yemeni women do indeed enjoy political rights and ordinary personal liberties denied to their more affluent sisters in the Gulf, none of whom are allowed to vote, and many of whom face much stricter legal restrictions on their public comportment or employment. The female franchise was reaffirmed in Yemen's 1997 parliamentary elections, when women accounted for a quarter of the electorate. Twenty-three women ran for election, but more of them were party candidates. Whereas in 1993 only two parties, the Socialists and the Ba'th, ran women candidates, now seven out of the eight parties — the exception being the Islah — ran women for parliament. Again two women entered parliament, again both from the South, but this time backed by Sana'a. While about a dozen female judges remained on the bench in southern courts, several female law graduates became practicing attorneys. Others were promoted to the rank (although not the position) of minister. A move toward gender-segregated colleges notwithstanding, women compete with men in most faculties.

For the several dozen women prominent in public life, then, success depends more on one's relationship to the national leadership than on gender as such. Women in powerful families enjoy the privileges, if not the direct political prowess, of the ruling class. For others politically active "in their own right," the possibilities are not necessarily less than civilian male counterparts of comparable family, education, wealth, and age. The current litmus test of "support for unity" is the same for both genders. Conversely, however, some are doubly victimized, by gender and by politics. Southern women suffer special indignities from northern soldiers whose indoctrination includes anticommunist propaganda about sexual promiscuity under the PDRY.

Western and northern Arab feminist advocacy through assistance programs for women operates obliquely in this environment. Mother and child health programs, for instance, offer essential medical services on a "cost-recovery" basis that may make them more expensive than comparable programs offered through Yemeni religious charities. Funds and training for microenterprises encourage marginally remunerative housewifery skills like needlecraft and food production, again no different from the neo-Islamist programs for girls, and short of traditional productive contributions. The availability of international funds for projects involving women in the electoral process is an inducement for Yemenis to found women's associations and for the government to guarantee a female voice inside parliament, but the lion's share of foreign money for these initiatives goes to a handful of English-speaking politicians. Western support for privatization, marketization, and other "post-socialist" reforms unwittingly fortifies those who associate gender equity with communism. American concern for the stability of the misogynist Saudi monarchy (not to mention their joint backing for the Afghan jihad) is at odds with statements and efforts on behalf of electoral participation by Yemeni women, for Riyadh contends that voting generally, female suffrage, is anti-Islamic, and spends good money broadcasting this message. Finally, the European, North American, or Mediterranean Arab visitors who address women's liberation in Yemen from a fashion perspective, as if there were a "right" to Western-style clothes, are puzzled by local women's responses. More than any of these things, Yemeni women are concerned about welfare and violence.

Some rather dire circumstances notwithstanding, South Arabian womanhood is not entirely helpless. Folk historiography reveres Queen Bilqis of Sheba (Saba') and the medieval Queen Arwa as its best-loved, wisest leaders. The courts do offer some legal protections under contract and property law.[7] The PDRY legacy cannot be wholly obliterated. The unified republic is committed to feminine electoral rights. Yemeni males are far more victim to physical violence and political repression than females, and their political and civil rights are also insecure. Given a certain brutality in the public political sphere and the economy, "withdrawal" — veiling, political alienation, dropping out of school, consenting to polygamous marriage, socializing only with women — may represent deliberate choices. Yet more and more females, especially but not exclusively those from families with wealth, power, and prestige, are finishing secondary school, graduating from the universities, pursuing careers, joining parties and civic associations, and entering the public sphere. Equally important the men who head all three main political tendencies — the Socialists, the Islamists, and the governing party — recognize the political advantages of empowering women politically: to distinguish Yemen as more progressive and republican than the neighboring monarchies, and to cultivate a voting constituency among the unarmed half of the population. Given its political and economic difficulties, Yemen would do well to do well by its women.

# The Political Economy of Female Employment in Postrevolutionary Iran

Fatemeh Etemad Moghadam

The status of women and their labor force participation have been subject to considerable change in Iran during the last four decades. Three distinct phases of government policy can be detected: 1960–1979, 1980–1989, and 1990 until the present. In the first phase, the explicit policy was utilization of female labor for economic growth. In the period immediately following the Revolution, the policy aimed at Islamization of the society, and a reversal of the "immoral and Westernized" policies of the Shah. While the "Islamization" policy objective has not been abandoned, it has been considerably modified since 1989. By examining labor participation during each of these three periods, I will argue that a host of complex factors, including government policy and ideology have affected employment.[1]

As indicated in Table 1, the share of women in total active labor more than doubled during the period 1956–76, and declined to nearly one half of its prerevolutionary level in 1986. Since 1986, however, there are indications of modest increases (Table 2). Occupational segregation increased for the period 1980–89. I will argue that the general decline in active female labor can be explained by the sluggish performance of the economy, education, and ideology. However, the increase in the intensity of occupational segregation is primarily an ideological factor.[2]

## Framework

Rising labor force participation of women is generally linked to increases in the level of educational attainments of women,

TABLE 1. Population in active labor force (%)

|         | 1956   | 1966   | 1976   | 1986   |
|---------|--------|--------|--------|--------|
| Males   | 90.45  | 86.73  | 79.73  | 89.73  |
| Females | 9.55   | 13.27  | 20.27  | 0.27   |
| Total   | 100.00 | 100.00 | 100.00 | 100.00 |

Source: International Labor Organization *Yearbook of Labor Statistics* (1967): 20; (1971): 28; (1982): 23; (1992): 31.

TABLE 2. Employment and education of population ages 10 years and older

|                        | 1956  | 1966  | 1976  | 1986  | 1991  |
|------------------------|-------|-------|-------|-------|-------|
| *Total populaton*      |       |       |       |       |       |
| (1000s)                | 12785 | 17000 | 23002 | 32874 | 38655 |
| Male                   | 6542  | 8794  | 11796 | 16841 | 19997 |
| Female                 | 6242  | 8206  | 11206 | 16033 | 18658 |
| *Total female (%)*     |       |       |       |       |       |
| Active                 | 9.2   | 12.6  | 12.9  | 8.2   | 8.7   |
| Employed               | 9.2   | 11.5  | 10.8  | 6.1   | 6.6   |
| Home-maker*            | 79.5  | 73.3  | 68.8  | 68.7  | 63.7  |
| Student                | 3.0   | 7.4   | 14.8  | 16.6  | 22.0  |
| *Total urban female (%)* |     |       |       |       |       |
| Active                 | 9.3   | 9.9   | 9.0   | 8.3   | 8.9   |
| Employed               | 9.2   | 9.6   | 8.5   | 5.1   | 6.9   |
| Home-maker             | 77.0  | 68.1  | 64.2  | 66.5  | 61.5  |
| Student                | 8.4   | 16.4  | 23.7  | 20.5  | 25.2  |
| *Total rural female (%)* |     |       |       |       |       |
| Active                 | .2    | 14.3  | 16.6  | 7.9   | 8.6   |
| Employed               | 9.1   | 12.7  | 13.0  | 6.3   | 6.1   |
| Home-maker             | 80.8  | 76.7  | 73.0  | 71.8  | 66.6  |
| Student                | 0.4   | 1.7   | 6.5   | 11.8  | 17.6  |

Source: *Salnameh Amary-e Keshvar: 1369* (Annual Statistics 1990) (Tehran: Markaz-e Amar-e Iran [Iran Statistical Center], 1990), 62–63; *Preliminary Results of 1991 Population Survey* (Tehran: Markaz-e Amar-e Iran [Iran Statistical Center], 1990), 2–3.
* This category is not exclusive to housewives and includes family members whose primary occupation is homemaking.

declines in fertility, and increases in the age of marriage. Structural changes in the economy — urbanization, growth of service and industrial sectors, and changes in the agricultural sector — also affect labor participation. The impact of growth, however, is less clear, and not always positive. There is no consensus on trends associated with development on women's participation.[3]

While sluggish growth may contribute to a decrease in the relative share of female employment, empirical findings are not conclusive.[4] Women workers are often clustered in certain jobs and their entry in others is slow. Factors contributing to occupational segregation include education, skills, and discrimination. Women generally have low levels of market oriented education and skills, and are clustered in lower skill and lower paying jobs.[5] Gender role perceptions lead to discrimination, with equally productive women workers being discriminated against in certain job categories. Cultural factors also impact employment: differences in the extent and type of patriarchal domination have different impacts on labor force participation.[6] I will examine women's labor participation and show that postrevolutionary ideological factors that were reflected in changes in fertility, age of marriage, legal status of women, access to higher education, and emphasis on traditional cultural values affected women's employment. As the ideological factor was more pronounced during the earlier stages of the Revolution, the impact was stronger. Over time, however, the ideological factor has been modified, and the impact is less pronounced. The data are primarily based on four available cross section population surveys for 1956, 1966, 1976, and 1986, and the results of a sample survey for 1991. Note that the data in general underestimates participation rates, particularly unpaid female labor in agriculture.[7] However, since the same data collection method is used for all surveys, the cross-section data are comparable. Unless otherwise stated, I have used the same definitions and categories of labor force as those provided by the International Labor Organization (ILO), *Yearbook of Labor Statistics.*

## The Economy

Performance of the Iranian economy has been generally poor since the revolution, with modest improvements since 1989. For the period 1976–86, the Gross Domestic Product grew on average by a negative 0.6 percent per annum, manufacturing by a negative 0.9, and the oil sector by a negative 11.5. Agriculture was the only sector showing a positive growth: 4.5 percent average annual. The period 1986–91, however, showed improvements: the GDP grew on the average by 4.1 percent per annum.[8]

A somewhat similar pattern is observed in female employment. The total number of active women in the population of ten years and older was about 1.45 million in 1976, fell to 1.31 million in 1986, and rose to 1.63 million in 1991. The percentage shares of active women in total female population of ten years and older were 12.9, 8.2, and 8.7 for 1976, 1986, and 1991 respectively. These numbers suggest that economic factors had an impact on employment. For the period 1976–1986, however, male employment grew by an average annual rate of nearly 4 percent (Table 2).[9] Thus female labor as a percentage of total active labor declined from 20.3 percent in 1976 to 10.3 percent in 1986, as the share of male labor increased (Table 1). The decline in active labor is clearly gender biased. Factors other than stagnation are likely to have impacted the decline.

To separate the impact of stagnation from other factors, in the subsequent sections I will make a sectoral and occupational examination of female employment, to see if the specific sectors that employed women were affected by stagnation.

Economic stagnation may indirectly affect female participation through cultural factors. In Iran, legally and culturally, men are expected to provide for their families. Thus in recessions employers may be sympathetic to employing men and discriminating against women. While postrevolutionary Iran placed a greater emphasis on traditional cultural factors, changes even in the absence of ideological economic stagnation would have contributed to increased discrimination against women. The indirect impact of stagnation — through cultural factors independent of the ideological changes — should not be overlooked.

## Ideology, Age of Marriage, and Fertility

Important changes were introduced in the family law after the Islamic revolution. Following early Islamic practices, the legal age of marriage for girls was reduced from 18 to 9 years, subject to the approval of a special court and the girl's guardian. These courts, however, are lenient in issuing the permits. On average each court spends a few minutes asking the girl if she is voluntarily getting married, and then issues the permit. When interviewed and challenged by the representative of the weekly magazine *Zan-e Rooz* on the ease of issuing permits, a judge answered that if a permit is refused by one court, it can easily be obtained from another.[10]

In 1976, the percentage share of married to all girls in the age category of ten to fourteen was nearly zero. This share, however, was about 2.5 and 2.2 for 1986 and 1991, respectively. The percentage of married girls in the total for the age category of 15 to 19 years is almost identical for 1976 and 1986, and there is a significant decline for 1991. If we compare the combined age category of 10 to 19 for these three years, the percentage shares are 12.76, 17.59, and 12.41 for 1976, 1986, and 1991 respectively, indicating a sharp decrease in the age of first marriage for 1986 and a modest increase for 1991. The drop in the age of first marriage for 1986 is one factor contributing to the decline in labor participation. Although child marriage continues to be legal, the data show a general tendency toward an increase in the age of first marriage for 1991. Since 1991, the available anecdotal information suggest a general increase in the age of first marriage.[11]

Another factor affecting employment is fertility. Average annual population growth rates are about 2.7, 3.9, and 3.28 percent for the periods 1966–76, 1976–86, and 1986–91 respectively.[12] The rate appears to have declined to about 2.2 percent in recent years. These changes reflect a change in government policy. After the revolution, abortion became illegal and other measures of population control were considered against the principles of an Islamic society.[13] The revolution vowed to protect the mostazafeen (oppressed). Promises of free urban housing for the mostazafeen were made, and it was declared that families with a larger number of children would have precedent. In mosques and through the media, the clergy urged people to get married and to have children.

The subsequent explosive population growth, however, was alarming. In 1989, just before his death, a fatwa (religious declaration) by Ayatollah Khomeini removed the prohibition on the use of contraceptives and sterilization. Since then the government has aggressively pursued a policy of population planning, accompanied with free distribution of contraceptives, as well as the active use of mosques, the media, and other sources to persuade people to have fewer children. Officially, abortion remains illegal, but legal loopholes and clerical interpretations have made abortion available free of charge in government hospitals and clinics. Legally, abortion can be performed if pregnancy is harmful to a woman's health. In practice, medical attestations are regularly signed.[14]

## Legal and Ideological Aspects of Female Employment

The Constitution of the Islamic Republic states that no one can be forced into a specific occupation, or exploited in the job market. Irrespective of race, language, and sex, people are entitled to equal access to employment, provided that such access is not contrary to Islamic principles, public welfare, and the rights of others.[15] While the Constitution is not explicitly gender biased, the reference to Islamic principles can be used as an obstacle to equal access to employment. According to the clergy, Islamic ideology emphasizes the complementary aspects of the biological differences between men and women, and considers family — not individual — as the basic social unit.[16] Thus it can be argued that the proper place for women is at home, that men as heads of households should be given priority to women in employment, and that women are biologically unfit for certain occupations. One of the main ideological objectives of the revolution was to force women to wear the veil. Veiling and segregation had important implications for employment. The government undertook a campaign to expel from work women considered "morally decadent," to *paksazy* (purify) the workplace. It also used incentives to persuade women to retire early. A 1979 law allowed workers to retire after 15 instead of 25 years of service. Although the law included male as well as female workers, more women than men retired.[17]

In recent years, however, the work environment has become more friendly to women.[18] In contrast to the earlier period when daycare centers in some government institutions were closed down,[19] many workplaces now have daycare facilities for their employees. A law passed in 1990 allows women to retire after 20, instead of 25, years in government service. While this law shows a pattern similar to earlier policies of keeping women at home, it was in response to demands of women in the public sector, and a recognition of the double burden of women. Furthermore, the law explicitly states that retirement should be voluntary and noncoercive.[20]

According to both pre- and postrevolutionary laws, a woman requires her husband's permission to work outside the home. Today women in growing numbers are challenging this requirement, and other employment restrictions. In an interview with the women's magazine *Zan-e Rooz,* Ostad Amid-e Zanjani, an elected representative of the *majles,* in defense of the law, argued that husbands are legally bound to provide *nafaqeh,* upkeep, for their wives. Therefore, women should need their husbands' permission to work outside the home.[21] The issue, however, is controversial. For example, according to Ayatollah Borujerdi, a man cannot prevent his wife from pursuing work outside the home and the law requiring the husband's permission is an incorrect interpretation of Islamic jurisprudence.[22] Furthermore, these and other legal and ideological issues are being challenged and debated by women's groups, and by women parliamentary representatives.

## Education

Primary and secondary education have expanded under the Islamic regime. The percentage of female students in the population of 10 years and older rose from 14.85 percent in 1976, to 16.58 and 22 percent for 1986 and 1991 respectively. This increase in part explains the decline in labor participation, especially that of teenage girls, as they go to school instead of work. The increase in the number of women students is more pronounced in the rural areas: 6.5, 11.8, and 17.6 percent for 1976, 1986, and 1991 respectively. However, the combined total percentage shares of female students and active female labor for 1976 (27.8 percent) — is larger than that of 1986 (24.7 percent), indicating that other factors also account for the decline in labor participation. However, this figure (30.7 percent) for 1991 is higher than the 1976 figure, suggesting that education is an important explanatory factor for the relatively lower labor participation rates for 1991 (Table 2).

In higher education there remains a gender-based discriminatory policy based on an ideological perception of the proper occupations for women. This position, however, has been modified in recent years. In general, women are considered suitable for the professions of teaching and health related services. Fields such as engineering are considered to be against the nature of women. In spite of a significant growth in secondary education, the level of tertiary female education remained constant in 1986. Because of the ideology of segregation, coeducational technical schools became single sex, denying women access to technical education. Women's technical schools specialized in hygiene, first aid, sewing, cooking, and knitting. In 1984–85, 54 percent of the fields of higher education were not available to women, mostly in the technical and scientific areas. In other areas women faced maximum quotas ranging from 20 to 50 percent. Marginal modifications were introduced in 1989, increasing the areas open to women by about 10 percent.[23] Subsequent changes in 1994 allowed women to participate in such fields as engineering and law that had been closed to them, and removed the gender-based quota system.

According to a 1985 law, women are also discriminated against for graduate studies abroad. They have to be married in order to qualify to go abroad for graduate studies.[24]

## Female Employment: A Sectoral and Occupational Examination

As indicated in Table 3, women's economic activities are heavily concentrated in agriculture, manufacturing, and public and private services for both 1976 and 1986. Since rural women were not an ideological target of the Islamic regime, and the data does not suggest that ideological changes were a factor, I will concentrate primarily on the manufacturing and service sectors.

### Manufacturing

By 1986 the absolute number of women in manufacturing had declined to one third of its 1976 level. This occurred while men's employment increased. While the decline occurred in all categories, a substantial part was in unpaid labor (Table 5).[25] In 1976, the absolute number of unpaid women workers was six and a half times that of 1986. The share of these workers in total manufacturing declined from 21.35 percent in 1976 to 3.7 percent in 1986. Note that unpaid male labor also declined. This decline can be explained by economic stagnation and the decline of the activities of small family workshops. Rural to urban migration was also a factor as many small carpet and other workshops were rural based.

The textiles industry was the largest employer of both paid and unpaid women workers. The number of women employed in this industry declined by 419,000 in 1986, accounting for 97.4 percent of the total decline in manufacturing. For the same period, male employment in the industry declined by only 16,000.[26]

Female wage labor in manufacturing also declined to one third of its 1976 level, and its share in total active labor in manufacturing dropped from 10.5 to 3.9 percent. For the same period, however, male wage labor rose and its share in total active labor increased from 43 to 52.2 percent.

Between 1976 and 1986, no significant changes in technology and use of machinery were introduced in the textiles industry, so the decline was not due to job obsolescence resulting from technological change.[27] It seems that the government, through a combination of institutional reorganization, harassment of women workers, early retirement, and other monetary incentives, contributed to the decline. The reorganization of factories into cooperatives also resulted in job loss for women. During the early postrevolutionary period, many large textile factories came under public control. In addition to the early retirement incentives, according to another law passed during the

TABLE 3. Distribution of employed women by economic sector (age 10 or older, 1000s)

|  | 1976 | | 1986 | |
|---|---|---|---|---|
|  | Total | % | Total | % |
| Total | 1212 | 100.0 | 975.3 | 100.0 |
| Agriculture and | 227.9 | 18.8 | 259.0 | 26.6 |
| industry | 639.1 | 52.7 | 210.8 | 21.6 |
| Public, social, and | 286.6 | 23.6 | 414.2 | 42.5 |
| private services |  |  |  |  |
| All other categories* | 58.4 | 4.8 | 91.3 | 9.4 |

Source: Mitra Baqerian, *Barressye vigegyhaye eshteqali dar Iran (1355–65)* (An examination of the specific characteristics of female employment in Iran: 1976–1986) (Tehran: Plan and Budget Organization, 1990), 87.
* In each economic sector included in this category, women's participation is less than 2 percent of the total. However, for 1986 the category "activity not classified" accounts for 4.6 percent of the total.

TABLE 4. Active population, agriculture, hunting, fishing, and forestry (%)

|  | 1956 | 1966 | 1976 | 1986 |
|---|---|---|---|---|
| *All categories* |  |  |  |  |
| Total | 100 | 100 | 100 | 100 |
| Males | 95.7 | 93.6 | 77.2 | 91.8 |
| Females | 4.3 | 6.4 | 22.8 | 8.2 |
| *Employers and own account workers* |  |  |  |  |
| Total | 54.9 | 58.1 | 48.2 | 75.6 |
| Males | 54.1 | 56.8 | 47.6 | 73.3 |
| Females | 0.8 | 1.3 | 0.5 | 2.3 |
| *Employees* |  |  |  |  |
| Total | 28.7 | 25.2 | 18.3 | 1.0 |
| Males | 27.7 | 23.1 | 16.2 | 9.4 |
| Females | 1.0 | 2.1 | 2.1 | 0.9 |
| *Unpaid family workers* |  |  |  |  |
| Total | 16.1 | 16.3 | 16.2 | 12.2 |
| Males | 13.6 | 13.4 | 12.5 | 7.3 |
| Females | 2.5 | 3.0 | 3.7 | 4.8 |
| *Not classified by status* |  |  |  |  |
| Males | 0.3 | 0.2 | 0.8 | 1.8 |
| Females | 0.0 | 0.0 | 16.5 | 0.1 |

Source: International Labor Organization *Yearbook of Labor Statistics* (1967): 128; (1971): 106; (1982): 106; (1992): 106.

TABLE 5. Economically active population in manufacturing

|  | 1976 | | 1986 | |
|---|---|---|---|---|
|  | Total (1000s) | % | Total (1000s) | % |
| *All categories* | | | | |
| Total | 1682.2 | 100.0 | 1460.1 | 100.0 |
| Males | 1035.8 | 61.6 | 1243.8 | 85.2 |
| Females | 646.4 | 38.4 | 216.3 | 14.8 |
| *Employers and own account workers* | | | | |
| Total | 357.6 | 21.3 | 505.4 | 34.6 |
| Males | 255.3 | 15.2 | 414.6 | 28.4 |
| Females | 102.3 | 6.1 | 90.8 | 6.2 |
| *Employees* | | | | |
| Total | 900.9 | 53.5 | 818.1 | 56.0 |
| Males | 724.5 | 43.1 | 761.7 | 52.2 |
| Females | 176.3 | 10.5 | 56.4 | 3.9 |
| *Unpaid family workers* | | | | |
| Total | 411.2 | 24.4 | 73.7 | 5.0 |
| Males | 52.2 | 3.1 | 18.4 | 1.3 |
| Females | 359.1 | 21.3 | 55.2 | 3.8 |
| *Not classified by status* | | | | |
| Total | 12.5 | 0.7 | 63.0 | 4.3 |
| Males | 3.7 | 0.2 | 49.1 | 3.4 |
| Females | 8.7 | 0.5 | 13.8 | 0.9 |

Source: International Labor Organization *Yearbook of Labor Statistics* (1967): 128; (1971): 106; (1982): 106; (1992): 106.

early postrevolutionary years, the husbands of women who resigned from their jobs became eligible for a lifetime salary increase of Rls. 10,000, roughly $100 at the time of the passage of the law, persuading many poor working women to resign from their factory jobs.[28] Thus government ideology and policy were important contributors to the decline of female wage labor in the industry.

*Services*

In contrast to agriculture and manufacturing, the absolute number of active women in the service sector increased by about 45 percent in 1986 as compared to 1976, mainly in the public sector. In 1986, 42 percent of employed

TABLE 6. Active population, community, social, and personal services

| | 1976 | | 1986 | |
|---|---|---|---|---|
| | Total (1000s) | % | Total (1000s) | % |
| Total | 1523.7 | 100 | 3050.9 | 100 |
| Males | 1236.1 | 81.1 | 2636.5 | 86.4 |
| Females | 287.6 | 18.9 | 414.4 | 13.6 |

Source: International Labor Organization *Yearbook of Labor Statistics* (1967): 128; (1971): 106; (1982): 106; (1992): 106.

women worked for the public sector, in contrast to 30 percent for 1976. Nevertheless, the share of women in total active labor in this category declined from about 18.9 percent in 1976 to 13.6 percent in 1986 (Table 6), as the growth in male employment was faster.[29] The increase in employment of women by the public sector was largely in teaching, and to a lesser extent in health services. About 83.2 percent of the women employed by the public sector were teachers, and 8.9 percent were in the health services. The following factors contributed to an increased demand for women teachers: the ideology of segregation; the young composition of the population; and the state's commitment to expand elementary and secondary education. Supply factors were also important. At the time of the revolution about one third of the university students were women. These women graduated and joined the labor force after the revolution.

The 1986 data indicate a slight increase in the very small share of women in the category of administrator, manager and executive: from 1356 (1976) to 1534.[30] For 1986, nearly all women in this category were school principals, and the number of women in any other managerial sector was near zero. In 1976, there were a variety in the positions held by women, including prestigious and high ranking positions in the government, such as two women cabinet ministers. It should also be noted that on the average women employed by the public sector are more educated than men. Thus their underrepresentation in managerial share is not due to the differences in human capital, but to discrimination based on ideology and culture. Anecdotal information indicates that the situation is changing and women are now occupying comparatively diverse positions in the public sector. For example, in recent years the earlier ruling of the Islamic regime barring women from being judges has been reversed, and there are now women judges. Furthermore, women can be seen in managerial and administrative positions such as mayors, or mid-level managerial positions in the government.[31]

## Conclusions

The data suggest that state ideology is an important factor affecting employment of women. In general the impact of Islamic ideology on employment has been negative. The decline in both wage and non-wage labor in agriculture was prompted by economic, demographic, education, and cultural factors in 1986. The decline in unpaid family labor in manufacturing was primarily due to economic factors. Altogether about 860,000 jobs lost in agriculture and manufacturing can be attributed primarily to economic, education, and cultural factors. This accounts for about 43.3 percent of the total active female labor force for 1976, or 65.2 percent that of 1986 (Tables 3, 4). Thus the impact of stagnation and other nonideological factors was substantial.

An assessment of the impact of ideological changes on female labor participation is more complex. Ideological factors seem to have been the primary contributors to the decline in wage labor in manufacturing, accounting for about 6 percent of the total active women for 1976, or 9.1 percent that of 1986 (Table 4). An assessment of the extent of ideological impact in other sectors is more difficult. For example, in the public sector many women were forced to resign, or persuaded to retire, but no quantitative estimates are available. Furthermore, ideological factors contributed to a substantial increase in fertility and a decline in the age of first marriage for 1986. The data, however, are not sufficiently refined to measure the impact of these factors on labor participation rates. In addition, discriminatory policies were used in higher education, but the impact cannot be quantified.

For 1986, there was an increase in the number of active women in the service category, largely in teaching and health related services. It is difficult to attribute this gain to the positive impact of the revolution and its ideology of segregation. While the number of students of ten years and older increased after the revolution, the trend in the earlier years was also that of increase in the number of students. Furthermore, the Iranian population is young, and the demand for schooling is strong. As teaching and health services have historically been female occupations, it is likely that in the absence of the ideological changes, there would have still been a substantial increase in the number of women teachers and health care providers. An appropriate assessment of a strict policy of segregation would be to argue that so many other occupations were closed to the professionally trained and educated women. Thus the net impact was probably negative.

The evidence also supports the hypothesis that ideological factors were the primary contributors to the increase in the intensity of occupational segregation. This was specially pronounced in the female quota in higher education, attempts to remove women from the textile factories, and the public sector employment policies.

Changes in the earlier policies of the Islamic Republic during the 1990s led to general improvement in the participation rates. Anecdotal information suggests that more changes are also occurring. This is an area in which more data and research is needed. Considering the highly dynamic and rapidly changing conditions in Iran, this is also an important area of research for the future.

# Notes

## Introduction

1. See in particular Hisham Sharabi, *Neopatriarchy: A Theory of Distorted Change in Arab Society* and Halim Barakat, *The Arab World: Society, Culture, and State.*

2. Islamic custom usually entitles daughters to half the share of sons. Many Middle Eastern and North African states have overridden this custom with laws requiring equal distribution to both. However, the laws are not always applied.

3. Suad Joseph, "Connectivity and Patriarchy Among Urban Working Class Arab Families in Lebanon."

4. Carol Pateman, *The Sexual Contract.*

5. Judith E. Tucker, *Women in Nineteenth-Century Egypt.*

6. Julia A. Clancy-Smith, *Rebel and Saint: Muslim Notables, Populist Protest, Colonial Encounters (Algeria and Tunisia, 1800–1904).*

7. Sharabi, *Neopatriarchy.*

8. Edward Said, *Orientalism.*

9. Rola Sharara, "Women and Politics in Lebanon."

## Women's Activism in the Middle East: A Historical Perspective

1. Margot Badran, "Competing Agenda: Feminists, Islam and the State in Nineteenth- and Twentieth-Century Egypt," 205.

2. Suad Joseph, "Elite Strategies for State-Building: Women, Family, Religion and the State in Iraq and Lebanon."

3. See for instance Nawal El-Saadawi, *The Hidden Face of Eve: Women in the Arab World* and Nawal El-Saadawi, "Women and Islam."

4. See for instance Fatima Mernissi, *Beyond the Veil: Male-Female Dynamics in Modern Muslim Society* and Mernissi, "Virginity and Patriarchy."

5. Valerie J. Hoffman, "An Islamic Activist: Zaynab al-Ghazali."

## Women and Politics in the Middle East

1. Most of the examples given in the text refer to the following articles, published in *Middle East Report* 138, 16, no. 1 (1986): Judith Tucker, "Insurrectionary

Women: Women and State in 19th Century Egypt"; Mary Elaine Hegland, "Political Roles of Iranian Village Women"; Julie Peteet, "No Going Back: Women and the Palestinian Movement" (see also this volume); and Sondra Hale, "The Wing of the Patriarch: Sudanese Women and Revolutionary Parties."

2. Mervat Hatem, "Egyptian Middle Class Women and Views of the Sexual Division of Labor in the Nationalist Personalized Patriarchal System"; Rola Sharara, "Women and Politics in Lebanon."

3. Raymonda Tawil, *My Home, My Prison.*

4. Deniz Kandiyoti, "From Empire to Nation State: Transformations of the Woman Question in Turkey"; Serin Tekeli, "Women in Turkish Politics"; Suad Joseph, "The Mobilization of Iraqi Women into the Wage Labor Force."

5. Michelle Rosaldo and Louise Lamphere, eds., *Women, Culture, and Society.*

6. Suad Joseph, "Working-Class Women's Networks in a Sectarian State: A Political Paradox," 1.

7. Ibid., 1–22.

8. Suad Joseph, "The Family as Security and Bondage: A Political Strategy of the Lebanese Urban Working Class."

9. Cynthia Nelson and Virginia Olesen, "Veil of Illusion: A Critique of the Concept of Equality in Western Thought."

10. Suad Joseph, "The Mobilization of Iraqi Women into the Wage Labor Force."

11. Kandiyoti, "From Empire to Nation State," argues that feminism was built into the nationalist agenda of the Turkish state from the nineteenth century. Tekeli argues, however, that this was solely in the interests of nation-building. Mounira Charrad, "The Politics of Family Law: The Tunisian Example," makes a similar point for the place of women in constructing the Tunisian state. Algerian women have on the whole been left out of the nationalist agenda in the interests of retaining the support of the Islamic clergy. See Marnia Lazreg, "You Don't Have to Work, Sisters! This Is Socialism."

12. Suad Joseph, "The Mobilization of Iraqi Women into the Wage Labor Force."

13. For example, the studies cited in note 1.

14. See Afaf Lufti al-Sayyid Marsot, "Revolutionary Gentlewomen in Egypt"; Eliz Sanasarian, *The Women's Rights Movement in Iran: Mutiny, Appeasement, and Repression from 1900 to Khomeini*; and Leila Ahmed, "Mysticism, Female Autonomy, and Feminism in Islam."

15. Also noted in Vanessa Maher, "Kin, Clients, and Accomplices: Relationships Among Women in Morocco"; and Barbara Aswad, "Women, Class and Power: Examples from the Hatay, Turkey."

16. Also noted in Barbara Aswad "Visiting Patterns Among Women of the Elite in a Small Turkish City"; Louise Sweet, "The Women of 'Ain ad Dayr"; Soraya Altorki, "Religion and Social Organization of Elite Families in Urban Saudi Arabia"; and Peter A. Lienhardt, "Some Aspects of the Trucial States."

## Women and Work in the Arab World

1. M. Chamie, "Labour Force Participation of Lebanese Women," 99.

2. Quoted in Nadia Hijab, *Womanpower: The Arab Debate on Women at Work,* 73.

3. The ILO redefined the economically active population to include "all persons of either sex who provide labour for the production of economic goods and services. All work for pay or in anticipation of profits included. In addition, the standard specifies that the production of economic goods and services includes all production and processing of primary products, whether for the market, for barter, or for home consumption." See United Nations, *Women: Challenges to the Year 2000,* 39.

4. United Nations Development Programme, *Human Development Report 1995,* 6.

5. In this essay, the Arab world comprises the members of the League of Arab States: Algeria, Bahrain, Djibouti, Egypt, Iraq, Jordan, Kuwait, Lebanon, Libya, Mauritania, Morocco, Oman, Palestine, Qatar, Saudi Arabia, Somalia, Sudan, Syria, Tunisia, United Arab Emirates, and Yemen.

6. UNDP, *Human Development Report 1998,* 164–65.

7. Ibid.

8. In 1990 the *Human Development Report* introduced a new way to measure the progress of nations, the Human Development Index, which is based on longevity, literacy and educational attainment, and purchasing power. This showed that countries with low gross national product could still have achieved greater benefits in terms of their people's well-being. Each year, the *Report* ranks all countries on the basis of their HDIs, and groups countries into low, medium and high human development categories. The 1998 *Report* had no figures for Djibouti and included neither Somalia nor Palestine in its tables.

9. 21.4 percent in the Arab region, as compared to 36.2 percent in Africa, 24.8 percent in South Asia, 37.7 percent in East Asia, 27.7 percent in Latin America and the Caribbean, and 38 percent in industrialized countries; *Human Development Report 1998,* 206.

10. United Nations, *Report of the Secretary General: Recommendations of Regional Intergovernmental Preparatory Meetings,* 40. ESCWA groups the Arab states of Western Asia as well as Egypt.

11. Ibid., 46.

12. Family law covers areas like marriage, divorce, custody, and so on, and in all Arab countries is derived from Islamic law. Tunisia is the only state to have achieved complete equality between men and women in this area, and maintains it did so within an Islamic framework.

13. UNDP *Human Development Report 1998,* 206.

14. Camillia Fawzi El-Solh and Nabiha Masmoudi Chaalala, "Women's Role in Arab Food Security: A Gender Analysis of Selected Agricultural Projects."

15. UAE 25.1 percent, Kuwait 36.8 percent, Syria 37 percent, Algeria 27.6 percent, Tunisia 35.6 percent, Jordan 28.7 percent, Egypt 29.5 percent, Morocco 31.3 percent, Sudan 28.8 percent. UNDP *Human Development Report 1999.*

The Politics of Gender and the Conundrums of Citizenship

1. On this last point see Marnia Lazreg, *The Eloquence of Silence: Algerian Women in Question*; Leila Ahmed, *Women and Gender in Islam: Historical Roots of a Modern Debate*.

2. Deniz Kandiyoti, *Women, Islam, and the State*; Kandiyoti, "Women, Islam, and the State."

3. See, for instance, Carol Pateman, *The Sexual Contract*. Suad Joseph endorses this critique and extends it to argue that the model of selfhood implicit in liberal political theory does not apply cross-culturally: Joseph, "Gender and Citizenship in Middle Eastern States."

4. For a comprehensive and illuminating discussion of different positions in this debate see Maxine Molyneux, "Feminism, Citizenship, and Democracy: Reflections on Contemporary Debates." Given the tendency to conflate the term citizenship with liberal individualist versions of it, Molyneux's article serves as a useful reminder of the highly contested nature of the concept within Western political theory itself.

5. Aziz al-Azmeh, *Islams and Modernities,* 1.

6. See Deniz Kandiyoti, "Contemporary Feminist Scholarship and Middle East Studies."

7. For a broader discussion of the place of women in processes of national reproduction, see Nira Yuval-Davis and Floya Anthias, eds., *Women, Nation, State.*

8. For an excellent account of these tensions in Indian nationalism see Amrita Chhachhi, "Forced Identities: The State, Communalism, Fundamentalism, and Women in India."

9. Deniz Kandiyoti, "Identity and Its Discontents: Women and the Nation."

10. For contrasting perspectives on this issue see Bartrand Badie, *Les deux états: Pouvoir et société en occident et en terre d'Islam*; Sami Zubaida, "Nations: Old and New," and Zubaida, *Islam, the People, and the State.*

11. Yahya Sadowski, "The New Orientalism and the Democracy Debate."

12. This consideration lies at the heart of critiques of modernity in both postcolonial scholarship and in anti-development discourse. As an example of the latter see Stephen Marglin and Frederique Marglin, eds., *Dominating Knowledge: Development, Culture, and Resistance.*

13. For a fuller discussion of this issue see Deniz Kandiyoti, "Beyond Beijing: Obstacles and Prospects for the Middle East."

14. Pertinent illustrations of these contradictory pressures in the cases of Egypt and Bangladesh may be found in Mervat Hatem, "Economic and Political Liberalization in Egypt and the Demise of State Feminism"; Naila Kabeer, "The Quest for National Identity." For a comprehensive treatment of the various reservations put forward to the Convention on the Elimination of All Forms of Discrimination Against Women (CEDAW) in Muslim countries, see Ann Elizabeth Mayer, "Rhetorical Strategies and Official Politics on Women's Rights: The Merits and Drawbacks of the New World Hypocrisy."

15. This is poignantly illustrated in the case of Algeria, where women may be killed for being unveiled or for being veiled. See Susan Slyomovics, "Hassiba Ben Bouali: If You Could See Our Algeria."

Similar observations may be made in relation to the activities of the Taleban militia in Afghanistan, who imposed a curfew on women, severely punishing any transgressors.

16. An extensive discussion of these questions may be found in Michael Hudson, "Obstacles to Democratization in the Middle East"; Gudrun Kramer, "Islamist Notions of Democracy"; John Waterbury, "Democracy Without Democrats? The Potential for Political Liberalization in the Middle East."

17. Timothy Mitchell, *Colonising Egypt*; Partha Chatterjee, *The Nation and Its Fragments.*

18. See Valentine Moghadam, "Development and Women's Emancipation: Is There a Connection?" for the positive view; Mervat Hatem, "Toward a Critique of Modernization: Narrative in Middle East Women's Studies," for the less positive.

19. Shirin Rai, "Women and the State in the Third World."

20. Ibid., 35.

21. See Joseph, "Gender and Citizenship in Middle Eastern States."

22. Hisham Sharabi, *Neopatriarchy: A Theory of Distorted Change in Arab Society.*

23. Partha Chatterjee, "Two Poets and Death: On Civil and Political Society in the Non-Christian World."

24. Women have achieved gains in personal status (Homa Hoodfar, "Women and Personal Status Laws in Iran: An Interview with Mehranguiz Kar"), but suffered reverses in the 1997 election when the Council of Guardians rejected all nine women candidates (*Observer,* 18 May 1997, p. 16). It is easy to see that women can achieve modest gains. What is important, however, is that they have kept the will to push for their agenda against phenomenal odds.

## Sex and Gender in the Maghrib

1. The theoretical framework in this chapter and the references in all but the last section remain the same as in my 1990 *Middle East Report* article. New information on the most important developments in legislation in the 1980s and 1990s has been included in the last section.

2. The framework on the relationship between state formation and kin-based tribal solidarities as shaping family law is presented in greater detail in Mounira M. Charrad, *Origins of Women's Rights: State and Tribe in Tunisia, Algeria, and Morocco.*

3. Charles Tilly, ed., *The Formation of National States in Western Europe*; Theda Skocpol, *States and Social Revolutions: A Comparative Analysis of France, Russia, and China*; and Peter Evans, Dietrich Rueschemeyer, and Theda Skocpol, eds., *Bringing the State Back In.*

4. As in the title of Clifford Geertz, ed., *Old Societies and New States: The Quest for Modernity in Asia and Africa.*

5. See several of the articles in Ghassan Salame, ed., *The Foundations of the Arab State.*

6. Germaine Tillion, *The Republic of Cousins: Women's Oppression in Mediterranean Society.*

7. For example, Jean Cuisenier, *Economie et parenté,* and Hildred Geertz, "The Meaning of Family Ties."

8. The analysis here focuses on the doctrine of the law. What matters here is how the legal doctrine defines gender and kinship relations for the collectivity as a whole. In everyday life, legal regulations are usually mitigated by individual practices.

9. For a detailed analysis of legal reforms in Tunisia and Morocco, see Maurice Borrmans, *Statut personnel et famille au Maghreb de 1940 à nos jours*; and on Algeria, Maurice Borrmans, "Le nouveau code algerien de la famille dans l'ensemble des codes musulmans de statut personnel, principalement dans les pays arabes."

10. More drastic reforms of inheritance laws were contemplated at various times, but rejected for fear of widespread opposition.

11. Lisa Anderson, *The State and Social Transformation in Tunisia and Libya, 1830–1980*; Elbaki Hermassi, *Leadership and National Development in North Africa*; Allan Christelow, *Muslim Law Courts and the French Colonial State in Algeria*; Mounira M. Charrad, "Review of Christelow"; Ernest Gellner and Charles Micaud, eds., *Arabs and Berbers: From Tribe to Nation in North Africa.*

12. République Tunisienne, *Code du statut personnel.* On divorce law and its application, see Mounira M. Charrad, "Repudiation Versus Divorce: Responses to State Policy in Tunisia." The 1993 reforms in Tunisia also changed some of the dispositions on citizenship, an issue related to personal status but separate from it. The changes made it easier for the child of a Tunisian mother and a foreign father to obtain Tunisian citizenship: Mounira M. Charrad, "Becoming a Citizen: Lineage Versus Individual in Tunisia and Morocco."

13. Mohamed Chafi, *Code du statut personnel annoté: textes législatifs, doctrine et jurisprudence.*

14. On unregistered marriages in the 1980s in Morocco, see Ziba Mir-Hosseini, *Marriage on Trial: A Study of Islamic Family Law — Iran and Morocco Compared.*

15. On women's agency in Tunisia, Algeria, and Morocco, see Rahma Bourqia, Mounira M. Charrad, and Nancy Gallagher, eds., *Femmes: culture et société au Maghreb,* vol. 2, *Femmes: pouvoir politique et développement*; M. M. Charrad, "Policy Shifts: State, Islam, and Gender in Tunisia, 1930s–1990s"; and "Cultural Diversity Within Islam: Veils and Laws in Tunisia"; Marnia Lazreg, *The Eloquence of Silence: Algerian Women in Question,* ch. 10; Boutheina Cheriet, "Islamism and Feminism: Algeria's 'Rites of Passage' to Democracy"; Cherifa Bouatta, "Feminine Militancy: Moudjahidates During and After the Algerian War"; and Laurie A. Brand, *Women, the State, and Political Liberalization: Middle Eastern and North African Experience.*

## Sex, Lies, and Television: Algerian and Moroccan Caricatures of the Gulf War

1. On the background and evolution of the yellow ribbon as a symbol of families separated by wars, see Gerald E. Parsons, "How the Yellow Ribbon Became a National Folk Symbol."

2. See Reinhold Aman, "Hussein and the War"; Alan Nadel, "A Whole New (Disney) World Order: *Aladdin,* Atomic Power, and the Muslim Middle East"; Robert Stam, "Mobilizing Fictions: The Gulf War, the Media, and the Recruitment of the Spectator"; and Anne Norton, "Gender, Sexuality, and the Iraq of Our Imagination."

3. For an excellent historical overview of Egypt in cartoons, see the collection of essays from the CEDEJ conference held in Cairo: Jean-Claude Vatin, ed., *Images d'Egypte: de la fresque à la bande dessinée.*

4. See Lisa Wedeen for an excellent contextualization of the work of Syrian cartoonist, Ali Farzat, in her *Ambiguities of Domination: Politics, Rhetoric and Symbols in Contemporary Syria* 107–112. She notes: "No Syrian paper has ever printed even a favorable cartoon of [President Hafiz al-] Asad."

5. The relationship between the censored television broadcasts and a free, or freer, space for cartoons during the Gulf War has been analyzed in Susan Slyomovics, "Algeria Caricatures the Gulf War," and Slyomovics, "Cartoon Commentary: Algerian and Moroccan Caricatures from the Gulf War." This essay is a revised and expanded version of these two earlier articles.

6. Allen Douglas and Fedwa Malti-Douglas, *Arab Comic Strips: Politics of an Emerging Mass Culture,* 174–97.

7. Some examples are characters' names in Malek Zirout's oeuvre: the evil judge Bou F'tou, French for *bouffe-tout* or "eats all," and the governor Ben Efis, French *bénéfice* or "profit." See Malek Zirout, *La route de sel.*

8. Slyomovics, "Cartoon Commentary," 94–95.

9. Douglas and Malti-Douglas, *Arab Comic Strips,* 188.

10. It is noteworthy that these cartoons were appreciated, circulated, and reprinted in the Arab world along with other Algerian publications. Though some have reappeared in specialized American journals and publications such as *Middle East Report,* American newspaper editors rejected them on the grounds that they were too strongly "anti-Arab." Nadjib Berber, interview with author.

11. See David Pollock, "Reporting the Middle East: An Overview."

12. Samuel Weber, "The Media and the War."

13. Cynthia Enloe, *The Morning After: Sexual Politics at the End of the Cold War* 166.

14. Nadjib Berber, Cartoon, *Révolution africain* 1406 (7–13 February 1991).

15. See Fatima Mernissi's discussion on American women soldiers in *Islam and Democracy: Fear of the Modern World,* especially 114–15.

## Women on Women: Television Feminism and Women's Lives

1. This and the names of other village women are pseudonyms.

2. All quotations from an interview on June 26, 1993. For more on Egyptian

feminist views of marriage, see my "The Marriage of Feminism and Islamism in Egypt: Selective Repudiation as a Dynamic of Postcolonial Cultural Politics."

3. See Lila Abu-Lughod, "The Objects of Soap Opera: Egyptian Television and the Cultural Politics of Modernity," for further discussion of the gaps between producers and consumers of television serials.

4. Martina Rieker, "The Sa'id and the City: The Politics of Space in the Making of Modern Egypt."

5. For a discussion of literacy classes, see Lila Abu-Lughod, "Television and the Virtues of Education."

6. Marnia Lazreg, "Feminism and Difference: The Perils of Writing as a Woman on Women in Algeria"; Chandra Talpade Mohanty, "Under Western Eyes: Feminist Scholarship and Colonial Discourses."

7. Margot Badran's comprehensive historical study of the Egyptian feminist movement, *Feminists, Islam, and Nation: Gender in the Making of Modern Egypt*, gives numerous examples of this patronizing attitude toward the lower classes and rural women. Omnia Shakry, "Schooled Mothers and Structured Play: Child-Rearing in Turn of the Century Egypt," critically analyzes the sources and implications of such attitudes.

8. For more on these feminist projects in Egypt, see Abu-Lughod, ed. *Remaking Women*; Leila Ahmed, *Women and Gender in Islam*; Badran, *Feminists, Islam, and Nation*; Beth Baron, *The Women's Awakening in Egypt: Culture, Society, and the Press*; Marilyn Booth, "May Her Likes Be Multiplied: 'Famous Women' Biography and Gendered Prescription in Egypt, 1892–1935"; Mervat Hatem, "Economic and Political Liberalization in Egypt and the Demise of State Feminism"; and Cynthia Nelson, *Doria Shafik, Egyptian Feminist: A Woman Apart.*

## Sudanese Women and the Islamist State

1. For more about zar, see Sondra Hale, "The Wing of the Patriarch: Sudanese Women and Revolutionary Parties." cf. 70, 207, 210.

2. Sondra Hale, *Gender Politics in Sudan: Islamism, Socialism, and the State.*

## For the Common Good: Gender and Social Citizenship in Palestine

1. Over a year after the Legislative Council was inaugurated, no major piece of legislation had been passed by the Council and ratified by the President, reflecting conflict between the legislative and the executive, as well as the political problem of developing legal frameworks for the transitional phase when the political outcome is undetermined. Only minor pieces of legislation were passed during the five years of the transitional period; the Basic Law was not passed.

2. Islah Jad, "A Feminist Analysis of Tribalism and 'Municipal Elections."

3. For an analysis of the gendering of social assistance programs in Palestine,

see Penny Johnson, *Palestinian Women: A Status Report,* vol. 5., *Social Support: Gender and Social Policies in Palestine.*

4. In examining similar networks of social support in the Lebanese context, Suad Joseph has proposed a construct of "relational rights" gained through investment in relationships and an active process of negotiation and mediation. While, we have questions about the implications of placing these informal systems of claims within a rights discourse, her intervention is helpful in analyzing the Palestinian context.

5. World Bank, *Developing the Occupied Territories: An Investment in Peace,* vol. 2, *The Economy.*

6. A phrase used by economist Diane Elson to characterize assumptions about women's labor.

7. International Labor Organization, *Capacity Building for Social Development: Programme of Action for Transition in the Occupied Palestinian Territories.*

8. Geir Ovenson, *Responding to Change: Trends in Palestinian Household Economy,* 129.

9. World Bank, *Developing the Occupied Territories,* vol. 6, *Human Resources and Social Policy,* 49.

10. Deniz Kandiyoti pointed out this global trend in a discussion during a November 1994 workshop on "Palestinian Women in Society: State of Research and New Directions," held at Birzeit University by the Women's Studies Program.

11. The authorship of this study, written in Arabic, is given only as the "PLO Department of Economics and Planning," but the general editor is known to be the distinguished economist Yusif Sayigh. A more detailed review may be found in our article "Gender and Public Policies."

12. We have benefited from the analysis of "the two-track welfare system" provided by Linda Gordon and Nancy Fraser in their article "Dependency Demystified: Inscriptions of Power in a Keyword of the Welfare State," despite the great difference in context in examining Palestinian policies.

13. Palestinian Central Bureau of Statistics.

14. World Food Programme, "Closure Underlines Structural Dependency of Palestinian Economy," September 9, 1996, 8.

15. For data, see Palestinian Central Bureau of Statistics, *The Demographic Survey in the West Bank and Gaza: Preliminary Report.* For analysis, see Rita Giacaman, *Palestinian Women: A Status Report,* vol. 2, *Population and Fertility: Population Policies, Women's Rights and Sustainable Development.*

## Women and the Palestinian Movement: No Going Back?

1. Lt. Col. W. F. Stirling, "Palestine: 1920–1923" in Walid Khalidi, ed., *From Haven to Conquest: Readings in Zionism and the Palestinian Problem Until 1948.*

2. See Roger Keesing, "Kwaio Women Speak: The Micropolitics of Autobiography in a Soloman Island Society," for a discussion of women as representatives of colonized, or postcolonial cultures.

3. Julie Peteet, "From Refugees to Minority: Palestinians in Post-War Lebanon."

4. For the best analysis of this series of events see Reema Hammami, "Women, the Hijab and the Intifada."

5. Julie Peteet, " 'They Took Our Blood and Milk': Palestinian Women and War."

6. Julie Peteet "Icons and Militants: Mothering in the Danger Zone."

7. Ibid.

## Searching for Strategies: The Palestinian Women's Movement in the New Era

1. Interview with the authors, Ramallah, 1995.

2. Interview with the authors, Ramallah, 1995.

3. Marianne Heiberg et al., *Palestinian Society in Gaza, West Bank and Arab Jerusalem: A Survey of Living Conditions.*

4. Interview with the authors, Ramallah, 1995.

5. For a discussion of political views of Palestinian women activists who oppose this agreement, see Maya Rosenfeld, "Interview with Maha Nassar and Aida Issawi."

6. Interview with the authors, Birzeit, 1996.

7. Interview with the authors, Jerusalem, 1997.

8. "Women Under the Palestinian Authority," interview with Rema Hammami.

## Gender and Citizenship: Considerations on the Turkish Experience

1. Quotations from Filiz Koçali and Serpil Gülgün, "Binenaleyh Tansu Çiller," 55.

2. Ibid., 59–60.

3. For a critical discussion of the difference between citizenship from above and below, see Bryan Turner, "Outline of a Theory of Citizenship."

4. For a feminist critique of the liberal concept of citizenship, see Carol Pateman, *The Sexual Contract*; Kathleen Jones, "Citizenship in a Woman Friendly Polity"; Mary Dietz, "Context Is All: Feminism and Theories of Citizenship."

5. State Planning Organization (SPO), "Turkish Family Structure, 1992," 61.

6. State Institute of Statistics, *1990 General Population Census and Formal Education Series.*

7. SPO, "Turkish Family Structure, 1992," 6–7.

8. Suad Joseph, "Problematizing Gender and Relational Rights: Experiences from Lebanon."

9. Günseli Berik, "Born Factories: Women's Labor in Carpet Workshops in Rural Turkey."

10. Deniz Kandiyoti, "Bargaining with Patriarchy."

11. Yeşim Arat, "Islamic Fundamentalism and Women in Turkey."

12. Sivas bu kez 'turban' yuzunden gerginlik yasiyor (Sivas is tense this time due to turban) *Milliyet* (2 September, 1996) 1, 15.

13. On Egyptian feminism, see Margot Badran, *Feminists, Islam, and Nation: Gender in the Making of Modern Egypt.* On contemporary feminists in Turkey, see Yeşim Arat, "Towards a Democratic Society: Women's Movement in Turkey."

14. See the April, May, June, and July 1995 issues of the feminist monthly *Pazartesi.*

## Women in Saudi Arabia: Between Breadwinner and Domestic Icon?

1. Rida Muhammad Lari, "Women Are Not Allowed to Take Cabs."

2. Author's interview with Council member Abd al-Aziz al-Fayidh, Chicago, 5 December 1998.

3. U.S. Department of State, *Saudi Arabia Human Rights Practices, 1995.*

4. "Ulama Reject Cairo Conference," *al-Nadwa* (1 September 1994), 1, 5.

5. Ibid.

6. "Ibn Baz: 'Women's Work Is Quick Road to Adultery.' "

7. Muhammad bin Abdul-Aziz Al Musnad, comp., *Islamic Fatawa Regarding Women,* 45.

8. Ibid., 338–39.

9. Ibid., 341.

10. Committee for the Defense of Legitimate Rights, *CDLR Monitor,* 107, (8 February, 1996).

11. Anonymous ("a female correspondent"), "Report on 'Security' of Saudi Women," 21.

12. "Chamber of Commerce Urges Dialogue on Saudi Woman's Role," 2. The percentage of employed women is very low when compared to all other Middle Eastern countries outside the Gulf. In Morocco, for example, in 1991 25.5 percent of women were employed; in Tunisia, almost 21 percent, with 28.8 percent in Egypt, and 17.7 percent in Syria. Valentine Moghadam, *Women, Work, and Economic Reform in the Middle East and North Africa,* table 3.4, 5.1, and 6.5. The World Bank gives a higher figure (10 percent in 1995) for women as a percentage of all working-age women in the labor force, but this figure probably includes foreign workers: the World Bank also gives a figure of 8 percent for the percentage of women in the total labor force in 1992. Willem van Eeghen, *Education in MENA: Benefits and Growth Pay-Offs Now and Then,* table 19, "Labor Force in 1995," 53; Table 20, "Women in the labor force," p. 54.

13. "Chamber of Commerce Urges Dialogue on Saudi Woman's Role."

14. Hamad Al Salloom, *Education in Saudi Arabia,* 45–46, 69.

15. Javid Hassan, "Saudi Women Given Green Light in Hotel Industry."

16. Abid Khanzandar, "The Woman and the Computer."

17. Dr. Ali Abd al-Aziz al Abd al-Qadir, "The Saudi Woman, the Finance and Business Sectors, and University Curricula." The lower figure is reported in "Chamber of Commerce Urges Dialogue on Saudi Woman's Role."

18. Thurayya al-ʾUrayyid, "In Her Own Voice Without a Go-Between," Haya ʿAbd al-ʿAziz al-Maniʿ, "Writer Pleads Case for Women's Involvement in Planning."

19. Amir Taheri, "Role of Saudi Women on the Eve of New Century."

20. Charles Hanley, AP Special Correspondent, Riyadh, "Slide over Saudi Economy," Associated Press, April 13, 1997.

21. Ibid.

22. Hammad bin Hamid al-Salimi, "Where Is the Saudi Woman?"

23. Jamal Khashoggi, "Dialogue on Women's Role Urged."

## Women's Organizations in Kuwait

1. See Haya al-Mughni, *Women in Kuwait: The Politics of Gender.*

2. Kuwait Ministry of Planning, *al-Siyassah al-Ijtima'ya fi Araba' Sanawat* (Social Policy in Four Years).

3. For a more in depth analysis, see Mary Ann Tetreault and Haya al-Mughni, "Gender, Citizenship and Nationalism in Kuwait."

4. See Shafiq Ghabra, "Voluntary Associations in Kuwait: The Foundation of a New System?"

5. S. M. al-Sabah, *Kuwait: Anatomy of a Crisis Economy,* 25.

6. Women's Cultural and Social Society, *Women's Cultural and Social Society 1963–1994.*

7. WCSS, *Masirat al-Jam'iya* (March of the Society).

## The Dialectics of Fashion: Gender and Politics in Yemen

1. Helen Lackner, "Women and Development in the Republic of Yemen."

2. Sheila Carapico and Richard Tutwiler, *Yemeni Agriculture and Economic Change.*

3. Cynthia Myntti, *Women and Development in the Yemen Arab Republic.*

4. Maxine Molyneux, "The Law, the State, and Socialist Policies with Regard to Women: The Case of the People's Democratic Republic of Yemen, 1967–1990."

5. Sheila Carapico and Cynthia Myntti, "A Tale of Two Families: Change in North Yemen 1977–1989."

6. Martha Mundy, *Domestic Government: Kinship, Community, and Polity in North Yemen.*

7. Anna Wuerth, "A Sana'a Court: The Family and the Ability to Negotiate."

## Female Employment in Postrevolutionary Iran

1. Other studies on women's employment in postrevolutionary Iran have not focused on ideological issues, and have treated them only marginally. See, for example, Valentine M. Moghadam, "Women's Employment Issues in Contemporary Iran: Problems and Prospects in the 1990s."

2. For an examination of female labor participation in Iran see Mitra Baqerian, "Eshteghal va bikary-e zanan az did-gah tose'e" (Employment and Unemployment

of Women from the Perspective of Development); Valentine Moghadam, "Women, Work, and Ideology in the Islamic Republic"; Fatemeh Etemad Moghadam, "Commoditization of Sexuality and Female Labor Participation in Islam: Implications on Iran 1960–1990."

3. Donald J. Treiman and Heidi Hartmann, eds., *Women, Work, and Wages: Equal Pay for Jobs of Equal Value.* Some writers have argued that during the earlier years of industrialization and growth female employment actually declines, as younger women go to school instead of working in farms or workshops. At later stages, however, it begins to rise again, so that the shape of female employment over time looks like a U. See Nilufer Cagatay and Sule Ozler, "Feminization of the Labor Force: The Effects of Long Term Development and Structural Adjustment."

4. T. Paul Schultz, "Women's Changing Participation in the Labor Force: A World Perspective"; Ester Boserup, *Women's Role in Economic Development,* 53.

5. Treiman and Hartmann, eds., *Women, Work, and Wages.*

6. Francine D. Blau, "Gender."

7. On each survey, the respondents were asked if they worked on a farm during the last ten days, and only one annual visit was undertaken by the survey team. If, for seasonal reasons, women did not perform agricultural tasks, their overall participation was not reported. By contrast, in Turkey, for each survey more than one visit during different seasons was carried out. Thus the latter may reflect a more accurate picture of labor participation.

8. *Salnameh Amary-e: 1370* (Annual Statistics, 1991), 606–7; International Monetary Fund, "Islamic Republic of Iran: 1993."

9. Estimates by Baqerian are about 3.2 percent average annual rate (Mitra Baqerian, "Barressye vigegyhaye eshteqale zanan dar Iran (1355–65). (An examination of the specific characteristics of female employment in Iran: 1976–1986)."

10. *Zan-e Rooz,* 1235 (September 29, 1989); 1236 (October 6, 1991): 14–15, 54–55.

11. This information can be detected from various articles in the daily newspaper *Ettella't,* as well as *Zan-e Rooz,* in which young people and their parents complain about problems of housing, inflation, and heavy initial costs of weddings as obstacles to marriage.

12. *Iran dar Ayineye Amar,* 11; *Salnameh Amary-e 1370* (Annual Statistics, 1991), 34; *Gozydeh-e Mataleb-e Amary,* 41.

13. Homa Hoodfar, "Devices and Desires: Population Policy and Gender Roles in the Islamic Republic.

14. Ibid.

15. Constitution of the Islamic Republic of Iran, amendment 4, principle 43; amendment 2, principles 19, 20, 21, cited in Kar, "Female Labor Laws."

16. Sayyed Hossein Nasr, *Traditional Islam in the Modern World,* 47–53.

17. Mitra Baqerian, "An Examination," 75–76.

18. Personal observations and comparisons between my visits to Iran in 1989, 1992, and 1994.

19. For example the Agricultural Development Bank had a daycare system that was closed after the revolution.

20. *Zan-e Rooz,* Mehr 1369, no. 1286; Esfand 1369 (1990), no. 1304, 6–10.

21. *Zan-e Rooz,* 4 Mah 1372 (1993), no. 1440, 14–15. This point was also reiterated by Ayatollah Yazdi 18 Ordibeheshet 1372, (1993), no. 1407, 4–6.

22. *Zan-e Rooz,* 2 Bahman 1372 (1993), no. 1444, 10–11.

23. Hammed Shahidian, "The Education of Women in the Islamic Republic of Iran."

24. Ibid.

25. The two population censuses (1976 and 1986) used identical definitions and methods of data collection. The changes cannot be attributed to different methods of data collection.

26. Baqerian, "An Examination," 74–76.

27. Ibid.

28. Ibid., 21, 34, 37.

29. Ibid. Note that male employment rose by an average annual rate of 8 percent.

30. For both 1976 and 1986, the total share of women in this category is about 1 percent (International Labor Organization, *Yearbook of Labor Statistics*).

31. Personal observations, trips to Iran in 1995 and 1997.

# Bibliography

Abu-Lughod, Lila. "The Interpretation of Culture(s) After Television." *Representations* 59 (Summer 1997): 109–34.

———. "The Marriage of Feminism and Islamism in Egypt: Selective Repudiation as a Dynamic of Postcolonial Cultural Politics." In *Remaking Women: Feminism and Modernity in the Middle East,* edited by Lila Abu-Lughod, 243–69. Princeton, N.J.: Princeton University Press, 1998.

———. "The Objects of Soap Opera: Egyptian Television and the Cultural Politics of Modernity." In *Worlds Apart: Modernity Through the Prism of the Local,* edited by Daniel Miller, 190–210. London and New York: Routledge, 1995.

———, ed. *Remaking Women: Feminism and Modernity in the Middle East.* Princeton, N.J.: Princeton University Press, 1998.

———. "Television and the Virtues of Education." In *Directions of Change in Rural Egypt,* edited by Nicholas S. Hopkins and Kirsten Westergaard, 147–65. Cairo: American University in Cairo Press, 1998.

Ahmed, Leila. "Mysticism, Female Autonomy, and Feminism in Islam." Paper presented at the Middle East Studies Association annual meeting, San Francisco, 1984.

———. *Women and Gender in Islam: Historical Roots of a Modern Debate.* New Haven, Conn.: Yale University Press, 1992.

al-Azmeh, Aziz. *Islams and Modernities.* London: Verso, 1993.

al-Hibri, Azizah, ed. *Women and Islam.* Oxford: Pergamon Press, 1982.

al-Mani', Haya 'Abd al-'Aziz. "Writer Pleads Case for Women's Involvement in Planning." *Al-Riyadh,* 23 January 1997, 12. (Quoted in Foreign Broadcast Information Service FBIS-NES-97-017.)

al-Mughni, Haya. *Women in Kuwait: The Politics of Gender.* London: Saqi Books, 1993.

al-Musnad, Muhammad bin Abdul-Aziz, comp. *Islamic Fatawa Regarding Women.* Riyadh: Darussalam Publishers, 1996.

al-Qadir, Ali Abd al-Aziz al Abd. "The Saudi Woman, the Finance and Business Sectors, and University Curricula." *Al-Yawm,* 15 May 1999, 7. (Quoted in Foreign Broadcast Information Service 19990518000258.)

al-Sabah, S. M. *Kuwait: Anatomy of a Crisis Economy.* London: Eastlords Publishing Ltd., 1984.

al-Salimi, Hammad bin Hamid. "Where Is the Saudi Woman?" *Al-Jazirah,* 3 May 1999, 13. (Quoted in Foreign Broadcast Information Service FTS 19990509000502.)

Al-Salloom, Hamad. *Education in Saudi Arabia.* Washington, D.C.: Amana, 1995.

Altorki, Soraya. "Religion and Social Organizations of Elite Families in Urban Saudi Arabia." Ph.D. diss., University of California, Berkeley, 1973.

al-'Urayyid, Thurayya. "In Her Own Voice Without a Go-Between." *Al-Jazirah,* 16 November 1996, 5. (Quoted in Foreign Broadcast Information Service FBIS-NES-96-230.)

Aman, Reinhold. "Hussein and the War." *Maledicta Monitor* 2 (1990): 1–2.

Anderson, Lisa. *The State and Social Transformation in Tunisia and Libya, 1830–1980.* Princeton, N.J.: Princeton University Press, 1986.

Arat, Yeşim. "Islamic Fundamentalism and Women in Turkey." *Muslim World* 80, no. 1 (1990): 17–23.

——. "Towards a Democratic Society: Women's Movement in Turkey." *Women's Studies International Forum* 17, no. 2/3 (1994): 241–48.

Aswad, Barbara. "Visiting Patterns Among Women of the Elite in a Small Turkish City." *Anthropological Quarterly* 47 (1974): 9–27.

——. "Women, Class, and Power: Examples from the Hatay, Turkey." In *Women in the Muslim World,* edited by Lois Beck and Nikki Keddie, 473–81. Cambridge, Mass.: Harvard University Press, 1978.

Badie, Bartrand. *Les deux états: Pouvoir et société en occident et en terre d'Islam.* Paris: Fayard, 1986.

Badran, Margot. "Competing Agenda: Feminists, Islam, and the State in Nineteenth- and Twentieth-Century Europe." In *Women, Islam, and the State,* edited by Deniz Kandiyoti, 201–36. Basingstoke: Macmillan; Philadelphia: Temple University Press, 1991.

——. *Feminists, Islam, and Nation: Gender in the Making of Modern Egypt.* Princeton, N.J.: Princeton University Press, 1995.

Baqerian, Mitra. *Barressye vigegyhaye eshteqale zanan dar Iran (1355–65)* (An examination of the specific characteristics of female employment in Iran: 1976–1986). Tehran: Plan and Budget Organization, 1990.

——. "Eshteghal va bikary-e zanan az did-gah tose'e" (Employment and Unemployment of Women from the Perspective of Development). *Zanan* 1, no. 1 (1992): 4–10.

Barakat, Halim Isber. *The Arab-World: Society, Culture, and State.* Berkeley: University of California Press, 1993.

Baron, Beth. *The Women's Awakening in Egypt: Culture, Society, and the Press.* New Haven, Conn.: Yale University Press, 1994.

Berik, Günseli. "Born Factories: Women's Labor in Carpet Workshops in Rural Turkey." In *Working Paper 177.* East Lansing: Michigan State University, 1989.

Blau, Francine D. "Gender." In *The New Palgrave: A Dictionary of Economics,* edited by John Eatwell, Murray Milgate, and Peter Newman, 2:492–98. London: Macmillan, 1987.

Booth, Marilyn. "May Her Likes Be Multiplied: 'Famous Women' Biography and Gendered Prescription in Egypt, 1892–1935." *Signs* 22 (1997): 827–90.

Borrmans, Maurice. "Le nouveau code algerien de la famille dans l'ensemble des codes musulmans de statut personnel, principalement dans les pays arabes." *Actualités et Informations* 38, no. 1 (1986): 133–39.

———. *Statut personnel et famille au Maghreb de 1940 à nos jours.* Paris and the Hague: Mouton, 1977.

Boserup, Ester. *Women's Role in Economic Development.* London: Allen and Unwin, 1970.

Bouatta, Cherifa. "Feminine Militancy: Moudjahidates During and After the Algerian War." In *Gender and National Identity: Women and Politics in Muslim Societies,* edited by Valentine M. Moghadam, 18–39. London: Zed Books, 1994.

Bourqia, Rahma, Mounira M. Charrad, and Nancy Gallagher, eds. *Femmes, culture et société au Maghreb.* Vol. 2, *Femmes, pouvoir politique et développement.* Casablanca: Afrique Orient, 1996.

Brand, Laurie A. *Women, the State, and Political Liberalization: Middle Eastern and North African Experience.* New York: Columbia University Press, 1998.

Cagatay, Nilufer, and Sule Ozler. "Feminization of the Labor Force: The Effects of Long Term Development and Structural Adjustment." *World Development* 23, no. 11 (1995): 1883–1884.

Carapico, Sheila, and Cynthia Myntti. "A Tale of Two Families: Change in North Yemen 1977–1989." *Middle East Report* 170, 21, no. 3 (1991): 24–29.

Carapico, Sheila, and Richard Tutwiler. *Yemeni Agriculture and Economic Change.* Milwaukee: American Institute for Yemeni Studies, 1981.

Chafi, Mohamed. *Code du statut personnel annoté: Textes législatifs, doctrine, et jurisprudence.* Marrakech: Imprimerie Walili, 1996.

"Chamber of Commerce Urges Dialogue on Saudi Woman's Role." *Saudi Gazette,* 3 May 1999, 2. (Quoted in Foreign Broadcast Information Service 1999050500635.)

Chamie, Mary. "Labour Force Participation of Lebanese Women." In *Women, Employment, and Development in the Arab World,* edited by Julinda Abu Nasr, Nabil F. Khoury, and Henry T. Assam, 73–102. Berlin: Mouton, 1985.

Charrad, Mounira M. "Becoming a Citizen: Lineage Versus Individual in Tunisia and Morocco." In *Gender and Citizenship in the Middle East,* edited by Suad Joseph. Syracuse, N.Y.: Syracuse University Press, in press.

———. "Cultural Diversity Within Islam: Veils and Laws in Tunisia." In *Women in Muslim Societies: Diversity Within Unity,* edited by Herbert L. Bodman and Nayereh Tohidi, 63–79. Boulder, Colo.: Lynne Rienner, 1998.

———. *The Origins of Women's Rights: State and Tribe in Tunisia, Algeria, and Morocco.* Berkeley: University of California Press, in press.

———. "Policy Shifts: State, Islam, and Gender in Tunisia, 1930s–1990s." *Social Politics* 4, no. 2 (1997): 284–319.

———. "The Politics of Family Law: The Tunisian Example." Paper presented at the Middle East Studies Association annual meeting, San Francisco 1984.

———. "Repudiation Versus Divorce: Responses to State Policy in Tunisia." In *Women, the Family and Policy: A Global Perspective,* edited by Esther Nganling Chow and Catherine White Berheide, 51–69. Albany: State University of New York Press, 1994.

———. Review of Christelow. *Middle East Journal* 41, no. 2 (1987): 281–82.

Chatterjee, Partha. *The Nation and Its Fragments.* Princeton, N.J.: Princeton University Press, 1994.

———. "Two Poets and Death: On Civil and Political Society in the Non-Christian World." Paper presented at the Nation Building After Independence in Central Asia and the Middle East Conference, Tashkent, October 1996.

Cheriet, Boutheina. "Islamism and Feminism: Algeria's "Rites of Passage" to Democracy." In *State and Society in Algeria,* edited by John P. Entelis and Phillip C. Naylor, 171–215. Boulder, Colo.: Westview Press, 1992.

Chhachhi, Amrita. "Forced Identities: The State, Communalism, Fundamentalism, and Women in India." In *Women, Islam, and the State,* edited by Deniz Kandiyoti, 144–75. Basingstoke: Macmillan; Philadelphia: Temple University Press, 1991.

Christelow, Allan. *Muslim Law Courts and the French Colonial State in Algeria.* Princeton, N.J.: Princeton University Press, 1985.

Clancy-Smith, Julia A. *Rebel and Saint: Muslim Notables, Populist Protest, Colonial Encounters (Algeria and Tunisia, 1800–1904).* Berkeley: University of California Press, 1994.

"Closure Underlies Structural Dependency of Palestinian Economy." *World Food Programme Journal* 37 (1996): 8.

Cuisenier, Jean. *Economie et parenté: Leurs affinités de structure dans le domaine arabe.* Paris and the Hague: Mouton, 1975.

Dietz, Mary. "Context Is All: Feminism and Theories of Citizenship." *Daedalus* 116, no. 4 (1987): 1–24.

Douglas, Allen, and Fedwa Malti-Douglas. *Arab Comic Strips: Politics of an Emerging Mass Culture.* Bloomington: Indiana University Press, 1994.

El-Saadawi, Nawal. *The Hidden Face of Eve: Women in the Arab World.* London: Zed Press, 1980.

———. In *Women and Islam,* edited by Azizah al-Hibri, 193–206. Oxford: Pergamon Press, 1992.

El-Solh, Camilla Fawzi, and Nabiha Masmoudi Chaalala. *Women's Role in Arab Food Security: A Gender Analysis of Selected Agricultural Projects.* New York: United Nations Development Programme, Regional Bureau for Arab States, 1992.

Enloe, Cynthia. *The Morning After: Sexual Politics at the End of the Cold War.* Berkeley: University of California Press, 1993.

Evans, Peter B., Dietrich Rueschemeyer, and Theda Skocpol, eds. *Bringing the State Back In.* New York: Cambridge University Press, 1985.

Geertz, Clifford, ed. *Old Societies and New States: The Quest for Modernity in Asia and Africa.* New York: Free Press, 1963.

Geertz, Hildred. "The Meaning of Family Ties." In *Meaning and Order in Moroccan Society,* edited by Clifford Geertz, Hildred Geertz, and Larry Rosen, 315–91. Cambridge: Cambridge University Press, 1979.

Gellner, Ernest, and Charles Micaud, eds. *Arabs and Berbers: From Tribe to Nation in North Africa.* Lexington, Mass.: D.C. Heath, 1972.

Ghabra, Shafiq. "Voluntary Associations in Kuwait: The Foundation of a New System?" *Middle East Journal* 45, no. 2 (1991): 199–215.

Giacaman, Rita. *Palestinian Women: A Status Report.* Vol. 2, *Population and Fertility: Population Policies, Women's Rights, and Sustainable Development.* Ramallah: Birzeit University Women's Studies Program, 1997.

Giacaman, Rita, Islah Jad, and Penny Johnson. "Gender and Public Policies." In *Working Paper No. 2.* Ramallah: Women's Studies Program, Birzeit University, 1995.

Gordon, Linda, and Nancy Fraser. "Dependency Demystified: Inscriptions of Power in a Keyword of the Welfare State." *Social Politics* 1, no. 1 (1994): 5–31.

*Gozydeh-e Mataleb-e Amary.* Tehran: Markaz-e Amar-e Iran (Iran Statistical Center), 1992.

Hale, Sondra. *Gender Politics in Sudan.* Boulder, Colo.: Westview Press, 1996.

——. "The Wing of the Patriarch: Sudanese Women and Revolutionary Parties." *Middle East Report* 138, 16, no. 1 (1986): 25–30.

Hammami, Reema. "Women, the Hijab and the Intifada." *Middle East Report* 164–165, 20, no. 3–4 (1990): 24–28.

Hanley, Charles. "Slide over Saudi Economy." Associated Press, 1997 (cited 1999). Available from <AOLNewsProfiles@aol.net>.

Hassan, Javid. "Saudi Women Given Green Light in Hotel Industry." *Internet Arab View in English,* 28 February 1997. (Quoted in Foreign Broadcast Information Service FBIS-NES-97-070.) Available from <www.arab.net/arabview/articles/hassan1.html>.

Hatem, Mervat. "Economic and Political Liberalization in Egypt and the Demise of State Feminism." *International Journal of Middle East Studies* 24 (1992): 231–51.

——. "Egyptian Middle Class Women and Views of the Sexual Division of Labor in the Nationalist Personalized Patriarchal System." Paper presented at the Middle East Studies Association annual meeting, New Orleans 1985.

——. "Toward a Critique of Modernization: Narrative in Middle East Women's Studies." *Arab Studies Quarterly* 15 (1993): 117–22.

Hegland, Mary Elaine. "Political Roles of Iranian Village Women." *Middle East Report* 138, 16, no. 1 (1986): 14–19, 46.

Heiberg, Marianne et al. *Palestinian Society in Gaza, West Bank, and Arab Jerusalem: A Survey of Living Conditions.* Oslo: FAFO, 1993.

Hermassi, Elbaki. *Leadership and National Development in North Africa.* Berkeley: University of California Press, 1972.

Hijab, Nadia. *Womanpower: The Arab Debate on Women at Work.* Cambridge: Cambridge University Press, 1988.

Hoffman, Valerie J. "An Islamic Activist: Zaynab al-Ghazali." In *Women and the Family in the Middle East: New Voices of Change,* edited by Elizabeth W. Fernea, 233–54. Austin: University of Texas Press, 1985.

Hoodfar, Homa. "Devices and Desires: Population Policy and Gender Roles in the Islamic Republic." *Middle East Report* 190, 24, no. 5 (1994): 11–17.

——. "Women and Personal Status Laws in Iran: An Interview with Mehranguiz Kar." *Middle East Report* 198, 26, no. 1 (1996): 36–39.

Hudson, Michael. "Obstacles to Democratization in the Middle East." *Contention* 14 (1996): 81–106.

"Ibn Baz: Women's Work Is Quick Road to Adultery." *APS Diplomatic Recorder* 44, no. 24 (1996).

International Labor Organization. *Capacity Building for Social Development: Programme of Action for Transition in the Occupied Palestinian Territories.* Geneva: ILO, January 1994.

——. *Yearbook of Labor Statistics.* Geneva: ILO, various years.

International Monetary Fund. "Islamic Republic of Iran: 1993." In *Article IV, Consultation, 1993.*

*Iran dar Ayineye Amar.* Tehran: Markaz-e Amar-e Iran (Iran Statistical Center), 1989.

Jad, Islah. "A Feminist Analysis of Tribalism and 'Municipal Elections.' " *Al Quds,* 12 September 1995.

Johnson, Penny. *Palestinian Women: A Status Report.* Vol. 5, *Social Support: Gender and Social Policies in Palestine.* Ramallah: Birzeit University Women's Studies Program, 1997.

Jones, Kathleen. "Citizenship in a Woman Friendly Polity." *Signs: Journal of Women in Culture and Society* 15, no. 4 (1990): 781–812.

Joseph, Suad. "Connectivity and Patriarchy Among Urban Working Class Arab Families in Lebanon." *Ethos* 21 (1993): 452–84.

——. "Elite Strategies for State-Building: Women, Family, Religion, and the State in Iraq and Lebanon." In *Women, Islam, and the State,* edited by Deniz Kandiyoti, 176–200. Basingstoke: Macmillan; Philadelphia: Temple University Press, 1991.

——. "The Family as Security and Bondage: A Political Strategy of the Lebanese Urban Working Class." In *Towards a Political Economy of Urbanization in Third World Countries,* edited by Helen Safa, 151–71. New Delhi: Oxford University Press, 1982.

——. "Gender and Citizenship in Middle Eastern States." *Middle East Report* 198, 26, no. 1 (1996): 4–10.

——. "The Mobilization of Iraqi Women into the Wage Labor Force." *Studies in Third World Societies* 16 (1982): 69–90.

——. "Problematizing Gender and Relational Rights: Experiences from Lebanon." *Social Politics* 1, no. 3 (1994): 271–85.

——. "Working-Class Women's Networks in a Sectarian State: A Political Paradox." *American Ethnologist* 10 (1983): 1–22.

Kabeer, Naila. "The Quest for National Identity: Women, Islam, and the State of Bangladesh." In *Women, Islam, and the State,* edited by Deniz Kandiyoti, 115–43. Basingstoke: Macmillan: Philadelphia: Temple University Press, 1991.

Kandiyoti, Deniz. "Bargaining with Patriarchy." *Gender and Society* 2, no. 3 (1988): 274–90.

——. "Beyond Beijing: Obstacles and Prospects for the Middle East." In *Muslim*

*Women and the Politics of Participation,* edited by Mahnaz Afkhami and Erika Friedl, 3–10. Syracuse, N.Y.: Syracuse University Press, 1997.

——. "Contemporary Feminist Scholarship and Middle East Studies." In *Gendering the Middle East,* edited by Deniz Kandiyoti, 1–27. London: Tauris, 1996.

——. "From Empire to Nation-State: Transformations of the Woman Question in Turkey." Paper presented at the Forum on Current Research on Middle Eastern Women, University of California, Berkeley, 1984.

——. "Identity and Its Discontents: Women and the Nation." *Millennium* 20 (1991): 429–43.

——. "Women, Islam, and the State." In *Political Islam: Essays from Middle East Report,* edited by Joel Beinin and Joe Stork, 185–93. Berkeley and Los Angeles: University of California Press, 1997.

Kandiyoti, Deniz, ed. *Women, Islam, and the State.* Basingstoke: Macmillan; Philadelphia: Temple University Press, 1991.

Keesing, Roger. "Kwaio Women Speak: The Micropolitics of Autobiography in a Soloman Island Society." *American Anthropologist* 8, no. 1 (1985): 27–39.

Khanzandar, 'Abid. "The Woman and the Computer." *'Ukaz,* 28 May 1999, 6. (Quoted in Foreign Broadcast Information Service FTS19990601000159.)

Khashoggi, Jamal. "Dialogue on Women's Role Urged." *Arab News,* 21 April 1999.

Koçali, Filiz, and Serpil Gülgün. "Binenaleyh Tansu Çiller." *Kim* 15 (1993): 54–60.

Kramer, Gudrun. "Islamist Notions of Democracy." In *Political Islam: Essays from Middle East Report,* edited by Joel Beinin and Joe Stork, 71–82. Berkeley and Los Angeles: University of California Press, 1997.

Kuwait Ministry of Planning. *al-Siyassah al-Ijtima'ya fi Araba' Sanawat* (Social Policy in Four Years) Kuwait: Ministry of Planning, 1975.

Lackner, Helen. "Women and Development in the Republic of Yemen." In *Gender and Development in the Arab World: Women's Economic Participation: Patterns and Policies,* edited by Nabil F. Khoury and Valentine M. Moghadam, 71–96. London: Zed Books, 1995.

Lari, Rida Muhammad. "Women Are Not Allowed To Take Cabs." *Al-Bilad,* 15 September 1998, 5. (Quoted in foreign Broadcast Information Service, FTS19980921000085.)

Lazreg, Marnia. *The Eloquence of Silence: Algerian Women in Question.* New York: Routledge, 1994.

——. "Feminism and Difference: The Perils of Writing as a Woman on Women in Algeria." *Feminist Studies* 14 (1988): 81–107.

——. "You Don't Have to Work, Sisters! This Is Socialism." Paper presented at the Middle East Studies Association annual meeting, New Orleans 1985.

Lienhardt, Peter A. "Some Aspects of the Trucial State." In *The Arabian Peninsula: Society and Politics,* edited by Derek Hopwood, 219–29. London: Allen and Unwin, 1972.

Maher, Vanessa. "Kin, Clients, and Accomplices: Relationships Among Women in Morocco." In *Sexual Divisions and Society: Process and Change,* edited by Diana L. Barker and Sheila Allen, 52–75. London: Tavistock, 1976.

Marglin, Stephen, and Frederique Marglin. *Dominating Knowledge: Development, Culture, and Resistance.* Oxford: Clarendon Press, 1990.

Marsot, Afaf Lutfi al-Sayyid. "Revolutionary Gentlewomen in Egypt." In *Women in the Muslim World,* edited by Lois Beck and Nikkie Keddie, 261–76. Cambridge, Mass.: Harvard University Press, 1978.

Mayer, Ann Elizabeth. "Rhetorical Strategies and Official Politics on Women's Rights: The Merits and Drawbacks of the New World Hypocrisy." In *Faith and Freedom,* edited by Mahnaz Afkhami, 104–32. Syracuse, N.Y.: Syracuse University Press, 1995.

Mernissi, Fatima. *Beyond the Veil: Male-Female Dynamics in Modern Muslim Society.* Bloomington: Indiana University Press, 1987.

———. *Islam and Democracy: Fear of the Modern World.* New York: Addison-Wesley, 1992.

———. "Virginity and Patriarchy." In *Women and Islam,* edited by Azizah al-Hibri, 183–91. Oxford: Pergamon Press, 1982.

Mir-Hosseini, Ziba. *Marriage on Trial: A Study of Islamic Family Law — Iran and Morocco Compared.* London: Tauris, 1993.

Mitchell, Timothy. *Colonising Egypt.* Cambridge: Cambridge University Press, 1988.

Moghadam, Fatemeh Etemad. "Commoditization of Sexuality and Female Labor Participation in Islam: Implications on Iran 1960–1990." In *In The Eye of the Story: Women in The Islamic Republic of Iran,* edited by Mahnaz Afkhami and Erika Friedl, 80–97. Syracuse, N.Y.: Syracuse University Press, 1994.

Moghadam, Valentine M. "Development and Women's Emancipation: Is There a Connection?" In *Emancipations, Modern and Postmodern,* edited by Jan Nederveen Pieterse. London: Sage, 1992.

———. *Women, Work, and Economic Reform in the Middle East and North Africa.* Boulder, Colo.: Lynne Rienner, 1998.

———. "Women, Work, and Ideology in the Islamic Republic." *International Journal of Middle East Studies* 20 (1988): 221–43.

———. "Women's Employment Issues in Contemporary Iran: Problems and Prospects in the 1990s." *Iranian Studies* 28, no. 3–4 (1995): 175–202.

Mohanty, Chandra Talpade. "Under Western Eyes: Feminist Scholarship and Colonial Discourses." In *Third World Women and the Politics of Feminism,* edited by Chandra Talpade Mohanty, Ann Russo, and Lourdes Torres, 51–80. Bloomington: Indiana University Press, 1991.

Molyneux, Maxine. "Feminism, Citizenship, and Democracy: Reflections on Contemporary Debates." Paper presented at the UNAM Conference on Women, Civic Culture and Democracy, Mexico City, July 1996.

———. "The Law, the State, and Socialist Policies with Regard to Women: The Case of the People's Democratic Republic of Yemen, 1967–1990." In *Women, Islam, and the State,* edited by Deniz Kandiyoti, 237–71. Basingstoke: Macmillan; Philadelphia: Temple University Press, 1991.

Mundy, Martha. *Domestic Government: Kinship, Community, and Polity in North Yemen.* London: Tauris, 1995.

Myntti, Cynthia. *Women and Development in the Yemen Arab Republic.* Eschborn: German Agency for Technical Cooperation (GTZ), 1979.

Nadel, Alan. "A Whole New (Disney) World Order: *Alladin,* Atomic Power, and the Muslim Middle East." In *Visions of the East: Orientalism in Film,* edited by Matthew Bernstein and Gaylyn Studlar, 184–203. New Brunswick, N.J.: Rutgers University Press, 1997.

Nasr, Sayyed Hossein. *Traditional Islam in the Modern World.* London: Routledge, 1987.

Nelson, Cynthia. *Doria Shafik, Egyptian Feminist: A Woman Apart.* Gainesville: University Press of Florida, 1996.

Nelson, Cynthia, and Virginia Olesen. "Veil of Illusion: A Critique of the Concept of Equality in Western Thought." *Catalyst* 10–11 (1974): 8–36.

Norton, Anne. "Gender, Sexuality and the Iraq of Our Imagination." *Middle East Report* 173, 21, no. 6 (1991): 26–28.

Ovensen, Geir. *Responding to Change: Trends in Palestinian Household Economy.* Oslo: FAFO, 1994.

Palestinian Central Bureau of Statistics. *The Demographic Survey in the West Bank and Gaza: Preliminary Report.* Ramallah: Palestinian Central Bureau of Statistics, 1996.

Parsons, Gerald E. "How the Yellow Ribbon Became a National Folk Symbol." *Folklife Center News* (1991): 9–11.

Pateman, Carol. *The Sexual Contract.* Stanford, Calif.: Stanford University Press, 1988.

Peteet, Julie. "From Refugees to Minority: Palestinians in Post-War Lebanon." *Middle East Report* 200, 26, no. 3 (1996): 27–30.

——. "Icons and Militants: Mothering in the Danger Zone." *Signs: Journal of Women and Culture* 23, no. 1 (1997): 103–29.

——. "No Going Back: Women and the Palestinian Movement." *Middle East Report* 138, 16, no. 1 (1986): 20–24, 44.

——. "They Took Our Blood and Milk: Palestinian Women and War." *Cultural Survival* 19, no. 1 (1995): 50–53.

Pollock, David. "Reporting the Middle East: An Overview." Paper presented at the conference on The Media and the Gulf: A Closer Look, Berkeley, California, May 1991.

Rai, Shirin. "Women and the State in the Third World." In *Women and Politics in the Third World,* edited by Haleh Afshar. London: Routledge, 1996.

"Report on 'Security' of Saudi Women." *Al-Jazirah,* 26 May 1999, 21. (Quoted in Foreign Broadcast Information Service FTS 19990601000175.)

République Tunisienne. *Code du statut personnel.* Tunis: Imprimerie Officielle, 1997.

Rieker, Martina. "The Sa'id and the City: The Politics of Space in the Making of Modern Egypt." Ph.D. diss., Temple University, 1996.

Rosaldo, Michelle Zimbalist, and Louise Lamphere, eds. *Woman, Culture, and Society.* Stanford, Calif.: Stanford University Press, 1974.

Rosenfeld, Maya. "Interview with Maha Nassar and Aida Issawi." *Challenge* 22 (1993): 8–10.

Sadowski, Yahya. "The New Orientalism and the Democracy Debate." In *Political Islam: Essays from Middle East Report,* edited by Joel Beinin and Joe Stork, 33–50. Berkeley and Los Angeles: University of California Press, 1997.

Said, Edward. *Orientalism.* New York: Pantheon, 1978.

Salamé, Ghassan, ed. *The Foundations of the Arab State.* London and New York: Croom Helm, 1987.

*Salnameh Amary-e: 1370* (Annual Statistics, 1991). Tehran: Markaz-e Amar-e Iran (Iran Statistical Center), 1992.

Sanasarian, Eliz. *The Women's Rights Movement in Iran: Mutiny, Appeasement, and Repression from 1900 to Khomeini.* New York: Praeger, 1982.

Schultz, T. Paul. "Women's Changing Participation in the Labor Force: A World Perspective." *Working Paper* 272, no. 6 (1989): 6–9.

Shahidian, Hammed. "The Education of Women in the Islamic Republic of Iran." *Journal of Women's History* 2, no. 3 (1991): 6–38, 12–14, 17–20.

Shakry, Omnia. "Schooled Mothers and Structured Play: Child-Rearing in Turn of the Century Egypt." In *Remaking Women: Feminism and Modernity in the Middle East,* edited by Lila Abu-Lughod, 126–70. Princeton, N.J.: Princeton University Press, 1998.

Sharabi, Hisham. *Neopatriarchy: A Theory of Distorted Change in Arab Society.* New York: Oxford University Press, 1988.

Sharara, Rola. "Women and Politics in Lebanon." *Khamsin: Journal of Revolutionary Socialists of the Middle East* 6 (1978): 6–15.

"Sivas bu kez 'turban' yuzunden gerginlik yasiyor" (Sivas is tense this time due to "turban"). *Milliyet,* 2 September 1996, 1, 15.

Skocpol, Theda. *States and Social Revolutions: A Comparative Analysis of France, Russia, and China.* New York: Cambridge University Press, 1985.

Slyomovics, Susan. "Algeria Caricatures the Gulf War." *Public Culture* 4 (1992): 93–101.

———. "Cartoon Commentary: Algerian and Moroccan Caricatures from the Gulf War." *Middle East Report* 180, 23, no. 1 (1993): 21–24.

———. "Hassiba Ben Bouali: If You Could See Our Algeria." In *Political Islam: Essays from Middle East Report,* edited by Joel Beinin and Joe Stork, 211–19. Berkeley and Los Angeles: University of California Press, 1997.

Stam, Robert. "Mobilizing Fictions: The Gulf War, the Media, and the Recruitment of the Spectator." *Public Culture* 4, no. 2 (1992): 101–26.

State Institute of Statistics (Turkey). *1990 General Population Census and Formal Education Series.* Ankara: State Institute of Statistics, 1991.

State Planning Organization. "Turkish Family Structure, 1992." In *The Status of Women in Turkey: Turkish National Report to the Fourth World Conference on Women.* Ankara: State Planning Organization, 1994.

Stirling, W. F., Lt. Col. "Palestine: 1920–1923." In *From Haven to Conquest: Readings in Zionism and the Palestinian Problem Until 1948,* edited by Walid Khalidi, 227–35. Beirut: Institute for Palestine Studies, 1971.

Sweet, Louise. "The Women of 'Ain ad Dayr.' " *Anthropological Quarterly* 40, no. 3 (1967): 167–83.

Taheri, Amir. "Role of Saudi Women on the Eve of New Century." *Arab News,* 22 April 1999, 8.

Tawil, Raymonda Hawa. *My Home, My Prison.* London: Zed Press, 1983.

Tekeli, Serin. "Women in Turkish Politics." In *Women in Turkish Society,* edited by Nermin Abadan-Unat, 293–310. Leiden: Brill, 1981.

Tetreault, Mary Ann, and Haya al-Mughni. "Gender, Citizenship and Nationalism in Kuwait." *British Journal of Middle Eastern Studies* 22, no. 1, 2 (1995): 64–80.

Tillion, Germaine. *The Republic of Cousins: Women's Oppression in Mediterranean Society.* Translated by Quintin Hoare. London: Al Saqi, 1983. Originally published as *Le harem et les cousins.* Paris: Editions du Seuil, 1966.

Tilly, Charles, ed. *The Formation of National States in Western Europe.* Princeton: Princeton University Press, 1975.

Treiman, Donald J., and Heidi I. Hartmann, eds. *Women, Work, and Wages: Equal Pay for Jobs of Equal Value.* Washington, D.C.: National Academy Press, 1981.

Tucker, Judith E. "Insurrectionary Women: Women and the State in 19th Century Egypt." *Middle East Report* 138, 16, no. 1 (1986): 9–13.

Tucker, Judith E. *Women in Nineteenth-Century Egypt.* Cambridge: Cambridge University Press, 1985.

Turner, Bryan. "Outline of a Theory of Citizenship." In *Dimensions of Radical Democracy: Pluralism, Citizenship, Community,* edited by Chantal Mouffe, 33–62. London: Verso, 1992.

"Ulama Reject Cairo Conference." *Al-Nadwa,* 1 September 1994, 1, 5.

U.S. Department of State. *Saudi Arabia Human Rights Practices, 1995.* Washington, D.C.: U.S. Government Printing Office, 1996.

United Nations. *Report of the Secretary General: Recommendations of Regional Inter-Governmental preparatory meetings.* New York: United Nations, 1985.

———. *Women: Challenges to the Year 2000.* New York: United Nations, 1991.

United Nations Development Programme. *Human Development Report.* New York and Oxford: Oxford University Press, various years.

van Eeghen, Willem. *Education in MENA: Benefits and Growth Pay-Offs Now and Then,* 53–54. World Bank, Middle East and North Africa Region, 1997.

Vatin, Jean-Claude, ed. *Images d'Egypte: De la fresque à la bande dessinée.* Actes des journées d'études CEDEJ-IFAO. Cairo: CEDEJ, 1991.

Waterbury, John. "Democracy Without Democrats? The Potential for Political Liberalization in the Middle East." In *Democracy Without Democrats? The Renewal of Politics in the Muslim World,* edited by Ghassan Salamé, 23–47. London: Tauris, 1994.

Weber, Samuel. "The Media and the War." *Alphabet City* (1991): 22–26.

Wedeen, Lisa. *Ambiguities of Domination: Politics, Rhetoric, and Symbols in Contemporary Syria.* Chicago: University of Chicago Press, 1999.

Women's Cultural and Social Society. *Masirat al-Jam'iya* (March of the Society). Kuwait: WCSS Publications, 1994.

————. *Women's Cultural and Social Society, 1963–1994.* Kuwait: WCSS Publications, 1994.

"Women Under the Palestinian Authority." Interview with Reema Hammami. *Challenge* 42 (1997): 12.

World Bank. *Developing the Occupied Territories: An Investment in Peace.* Vol. 2, *The Economy.* Washington, D.C.: World Bank, 1993.

————. *Developing the Occupied Territories: An Investment in Peace.* Vol. 6, *Human Resources and Social Policy.* Washington, D.C.: World Bank, 1993.

Wuerth, Anna. "Sana'a Court: The Family and the Ability to Negotiate." *Islamic Law and Society* 2, no. 3 (1995): 320–40.

Yuval-Davis, Nira, and Floya Anthias, eds. *Woman, Nation, State.* London: Macmillan, 1989.

Zirout, Malek. *La route de sel.* Algiers: Enterprise Nationale du Livre, 1984.

Zubaida, Sami. *Islam, the People and the State: Essays on Political Ideas and Movements in the Middle East.* London: Routledge, 1988.

————. "Nations: Old and New." *Ethnic and Racial Studies* 12 (1989): 329–39.

# Contributors

Lila Abu-Lughod is Professor of Anthropology and Women's Studies at Columbia University. She has written widely on women, gender, and popular culture in the Middle East. Her books include *Veiled Sentiments: Honor and Poetry in a Bedouin Society, Writing Women's Worlds: Bedouin Stories,* and an edited collection, *Remaking Women: Feminism and Modernity in the Middle East.*

Haya al-Mughni is a Kuwaiti sociologist with degrees from the University of Geneva, Switzerland, and the University of Exeter in Great Britain. She has published in both Arabic and English on issues relating to gender politics, citizenship, and women's groups. She is the author of *Women in Kuwait: The Politics of Gender.*

Yeşim Arat is a professor in the Department of Political Science and International Relations, Bogazici University, Istanbul, Turkey. She is the author of *Patriarchal Paradox: Women Politicians in Turkey*, coeditor with Barbara Laslett and Johanna Brenner of *Rethinking the Political: Gender, Resistance, and the State*, as well as numerous articles on Islamist women and feminist political activism in Turkey.

Sheila Carapico chairs the Editorial Committee of *Middle East Report* and the Political Science Department at the University of Richmond. She is the author of *Civil Society in Yemen: A Political Economy of Activism in Modern Arabia* and several articles and book chapters on Yemeni and Arab politics.

Mounira M. Charrad is Assistant Professor of Sociology and Middle East Studies at the University of Texas at Austin. She is the author of a comparative-historical study of the Maghrib, *The Origins of Women's Rights: State and Tribe in Tunisia, Algeria and Morocco.* She coedited and contributed to *Femmes, culture et société au Maghreb*, and has published articles in French and English on issues of state formation, culture, women's rights, and law.

Eleanor Abdella Doumato is the author of *Getting God's Ear: Women, Islam, and Healing in Saudi Arabia and the Gulf,* monographs on Arab communities in America, and numerous essays, encyclopedia articles, and book reviews on gender, human rights, Gulf politics, and Islam in the formative period. She has spent many years teaching and doing research in Lebanon, Saudi Arabia, and Iran before the revolution and is Adjunct Professor for International Studies (Research) at the Thomas J. Watson Institute for International Studies at Brown University.

Karim El-Gawhary is the Cairo based Middle East correspondent of the German daily *Berliner Zeitung* and other German, Austrian, and Swiss newspapers. He freelances for German Public Radio (ARD), works for the Portuguese daily *Publico,* and contributes regularly to *Middle East International* and *MERIP.*

Rita Giacaman is Director of the Institute of Community and Public Health, Birzeit University and a research associate at the Women's Studies Institute, Birzeit University. Her research areas include women's health, population policies, and fertility studies. She has published monographs, articles, and book chapters in the areas of women's health, health policy, disability rehabilitation, and the rational use of drugs. She is the author of *Life and Health in Three Palestinian Villages.*

Sarah Graham-Brown is a writer and researcher on the Middle East and on development issues. Her publications include *Sanctioning Saddam: The Politics of Intervention in Iraq, Education in the Developing World: Conflict and Crisis, Images of Women: The Portrayal of Women in Photography of the Middle East 1860–1950,* and *Education, Repression, and Liberation: Palestinians.*

Ellen Gruenbaum is Professor of Anthropology and Dean of the School of Social Sciences at California State University, Fresno. In the 1970s she spent five years in Sudan, where she conducted research and taught at the University of Khartoum, and returned for additional research in 1989 and 1992. She has published "Embrace and Resistance: Sudanese Rural Women and Systems of Power" in *Pragmatic Women and Body Politics, The Female Circumcision Controversy: An Anthropological Perspective* (University of Pennsylvania Press). She serves on the Committee for Human Rights of the American Anthropological Association.

Nadia Hijab is the author of *Womanpower: The Arab Debate on Women at Work* and of encyclopedia essays on subjects such as civil society, gender, and human rights, and coauthor of *Citizens Apart: A Portrait of Palestinians in Israel.* Before joining the United Nations Development Programme, she was editor of the London-based magazine *The Middle East,* and was a frequent commentator on the BBC and other British and

American media. At UNDP, she has helped elaborate approaches to development that are people-centered and sustainable, and contributed to the organization's major change in management process.

Islah Jad is Lecturer in Political Science, Cultural Studies Department and Women's Studies Center at Birzeit University. She is a founding member of Women's Studies Program at Birzeit University, founding member of an umbrella organization for mainstream women's organizations and centers in the West Bank and Gaza (WATC), and author of many articles on the Palestinian women's movement and on women's political participation. She is currently a visiting researcher at the Humanities Research Institute of the University of California, Irvine, working on Gender and citizenship in Muslim communities.

Penny Johnson is Assistant Director of the Women's Studies Center at Birzeit University and chairs the university's human rights committee. She has written on the Palestinian women's movement, human rights, and social policy issues in the Palestinian territories. Her current research interests are focused on Palestinian household composition, social support, children, and poverty. She was a representative of the Women's Studies Center on the National Poverty Commission and contributed to the research and writing of the National Poverty Report. She is a contributing editor to *Middle East Report.*

Suad Joseph is Professor of Anthropology and Women's Studies at the University of California, Davis. Her research raises questions of gender, family, children, citizenship, rights, and state in the Middle East. Her ethnographic work has focused mainly on her native Lebanon. Her publications include, as editor, *Intimate Selving in Arab Families: Gender, Self, and Identity* and *Gender and Citizenship in the Middle East* (in press); as coeditor with Najla Hamadeh and Jean Said Makdisi, *Gender and Citizenship in Lebanon* and with Walid Moubarak and Antoine Messarra, *Citizenship in Lebanon.*

Deniz Kandiyoti is Senior Lecturer in the Department of Development Studies, School of Oriental and African Studies, University of London. She is the editor of *Gendering the Middle East* (1996) and *Women, Islam, and the State* and author of *Women in Rural Production Systems* and *Concubines, Sisters, and Citizens.* She is currently working on post-Soviet Central Asia.

Fatemeh Etemad Moghadam is Professor of Economics and Department Chair at Hofstra University; President of the Middle East Economic

Association 1996–present and formerly Executive Secretary 1994–96. She is the author of *From Land Reform to Revolution: The Political Economy of Agricultural Development in Iran (1960–1979)* and of articles in *Economic Development and Cultural Change, Cambridge Journal of Economics,* and *Oxford Bulletin of Economics and Statistics.* Her areas of interest are women and development, political economy of agricultural development, and the Middle East and Iran.

Julie Peteet is Associate Professor and Chair of the Anthropology Department at the University of Louisville. She has published on gender, violence, and displacement, and is currently completing a book manuscript on refugee camps and identity.

Susan Slyomovics is Geneviève McMillan-Reba Stewart Professor of the Study of Women in the Developing World and Professor of Anthropology at the Massachusetts Institute of Technology. She is the author of *The Merchant of Art: An Egyptian Hilali Epic Poet in Performance* and *The Object of Memory: Arab and Jew Narrate the Palestinian Village* (University of Pennsylvania Press).

# Acknowledgments

Earlier versions of articles in this volume first appeared in the journal, *Middle East Report* (previously *MERIP Reports*) published by Middle East Report and Information Project (MERIP). We are especially grateful to *MERIP* editor Joe Stork, publishers Jim Paul and Peggy Hutchinson, assistant editor Martha Wenger, and the many contributing editors and staff over the decades who have participated in *MERIP* issues featuring gender perspectives, notably, Judith Tucker, Barbara Harlow, Julie Peteet, Joel Beinin, Esther Merves, Michelle Brouwers, Maggy Zanger, and Ann Schaub. Indeed our own involvement in MERIP as contributing editors has enriched our understanding of the region.

We thank Philip Khoury and the Dean's Office of the School of Social Sciences and Humanities at the Massachusetts Institute of Technology, who provided a publication subvention. Sheryl Yu Villa, funded by MIT's Undergraduate Research Opportunity Program (UROP), gave us her expertise in computers and bibliographical research. Patricia Reynolds Smith, our editor at the University of Pennsylvania Press, and her able staff guided this volume to publication.

Finally we thank our families — Sara Joseph, Nadjib and Iskandar Berber — for their support throughout this project.

Lila Abu-Lughod, "Islam and Public Culture: The Politics of Egyptian Television Serials," *MERIP* 180, 23, no. 1 (January–February 1993): 25–30. Adapted with permission from "The Interpretation of Culture(s) After Television," *Representations* 59 (Summer 1997): 109–34. Research supported by John Simon Guggenheim Memorial Foundation, NEH, American Research Center in Egypt, ACLS/SSRC Joint Committee on the Near and Middle East, New York University Research Challenge Fund.

Yeşim Arat, "Gender and Citizenship: Considerations on the Turkish Experience," *MERIP* 198, 26, no. 1 (January–February 1996): 28–31.

Sheila Carapico, "Women and Public Participation in Yemen," *MERIP* 173, 21, no. 6 (November–December 1991): 15.

Mounira M. Charrad, "State and Gender in the Maghreb," *MERIP* 163, 20, no. 2 (March–April 1990): 19–24; first presented as a paper, "State, Civil Society, and Gender: Examples from the Maghreb," at the conference on Retreating States and Expanding Societies: State Autonomy — Informal Civil Society Dialectic in the Middle East and North Africa, Joint Committee on the Near and Middle East, Social Science Research Council and American Council of Learned Societies, Aix-en-Provence, March 25–27, 1988.

Eleanor Abdella Doumato, "Women and the Stability of Saudi Arabia," *MERIP* 171, 21, no. 4 (July–August 1991): 26–30.

Karim El-Gawhary, "An Interview with Heba Ra'uf Ezzat," *MERIP* 191, 24, no. 6 (November–December 1994): 26–27.

Rita Giacaman, Islah Jad, and Penny Johnson, "For the Public Good? Gender and Social Citizenship in Palestine," *MERIP* 198, 26, no. 1 (January–March 1996): 11–17.

Rita Giacaman and Penny Johnson, "Searching for Strategies: The Palestinian Women's Movement in the New Era," *MERIP* 186, 24, no. 1 (January–February 1994): 22–25.

Sarah Graham-Brown, "Women's Activism in the Middle East: A Historical Perspective," *Women and Politics in the Middle East,* Women in the Middle East 2 (Washington, D.C.: MERIP, 1993).

Ellen Gruenbaum, "The Islamic State and Sudanese Women," *MERIP* 179, 22, no. 6 (November–December 1992): 29–32.

Nadia Hijab, "Women and Work in the Arab World," *Women and Work in the Arab World,* Women in the Middle East 3 (Washington, D.C.: MERIP, 1994).

Suad Joseph, "Women and Politics in the Middle East," *MERIP* 138, 16, no. 1 (January–February 1986).

Deniz Kandiyoti, "Women, Islam, and the State," *MERIP* 173, 21, no. 6 (November–December 1991): 9–14.

Haya al-Mughni, "Women's Organizations in Kuwait," *MERIP* 198, 26, no. 1 (January–March 1996): 32–35.

Julie Peteet, "No Going Back: Women and the Palestinian Movement," *MERIP* 138, 16, no. 1 (January–February 1986): 20–24.

Susan Slyomovics, "Cartoon Commentary: Algerian and Moroccan Caricatures of the Gulf War," *MERIP* 180, 23, no. 1 (January–February 1993): 21–24.